Praise for *Why Church History*

"Robert Rea has done something unique in this volume. He has dispelled the false notion that knowing the Bible makes understanding church history irrelevant. He has made church history a vital cornerstone for those who desire to serve the church well today and into the future. He has done this by taking the time to tie it deliberately and directly to the local church and practical ministry. Written by a veteran of the classroom and the church, this volume serves both venues well."

William R. Baker, professor of New Testament, Hope International University, and editor of *Stone-Campbell Journal*

"Robert Rea provides us with a passionate yet reasoned defense of church history in this thought-provoking study. Having been formed both intellectually and spiritually in a Protestant tradition that prioritized the Bible as the source of God's revelation to humankind, Rea discovered the wisdom of the church fathers and their successors in the course of his academic training. He presents in this book the fruit of years spent studying and teaching the ideas of Christian thinkers who flourished in the centuries after Jesus Christ and his apostles, with close attention to their historical circumstances. This is essential reading for all who teach or study church history or historical theology—two fields which Rea would prefer not to separate—since it offers not only an overview of the methods and concerns of theologians in the past but also important insights into how their work is received by Christian commentators in the present day."

Mary Cunningham, lecturer in historical theology, University of Nottingham, England

"Church history is the most important subject in the theological curriculum. I say this not only because I am a church historian but simply because it is true. Without a good grasp of the history of God's people through the ages one cannot understand the Bible, doctrine, ethics, ecumenism, spiritual formation or any other topic related to the life of faith. Robert Rea has given us here a readable and compelling statement of why that is so. This is a great primer for the study of Christian history in all of its multicolored meanings and forms."

Timothy George, founding dean, Beeson Divinity School of Samford University; general editor, *Reformation Commentary on Scripture*

"Robert Rea, who describes himself as a 'Bible-focused' Christian believer, wants others who focus on the Bible to take church history seriously. His careful, thought-provoking study shows why there is no biblical reason to fear 'tradition' properly understood, but every reason to heed believers from the past as guides to Christian life today. Most importantly, the book is successful in explaining why full commitment to Scripture demands close and respectful attention to the past."

Mark Noll, Francis A. McAnaney Professor of History, University of Notre Dame

ROBERT F. REA

Why Church History Matters

An Invitation to Love and Learn from Our Past

IVP Academic

An imprint of InterVarsity Press
Downers Grove, Illinois

InterVarsity Press
P.O. Box 1400, Downers Grove, IL 60515-1426
World Wide Web: www.ivpress.com
Email: email@ivpress.com

InterVarsity Press® is the book-publishing division of InterVarsity Christian Fellowship/USA®, a movement of students and faculty active on campus at hundreds of universities, colleges and schools of nursing in the United States of America, and a member movement of the International Fellowship of Evangelical Students. For information about local and regional activities, write Public Relations Dept., InterVarsity Christian Fellowship/USA, 6400 Schroeder Rd., P.O. Box 7895, Madison, WI 53707-7895, or visit the IVCF website at www.intervarsity.org.

Scripture quotations, unless otherwise noted, are from the New Revised Standard Version of the Bible, copyright 1989 by the Division of Christian Education of the National Council of the Churches of Christ in the USA. Used by permission. All rights reserved.

While all stories in this book are true, some names and identifying information in this book have been changed to protect the privacy of the individuals involved.

Cover design: David Fassett
Interior design: Beth Hagenberg
Images: Wooden staircase: Tom Merton/Getty Images
    Three Cappadocian Fathers: St Gregory of Nazianzus, St John Chrysostom and St Basil the Great, by an anonymous artist from the Byzantine school, De Agostini Picture Library. G. Dagli Orti. The Bridgeman Art Library
    Karl Barth: Horst Tappe Foundation / The Granger Collection, NYC. All rights reserved.
    Cathedral Saints: © suesmith2/iStockphoto
    Adam Clarke: © pictore/iStockphoto
    John Wesley: © Linda Steward/iStockphoto
    St. Teresa of Avila: © duncan1890/iStockphoto
    Gold frames: © winterling/iStockphoto; © wambi/iStockphoto; © JoKMedia/iStockphoto
    Wooden frame: © 1MoreCreative/iStockphoto

ISBN 978-0-8308-2819-7 (print)
ISBN 978-0-8308-6482-9 (digital)

Printed in the United States of America ♾

Library of Congress Cataloging-in-Publication Data

Rea, Robert F., 1953-
Why church history matters : an invitation to love and learn from our
past / Robert F. Rea.
   pages cm
Includes bibliographical references and index.
ISBN 978-0-8308-2819-7 (pbk. : alk. paper)
1. Church history—Miscellanea. I. Title.
BR148.R35 2014
270.01—dc23

                                                            2014012496

P	21	20	19	18	17	16	15	14	13	12	11	10	9	8	7	6	5	4	3	2	1
Y	32	31	30	29	28	27	26	25	24	23	22	21	20	19	18	17	16	15	14		

CONTENTS

Foreword 9

Abbreviations 11

Introduction 13

PART ONE: HOW WE UNDERSTAND THE TRADITION

1. What Is the Tradition? 23
>   What Are History and Christian History?
>   "Tradition," "tradition," "traditions" and "traditioning"
>   The Necessity and Dangers of Tradition
>   Tradition—Good or Bad?

2. How Have We Understood Tradition Historically? 35
>   Early Church
>   Middle Ages
>   Reformation Period
>   Since the Reformation
>   Recent Interest in Christian Tradition Among Bible-focused
>   Believers

3. How Do We Understand the Tradition Today? 59
>   Faith Groups Affirming Apostolic Succession
>   Faith Groups Not Affirming Apostolic Succession
>   Conclusion

PART TWO: EXPANDING CIRCLES OF INQUIRY

Introduction 81

4. Who Am I? Christian History and Christian Identity. 85
>   Identity Formation
>   Shared Identity
>   Identity Confirmation and Transformation

5. A Great Cloud of Witnesses 97
>   *Christian Community Across the Centuries*
>   The Human Desire for Community
>   How Historic Christian Community Helps

6. Accountability Partners 106
   Sharing Accountability with Historic Christians
   Accountability in Community
   How Do We Practice Accountability Across Centuries?
   Historic Examples
   Circles of Authenticity

7. Mentors and Friends 120
   Historic Christians Broaden Our Horizons and
   Fill Gaps in Our Understanding
   New Horizons and Filling Gaps
   Examples of Expanded Perspectives
   Authenticity and Certainty

PART THREE: TRADITION SERVING THE CHURCH

Introduction 133

8. Rightly Dividing the Word of Truth 134
   Christian Exegesis Across the Centuries
      Early Church
      Middle Ages
      Reformation Period
      Since the Reformation
      Recent Trends in Exegesis
   How Christian History Helps Bible Study
      Better Text and Translation
      More Balanced Exegesis
   Toward an Exegetical Model

9. Tradition and Ministry. 165
   Preaching and Teaching
   Systematic Theology
   Spirituality
   Worship
   Expansion: Mission
   Ethics
   Compassion
   Unity

    Cultural Engagement

    Making a Plan

Celebrate the Body of Christ 191

Recommended Resources for Ministry 195

Notes 201

Name and Subject Index 225

Scripture Index 233

FOREWORD

When I began teaching many years ago, I needed a textbook to help inspire inquiring students to study the Christian tradition. I began gathering materials for such a book. Thanks to much experience, and to IVP, that book is now a reality.

At times readers will come to other conclusions about some of the illustrations or about the theologians chosen as mentors and friends. I encourage you to consider each possibility and to reject any perspectives when they appear to run counter to Scripture especially, but also to the core values of tradition. But please do not dismiss the point being illustrated simply because the illustration itself does not meet your approval. The very fact that readers might disagree demonstrates the necessity and benefit of studying Christian history, for knowing the tradition empowers students to disagree reasonably.

I also invite readers to supplement my illustrations with others—that is a primary reason for the book. When our growing sensitivity to connect our identity, community and accountability with the past augments our unique collage of personal experiences, we discover illustrations that otherwise we would not see. Please extend the work in your own life, ministry and classroom.

Endnotes, in addition to giving reasons for points made in the text, are meant to provide resources for further study. I have cited resources that are more academic than popular, and wherever possible I favor resources written or translated into English, making them accessible to students. This should help students make a life plan for studying Christian history by preparing a list of resources to include as part of their regular reading.

Special appreciation to my professors, colleagues and students, for our study together helped to form in me what is reflected in this work. Thanks to all who evaluated the ideas and eventually the manuscript, and to IVP for believing in the project and encouraging its completion. I deeply appreciate the constant support of my wife, Mary Ann, who has been my partner for nearly three decades. Tremendous thanks to the sacrificial servants of God across the centuries, who many times have transformed my own thinking and challenged me to deeper spirituality. Finally, praise and glory be to God, whose presence and power, authority and word, grace and mercy—the redemptive plan, from eternity to eternity—are the reason why I want to face each new day.

Abbreviations

ACCS	Ancient Christian Commentary on Scripture (the series in general)
ACCSNT	Ancient Christian Commentary on Scripture: New Testament
ACCSOT	Ancient Christian Commentary on Scripture: Old Testament
ACR	*Australasian Catholic Record*
ACW	Ancient Christian Writers
ANF	Ante-Nicene Fathers
ASV	American Standard Version (1901)
AugStud	*Augustinian Studies*
BT	*Bible Translator*
CBQ	*Catholic Biblical Quarterly*
ChrCent	*Christian Century*
ChrTo	*Christianity Today*
CTHPT	Cambridge Texts in the History of Political Thought
CTJ	*Calvin Theological Journal*
CWS	Classics of Western Spirituality
EDNT	*Exegetical Dictionary of the New Testament*, ed. H. Balz and G. Schneider (3 vols.; Grand Rapids: Eerdmans, 1990–1993)
ERT	*Evangelical Review of Theology*
ESV	English Standard Version
FC	Fathers of the Church
HTR	*Harvard Theological Review*
HE	Eusebius, *Ecclesiastical History* (*Historia ecclesiastica*)
HeyJ	*Heythrop Journal*
JBL	*Journal of Biblical Literature*
JECS	*Journal of Early Christian Studies*
JETS	*Journal of the Evangelical Theological Society*
JTS	*Journal of Theological Studies*
KJV	King James Version
LCC	Library of Christian Classics
LCL	Loeb Classical Library
LF	Library of the Fathers
LXX	Septuagint

MSS	manuscripts
NASB	New American Standard Bible (1971)
NIDNTT	*New International Dictionary of New Testament Theology*, ed. C. Brown (4 vols.; Grand Rapids: Zondervan, 1975–1985)
NIV	New International Version
NovTSup	Supplements to Novum Testamentum
NPNF[1]	Nicene and Post-Nicene Fathers, series 1
NPNF[2]	Nicene and Post-Nicene Fathers, series 2
NRSV	New Revised Standard Version
NT	New Testament
NTS	*New Testament Studies*
OCA	Orientalia christiana analecta
OECT	Oxford Early Christian Texts
OSWC	Oxford Studies in World Christianity
OT	Old Testament
OTM	Oxford Theological Monographs
PP	Popular Patristics
PSTJ	*Perkins (School of Theology) Journal*
RBS	Resources for Biblical Study
RSV	Revised Standard Version (1952)
SBLGNT	Society of Biblical Literature Greek New Testament
SCES	Sixteenth Century Essays and Studies
SHCTh	Studies in the History of Christian Thought
SHCTr	Studies in the History of Christian Traditions
SMT	*Studii Montis Regii*
SVTQ	*St. Vladimir's Theological Quarterly*
TDNT	*Theological Dictionary of the New Testament*, ed. G. Kittel and G. Friedrich, trans. G. W. Bromiley (10 vols.; Grand Rapids: Eerdmans, 1964–1976)
TGl	*Theologie und Glaube*
ThTo	*Theology Today*
TLNT	*Theological Lexicon of the New Testament*, by C. Spicq, trans. and ed. J. D. Ernest (Peabody, MA: Hendrickson, 1994)
VE	*Vox evangelica*
WA	Weimar edition of *Luther's Works* (in German)
WTJ	*Westminster Theological Journal*

Introduction

"Why Are You Here?"

The next two hours would change the rest of my life. I had passed twelve hours of written exams. In just moments five scholars would determine my academic future. As a conservative Protestant from a free-church, Bible-only tradition, my horizons broadened considerably while studying historical theology at a Roman Catholic university in the Jesuit tradition. Now my Roman Catholic examiners would give their verdict. Four would question me on predetermined subjects. A fifth would ask about anything he chose.

The numerous and varied questions from the first three examiners proceeded quite well. My fourth examiner was to ask about Martin Luther. He first said, "Bob, we know you know about Martin Luther, so I want to ask some other questions." He then asked, "What is theology?" I swallowed hard. This was a shift from the agenda, and I wondered why. Were they coming after me? I answered, "Theology is the study of God, God's revelation, God's actions and God's people, including important documents, events, personalities, movements and doctrinal developments. I believe that theology should be Bible-based."

The examiner then asked some follow-up questions that seemed equally nebulous, and I struggled to answer. Finally I said, "I'm not sure how to answer your questions because I'm not sure what you're asking." My adviser, who chaired the exam, said that it was time for the next examiner, whose first question felt like an arrow into the dark. I remember feeling sick and saying, "I would love to answer, but I still don't know what you are asking." He then clarified, "Okay. If theology only comes from the Bible, and if we can get everything we need from the Bible, why are you here?" Aha! Finally I could see the purpose of their questions. They wanted to know why someone who simply needed to read the Bible to understand Christian theology would invest thousands of hours and even more dollars to study historical theology.

As I formulated my answers to those questions, little did I know that I was beginning to formulate an apologetic for the subject that I so deeply love and for a career as a seminary professor of church history/historical theology. Since that day, many Christians, from various backgrounds, have asked me the same question—Why are you here?—in one way or another. College students majoring in Bible ask why they should spend their time studying church history when they could spend that time studying the Scriptures. I suspect that some of my seminary students, savvy enough to realize such a question is presumptuous, silently wonder the same. Many seminarians have shared that they love the study of church history, but they fail to see how advanced study in historical theology is practical. Yet others say, "If I had known that there was so much theology and so much practical application from church history, I would have taken more classes, and I would have taken them early in my program."

This book, appearing some three decades after my appearance before the examiners, addresses these and similar questions. If the Bible is God's revelation, why spend time studying the history of the church's teaching and practice? Why should I care what Christians in other times and other places believed and how they acted? Aren't history and tradition more problems than solutions?

WHY DO WE NEED THIS BOOK?

We live in an era when church administration, counseling and technology dominate a pastor's time. Topics such as theology and tradition dwell near the bottom of the priority list at best, or are viewed with suspicion at worst. Church leaders, driven by perceived needs, and genuinely hoping to deepen their congregants' experience of the Christian life, have nonetheless inadvertently tended to steer church attention and activities away from the doctrines and teachings that are foundational to Christian experience through the centuries. This can leave us feeling shallow and unfulfilled. The problem is this: when we ignore centuries of God-loving Christians and the rich well of resources that they have passed on to us, sometimes ignoring even Scripture itself in the process, our perceived needs are often little more than mirrors of our fallen culture.

We need these earlier Christians. We need our brothers and sisters in Christ. Their wisdom and experience are foundational resources for Christian life and ministry. We can learn from their insights (and blind spots). We can grow by allowing them to instruct us. This book is a call to Christians who love the Bible to study historic Christians and their wisdom and experiences throughout the ages—to understand the Bible and theology better and to experience a fuller Christian life. I want contemporary Christians to embrace the entire Christian community by including not only Christians of the contemporary cultures in our current conversations but also Christians from previous cultures. This renewed relationship with our extended Christian family will help provide accountability for our faith and practices by allowing us to expand, nuance, confirm or correct our own convictions and assumptions. I hope to stimulate the study of church history among those who love God, love the Bible, love the church, love the truth and seek to know the truth and its application for life. I intend to help contemporaries discover the greater Christian community through their writings and the testimonies of their lives, while enjoying the fellowship of both those now living and those who have gone before us. When we invite into our contemporary fellowship the spiritual masters, scholars, pastors, preachers, educators and other Christian leaders who have gone before—often many centuries before—the study of our history greatly expands the number and variety of the church's teachers and mentors, research partners, ministerial fellowships, sermon preparation groups and academic cohorts.

Today we see among Christians an increasing desire to go back to this deep well. More and more believers look to the spiritual masters to deepen

> When we ignore centuries of God-loving Christians and the rich well of resources that they have passed on to us, our perceived needs often become little more than mirrors of our fallen culture.

their faith. These believers sense something missing in their own spiritual lives, and they have discovered that learning from great Christians throughout the centuries quenches a thirst and inspires them to serve others more effectively. This should come as no surprise, since Christianity is essentially historical. Christianity's background, emergence and development are deeply grounded in God's work in and through real people across real time and real space.

Israel remembered the mighty acts of God throughout their history. God, through leaders, prophets and the Scriptures, directed them to recall their historic moments with specific acts of remembrance, such as the Passover celebration. Hebrews recited to one another the stories of God's great acts, remembered their birth lineage, and recalled the prayers of their ancestors so that their faith would be true and grounded in the God who is not an idea or a wish but living and active.

Then, "in the fullness of time," God sent the only begotten of the Father to become a human being. The eternal creator of time became existence in time. The Word became flesh. The Son of God became Jesus, entering into the history that holds together in him. His miracles, healing and teaching were repeated again and again and then written down by the Gospel writers for posterity. His passion, death, resurrection and ascension were recorded for all to celebrate, to know that we find our identity and new life through participation in them with him. Christians remember these events through special dates in the Christian calendar and in weekly events, such as reading Scripture, preaching sermons and celebrating the Lord's Supper.

The character and the mission of the church likewise are fully historical, first referred to in the New Testament Epistles and recorded in the book of Acts (a crucial book for any Christian faith group to be able to understand their roots). Since the end of the writing of the Scriptures, but more extensively starting in the fourth century, Christian historians have intentionally endeavored to record the history of the church so that Christians can remember who they are, where they came from, and why they exist.

Because Christianity is essentially historical—grounded in the events of God leading up to the Messiah, in the life and redemption brought by the Messiah, in the founding of the church through apostolic leadership, and in the ongoing commitment to the faith and to its advance throughout the centuries—every Christian knows something of the history of Christianity. As we will see, one cannot "do" Christianity apart from the history of the church.

So, to ignore Christian history is always a huge loss to the church. It chokes Christian community by restricting our interaction with believers of our own time, who are already very much like us. The result is that we unknowingly overlook otherwise obvious blind spots in our view of the Christian landscape. We limit the breadth of our community, and we surrender opportunities for historical accountability. We also miss important opportunities in exegesis, spirituality, personal relationships, interchurch relationships and methods of practical ministry.

WHO SHOULD READ THIS BOOK?

The "ideal reader" of this book is a student who, throughout this book, is described as a "Bible-focused" Christian. Bible-focused students are simply those who hold the Bible dear and study it in order to know God and God's truth. This includes not only evangelicals, but also many mainstream Protestant believers and a growing number of Roman Catholics and Eastern Orthodox. I use this term because many alternative terms for Christians who focus their theology on the Bible as God's authoritative written revelation for the church's identity and mission carry connotations or limitations that exclude some who will benefit from the book. "Evangelical" is difficult to define and today sometimes includes those who themselves avoid the term. "Fundamentalist," while perhaps a good term at its onset, carries connotations of anti-intellectualism or legalism. "Protestant" is used in diverse ways as well. "Bible-focused," on the other hand, embraces those who are happy with one or more of the preceding terms, but it also includes believers who would never describe themselves in those ways but are Bible-focused nonetheless. If you, as a reader, do not feel that "Bible-focused" describes you well, I believe that this book will still be of great benefit in your Christian journey, and perhaps you will even change your mind somewhere along the way.

Why have Bible-focused Christians neglected the Christian tradition? In the sixteenth century Reformers such as Luther, Calvin, Zwingli and others raised serious questions about the church's departure from Scripture. This led to significant conflict. At the Council of Trent (1545–1563), the Roman Catholic Church responded by affirming both Scripture and tradition as

authoritative. Since the Council of Trent, most Protestants and Roman
Catholics have assumed a fairly strict dichotomy between Scripture and tradition. Many Protestants came to equate emphasis on tradition with rejection of the authority of Scripture, or at least pollution of the authority of
Scripture. Protestant leaders, especially those from more Bible-focused
groups, often have spoken of tradition as the antithesis of Scripture, even
though frequent recourse to individual denominational creeds rather than
Scripture seems inconsistent with such a position.

This prejudice against tradition has other consequences. First, it fosters
the tendency among Bible-focused groups to de-emphasize or ignore the
history of the church. This is true, as I have noted, at the congregational and
denominational levels, sometimes reinforced by the fact that unfortunate
educational experiences have left many with the distinct impression that the
only thing more boring than history is church history.

But this neglect is evident also in theological education. Most Bible-
focused educators give the nod to the importance of Christian history, but
few of them articulate convincing reasons as to why. Many college-level
ministerial training programs no longer require the traditional courses in
Christian history. Those who do so generally require only one course, which
sweeps through two thousand years in the blink of an eye, hitting the high-
lights and often missing the magic in the process. Most evangelical seminaries give heavy emphasis to biblical and practical courses with more ab-
breviated emphasis on historical and theological investigation.[1]

One way to address the problem is to offer more courses in Christian
history and to help students integrate their discoveries into their current
lives and future ministries. Another way is to make sure that Christian
history becomes one of the key theological lenses through which every
subject is examined—exegesis, systematic theology, ethics, Bible translation,
apologetics, preaching, teaching, counseling, worship, church growth, missions, and so on. What if historical theological considerations became an
integral aspect of every subject in Christian ministerial and vocational
training, especially in colleges and seminaries that consider themselves
Bible-focused?

A second consequence of the prejudice against tradition, it seems to me,
is that Protestant scholars tend to differentiate between church history as

one area of study and historical theology as another. This suggests that since absorbing names and dates and documents is difficult and often consumes the lion's share of our time and energy, we can bypass "history" and go straight to what matters, "theology." In other words, we study the past in order to understand the thinking of a few key people. This assumes that if we concentrate on their thoughts apart from the causes and contexts of their thoughts, we can get to the kernels of historical investigation without some of the difficulties of historical investigation.

For Roman Catholics and Eastern Orthodox, of course, such a differentiation makes no sense. I contend that they are correct. I have often been described as "not a church historian, but a historical theologian." Although I appreciate what I hope is intended as a compliment—"He doesn't just repeat the facts, but teaches theology that students can use"—such a separation for most students (and most believers) is artificial and can be misleading. How can we understand the development of Christian thought and practice apart from the contexts in which each developed? Rather than separating these perspectives, this book treats them as two names for the same thing, as "Martin" and "Luther" are two names for the same person. So for our purposes, "church history," "historical theology," "Christian history" and "Christian tradition" are synonymous phrases referring to a single discipline.

HOW IS THIS BOOK LAID OUT?

Bible-focused students of Christian history find addressed in one volume three major outcomes, reflected in the three parts of the book. Part 1 introduces history, Christian history and tradition by defining terms, by surveying the history of how tradition has been viewed and by explaining how major Christian faith groups view the tradition today. Part 2 provides rationale and motivation for the study of Christian history by explaining why Christian history is foundational for forming personal and corporate identity, for experiencing broad Christian community, for providing contemporary accountability, and for bringing theological balance by expanding horizons and filling theological gaps. Part 3 identifies specific ways church history can help in practical ministry in the study of Scripture (textual work, translation, exegesis) and in other areas (preaching, teaching, systematic theology, ethics, worship, spirituality, pastoral care, cultural transformation, ecumenical endeavors). The intent is to balance the scholarly and the practical, modeling scholarship in the service of the church. Students will also see how their current and future vocations can be enhanced by broadening their study to include great Christians, teachings, and developments from across the centuries.

Part One

How We Understand
the Tradition

1

WHAT IS THE TRADITION?

WHAT ARE HISTORY AND CHRISTIAN HISTORY?

History is the study of the past in order to understand the present and to improve the future. Historians examine significant physical remains, such as coins, artifacts and architecture, in order to reconstruct the framework of the past. They also looks at persons, events, documents, movements, developments and teachings to help individuals understand where they came from, how their cultures developed, why they hold to key values, and what assumptions and presuppositions from the past formulate their understanding of reality in the present. Historians also examine this data to help contemporary communities understand the various factors that contribute to each group's identity, purpose and values. In the process, history helps us understand and evaluate our worldview—the collection of basic values that drives one's foundational outlook about everything in the world.

History is not merely the collection of data. We do not simply stockpile information and then call the collected data "history." Not every person, event, document, movement, development or teaching is historic. Instead, history is the endeavor

> History is the study of the past in order to understand the present and to improve the future.

to provide accountability to the present in light of the past—to search out people, events, movements, artifacts and so on that have particular significance for the present and the future. Not all people and events carry the same relevance for history. For example, nearly every student of world history knows what happened on December 7, 1941, whereas few people know what happened on December 5, 1941. Yet both days had twenty-four hours and innumerable pieces of data. We remember December 7, 1941, however, because the attack on Pearl Harbor changed the world then and in many ways determined movements, relationships and identities for today and the future.

Christian history, or historical theology, is the study specifically of the church's past in order to understand the church's present and to improve the church's future. Church historians examine artifacts that shed light on times and places. Church historians also look at significant persons, events, documents, movements, developments and teachings in the history of the church to help individual Christians and groups of Christians understand where they came from, where other Christian groups came from, why they hold particular commitments, and what assumptions and presuppositions from the past formulate their Christian worldview in the present. One major difference between history and Christian history, at least among Christian historians, is that believers also look for the presence, actions, will and heart of God in past events in order to try to discern God's will for the present and the future.

Some have said that history never changes. This is simply untrue. The data of history—the actual artifacts, persons, events, documents, movements, developments and teachings from the past—do not change, except that new discoveries add more information or correct misinformation of the past. But how those persons and developments are understood—the identified significance of past developments—does change.

In other words, the personal or community identity and values that we bring to the data help determine what we interpret as significant. No one comes to the study of history with complete objectivity. For example, I am an Anglo, middle-class American male who grew up as a lower-class boy in a declining urban neighborhood. I will never be a tribal African woman who grew up in a small village. I will never be a disenfranchised Latino man who grew up on the outskirts of Mexico City. If the three of us were to discuss the significance of historical events, we would bring three very diverse perspectives to the historical data. Each of us would see particulars within those events that the others would not see. Occasionally, our understandings of events may conflict, but in most cases we would understand events in much the same way, emphasizing different aspects of the events.

In other cases changing times and changing cultural perspectives alter or augment the previous understanding of historical persons, events and developments. Here I offer an example from more recent world history. During World War II many American men joined the armed forces, leaving their production jobs vacant. Thousands of American women sacrificially left their homes to work in jobs previously thought to be exclusively for men. The women demonstrated competence in those positions, but when the war was over, nearly all of them, with little regret, returned to the places in life that they considered to be for women. But they told their daughters that they could grow up to be anything they wanted to be. Those daughters grew up to tell their daughters the same. Today women do not assume that their gender precludes them from becoming doctors, lawyers, plumbers, construction workers, soldiers or corporate executives. In the years immediately following World War II no historian would have considered the war a liberator of women in the realm of occupation. The significance of World War II was about political boundaries and the exchange of world power. But today we must recognize that one of the most significant developments in World War II for contemporary American life and culture was the sacrifice of those women who changed their world. The data of what happened did not change, but the interpretation of the data—the significance for today and tomorrow understood from that data—has changed. In other words, history has changed.

We could add to this a number of examples of how newly emphasized values can alter the perceived importance of characters and movements in the history of the church. Historical evaluations of fourth-century Roman emperor Constantine have moved from almost universal laud as the great Christian emperor to a variety of critical positions that take issue with his claim to Christian faith. Western Christians are currently reassessing the grace theology of fifth-century church father John Cassian—long considered a saint by Eastern Orthodox—who advocated that both God and the human individual work in every act of salvation and sanctification.

This is why it is so difficult to make lasting historical judgments until years after an event or movement. What contemporaries and those immediately after an experience think of the event's significance may differ greatly from how their children and grandchildren see the event. Sometimes the most unpopular political leaders are later highly esteemed.

This is not to say that there is no absolutely objective understanding of history and historical theology. God, who knows all things, has all the actual and potential perspectives of every person and event of history, including church history. But only God has that objectivity, because God is infinite. Father, Son and Holy Spirit know everything and can therefore see objectively. God knows absolute truth absolutely.

We humans, on the other hand, are finite and therefore always subject to the limitations of finitude—we have limited perspective, limited experience, limited intelligence, limited understanding of reality. We have degrees of objectivity, but not absolute objectivity. We can have enough objectivity to make a fair evaluation of the evidence. We can be objective enough to understand past persons, events and developments so that we see who they are, where they came from, why events occurred, and how current groups and emphases came to be.

Actually, "objective enough" is the functional standard in nearly every field of endeavor. Human blood, for example, already has all of the elements of human blood, many of which we probably have yet to discover. Early "objective" tests of human blood determined blood type. Then we added Rh factor. Today a standard blood test can measure scores of factors that we know to relate to various aspects of health. Particular blood tests target particular pathologies or profiles. The point is that long ago, when we knew precious little about human blood, we could be objective enough to determine what we sought—blood type. Then we were objective enough to determine Rh factor. Today we are objective enough to determine blood sugar levels, lipid profiles, liver enzymes, red and white blood cell levels, blood gases, DNA and more. In the future we will discover that there is much more diagnostic information available in human blood, and we will learn to test in a way which is objective enough to make reliable decisions.

In the same way, finite human beings can never be fully objective. But individuals and groups can be objective enough to make determinations in areas of investigation. In history, as in medicine, broadly universal agreement will give us functional objectivity. But fully aware of our finite limitations, we must always approach history with humility, for we must always recognize that our perspectives are limited.

In summary, we must recognize that real artifacts, persons, events, documents, movements, developments and teachings have actually occurred. The real facts change only in that we discover more information or correct previous inaccurate reports. Real events occurred, and real people lived in real situations. Only God, who is infinite, has a fully objective knowledge of these real events and real people. God is objective. We humans are finite, and thus we are never absolutely objective. But we can be objective enough to understand the past so that it can inform the present and improve the future. Our finitude, however, requires that we learn in community, and in regard to church history this community must include contemporary Christians and historic Christians.

The way we understand the significance of the past for today and for the future does change. I must insert a word of caution here, however. In recent years some historians have proposed that the data itself is insignificant, except insofar as it can be construed or misconstrued to establish or advance what the historian wants to promote. In other words, what really happened matters most when it supports the historian's agenda. These historians contend that since data is always subject to interpretation, and since cultural presuppositions determine the data's meaning, we should admit our intentions from the beginning and either reconstruct the historical data to make it support our case or even invent connections that never existed to support our case.[1]

This intentional reconstruction of historical data should not be the intent of Bible-focused Christians at any level. We endeavor to understand what actually happened and to understand the significance of what happened for our time and for our future, though we recognize that our own ideas and culture may focus our attention on certain perspectives of history or limit our ability to see important aspects of history. We recognize that we come to these events with a finite set of values, methods and assumptions.

This leads to one of the key reasons for this book. When we consult resources to help us understand history and theology, we must be careful not to limit our resources to authors who share our cultural perspectives and intellectual commitments. We need the points of view offered by contemporaries of various perspectives and various cultures. But also, we cannot hope to approach "objective enough" unless we also consider the points of view offered by historical figures who lived godly Christian lives and who endeavored to understand the truth with open hearts in times and cultures very different from our own. Only then can we expand our own limited understandings to approach a fuller and fairer analysis of the past in order to understand the present and improve the future.

"TRADITION," "TRADITION," "TRADITIONS" AND "TRADITIONING"

The words *tradition*, *Tradition* and *traditions* are classic terms to describe perspectives or approaches to understanding developments in the Church's history. The word *tradition* is used in a number of ways. In less technical contexts it is the general category or milieu for everything that has developed in Christian history. This includes major persons, events, documents, doctrines, controversies, councils, conflicts, movements, and much more.

In a more technical sense, when church leaders use the word *Tradition* (note the capital T), most often they are referring to the Roman Catholic and Eastern Orthodox view. In this view, God's revelation through prophets and apostles is preserved in Scripture, so Scripture receives double honor, so to speak; but the Holy Spirit is believed to reveal the repository of truth further and develop scriptural revelation further through the faith and practices of the church. The collection of revealed truth, the revealed authority, in Scripture and the post-Scripture faith and practice of the church, is called "Tradition." Roman Catholics and Eastern Orthodox sometimes differ on teachings that they include in the Tradition.

Some Protestants also use the term *Tradition* (with a capital T) when they affirm the teachings, doctrines and practices upon which believers throughout the world and over the centuries agree—a uniformity of belief and practice in the church that affirms teachings and practices in nearly every place and age. Of course, these Protestants do not include in the Tradition all of the same teachings that either Roman Catholics or Eastern Orthodox include. But there is much overlap, particularly in the major doctrines of Christianity, such as the doctrines of God (Trinity) and Christ (Christology). Other Protestants avoid using "Tradition" (capital T) and instead use "tradition" (lowercase t) to mean pretty much the same thing. For Protestants, this tradition, though not revelational and not nonnegotiable, has an authoritative aspect because committed believers have affirmed it across temporal, cultural and ecclesiastical lines. This common belief by the larger community of believers—the *consensus fidelium*—lends it credibility for all believers. To avoid confusion, from here on *Tradition* (capital T) will be used only for Roman Catholics and Eastern Orthodox and only when referring to the whole body of tradition taken together, which they consider to be revealed by God.

When church leaders use the word *traditions*, they refer to developing teachings, doctrines, events, churches and so forth within specific centuries, specific cultures and specific church groups. These are practices that the church as a whole or specific church groups have chosen to meet specific needs or desires in specific times or places. These traditions are understood to be dependent upon one culture or one set of philosophical presuppositions and to fade when new situations arise. They often depend upon or result in denominational distinctives. Hence, they are seen as helpful but not universally authoritative.

More recently an alternative use of the word *tradition* was included in the 1963 Faith and Order Commission Report, presented at Montreal. This use of "tradition" refers to the activity of tradition, or the dynamic of traditioning—the means by which some specific item of faith is transmitted.[2] Knowing how tradition emerges and is transmitted is important for understanding the value of tradition for contemporary Bible-focused Christians as well. For the sake of clarifying between "tradition" above and this use, I describe this fourth use as "traditioning."

In this book "tradition" is most often used in the general sense as a synonym for Christian history, church history or historical theology and includes all of the above: (1) "Tradition" or "tradition," (2) "traditions" and (3) "traditioning." Some sections will lend themselves naturally to including the first more than the others, but all are valuable for contemporary Bible-focused Christians.

Some tend to limit the period in which tradition has a normative nature. D. H. Williams, for example, has said, "The apostolic and patristic tradition is foundational to the Christian faith in *normative* ways that no other period for the church's history can claim. A theologian or pastor may agree or disagree with the patristic legacy, but it is functioning nonetheless as a rule by which such agreement or disagreement occurs."[3] Williams limits the primary period of tradition to the patristic period. I am tempted to affirm this position, since most issues of extreme importance were discussed in this period. But this position suffers the same critique as those that limit the tradition of significant value to the first century. Many important developments occur after the patristic period as well.

Still others, whether intentionally or accidentally, tend to limit tradition's value to the period that produced their own faith group. They may not say it directly, but they act and teach as though their favorite period or favorite movement is normative. Protestants, for example, often have paid particular attention to the fifteenth, sixteenth and seventeenth centuries, since the great Reformers who produced Protestantism lived and taught in that period. Many other examples could be given.

THE NECESSITY AND DANGERS OF TRADITION

Tradition is inevitable. Every sociological group develops standard practices and approaches that become, whether intentionally or accidentally, the normal or even the "right" way to live out their theory and practice. At the same time, each group must continue to weigh those traditions carefully to be sure that the traditions that either emerged or were designed to improve their lives and to implement their mission do not come to impede their mission. This is true with the church as a whole and with each faith group that is part of the church.

Christianity is a world religion dependent upon and explicitly concerned with tradition, because the entirety of Christian identity depends upon real events in history. God really acted in creation, in Abraham, Isaac and Jacob, in delivering Israel from slavery, and in preparing Israel for the Christ. The Son of God really became incarnate in a virgin woman, was born in Bethlehem, lived an exemplary life, died, was buried, was resurrected, and ascended. Apostles and others really spread the gospel throughout the world, with various practices being prescribed and others simply emerging. Yet in a variety of practices Christians served one God and one Christ through one Spirit. This continues today.

So in Christianity, not only do we stand on the tradition, but also in many ways we *are* the tradition. This means that *you* are the tradition. You have had Christianity passed on to you, in a particular form, at a particular time; you did not come up with the idea. Tradition informs you, your priorities, your points of view, your worldview. Tradition also guides the emphases, practices and commitments of your faith group, your congregation and even your circle of congregational friends. This is what the Bible teaches us. The Bible itself is part of Christian tradition, and at the same time it is foundational for Christianity.

Already in Galatians 1:8 the apostle Paul warns, "But even if we or an angel from heaven should proclaim to you a gospel contrary to what we proclaimed to you, let that one be accursed!" (NRSV). It mattered then and matters now what "gospel" is preached, for there can be a false gospel. Paul's readers were to believe only the proper tradition that had been preached to them by the apostles. George Tavard says it well: "Thus understood, tradition is the art of passing on the Gospel. It is not distinct from the Good News of Christ. Rather it is the power of the Gospel itself which inspires the devotion and loyalty of the men and Churches responsible for its transmission."[4]

When sincere Christians try to live the truth faithfully as their Christian community understands it, they develop normative strategies and practices to live, love, worship and serve together—they develop traditions. Intended to be grounded in Scripture, these traditions sometimes encompass core Christian practices, but often they are simply this or that particular Christian community choosing the best of several available options for their own setting. Each of these helpful choices of method, practice or preference, while not essential to the core of Christian faith, is necessary to carry out the core of Christian faith. For example, nearly every faith group has developed its own set of traditions for how to celebrate the Lord's Supper. The celebration itself, commanded by Jesus, is at the core of Christian faith; *how* the celebration is conducted is not. While each Christian community's traditions are meaningful, each can also learn from the rich practices of others.

This means that although Protestants often have declared their distaste for tradition, they have nonetheless developed traditions that are necessary to their ability to implement Christian faith and practice. Tradition helps them preach the gospel. Harold Brown observes, "From the Protestant perspective it is necessary to tone down the polemic against tradition as though it were necessarily a falsification of simple Christian truth. To do this we must recognize and acknowledge the role that tradition plays in our own worship and life. This should help us gain a tolerance for the importance of tradition in other communities."[5]

At the same time, we must recognize the dangers of tradition. Past Christians have had good reason to suspect the tradition, as we will see. Blind following of tradition has led to many travesties among Christians, as all Christian groups would admit. Jesus decried traditions that impede obedience to the very commands of God. He was clear that loyalty to traditions rather than loyalty to what is written in Scripture is not only counterproductive but also an affront to God.

Tradition can proliferate and come to hide the vital truths of the gospel. Tradition can lead us to trust our own practices and perspectives rather than Jesus Christ. Tradition can dull our sensitivity to insights that God may be helping us to discover. Traditions can incline us toward legalistic attitudes and actions in issues that are not at the core of the gospel. Extrabiblical traditions among various geographic locations or faith groups can lead us to consider our own group's or our own location's experience as normative for all times and places or even as essential to salvation. Loyalty to these parochial traditions can cause us to reject or devalue other Christians and their parochial traditions. Often traditions help faith groups identify their own members, but this can happen in such a way that the traditions rather than the gospel itself become their standard and consequently a cause of division among Christians.

Worst of all, the body of traditions can become so important to us that we neglect the real heart of the gospel, even granting assurance to some that they are Christians when indeed they are not. This was Martin Luther's fear—Roman Catholic traditions would lead people to believe they were saved when they did not have what Luther understood to be saving faith. This is the fear of nearly every major reformer—people following their traditions are not really on the path of salvation. Of course, each reformer ends up beginning another group—a group that recovers rich Christian emphases but at the same time begins to develop new traditions.

So on the one hand, tradition is not only inevitable but also beneficial. Tradition helps us connect with God and identify with one another in authentic faith. Tradition helps us experience God and Christian fellowship. Tradition helps us live the Christian life. In that sense, we are the tradition, the living gospel, and we believe that the true preaching of Jesus Christ, the proper tradition, is necessary for others to find saving faith. No substitute will do. On the other hand, tradition can be dangerous. When we elevate extrabiblical teachings and practices to the level of essential Christian faith, we are drawn from the gospel to something that we substitute for the gospel. When this happens, the results can be scandalous.

TRADITION—GOOD OR BAD?

God created human beings in time and in order to grow, making the records of human development and growth in the church part of God's plan. The Holy Spirit has worked in and through believers of all centuries. Much tradition has been very helpful to the church. At the grander levels, we owe much to those who clarified doctrines such as the canon of Scripture, the Trinity, Christology and many others. So we need the truth of Christ and historical theology as we evaluate our own Christian lives and practices.

But not every act or every movement of previous believers can be adopted as appropriate. Heresies and false teachings have been present in all centuries. Some tradition has been harmful, distracting the church from what is most important in the church's life and mission. Human motives are often questionable, and poor motives can lead to poor actions that turn the church in wrong directions.

The reality and the presence of tradition itself, therefore, are very good. Particular traditions, however, can be good or bad—either helpful in understanding and implementing God's will or counterproductive. When what is passed on to us is godly and biblical and produces in us salvation and godliness, such traditions are very good. But when what is passed on to us is corrupt or ungodly or contrary to Scripture, such traditions must be rejected.

Discerning when believers were moved by the Holy Spirit and when they were moved by other factors is a significant challenge. Complicating this task is that most often both historic believers and contemporary evaluators are motivated by a combination of factors, some likely divine and others human. Yet these decisions can have great impact on our contemporary understanding and on our future.

We appeal to the tools and reflections of tradition to evaluate particular traditions. For Bible-focused Christians, this begins with Scripture, but we recognize that even our understanding of Scripture is grounded in our own tradition. So tradition is always necessary as we evaluate our current situation, the events and persons and movements that helped make us who we are, and our future life investments. In other words, tradition is necessary to evaluate traditions. We decide whether particular traditions are helpful depending on whether they conform to God's will as we understand it through Scripture and theology, both understood with the aid of tradition.

The classic question of whether tradition itself is good or bad may actually be the wrong question. Tradition is both necessary and inevitable: as soon as the Christian community expresses their faith, they reflect the gospel as they received it and formulate models for expressing the gospel in the future. For this reason, among many others, contemporary Bible-focused Christians need a more focused and intentional study of the tradition. The fact that we may disagree with earlier decisions or the conclusions of our contemporaries does not diminish the value of the work, for we need each other, past and present. Scripture is paramount for understanding truth and God's will for the Christian life, but tradition empowers Christians to study Scripture more effectively, understand theology in dialogue with the historic Christian community, and express their faith more intentionally.[6]

> Tradition is both necessary and inevitable.

Our awareness of the emergence of tradition in the past reminds us to be careful in our decisions for current faith and practice, for what we do today could become tomorrow's "traditions." We embrace Scripture while at the same time providing ourselves the accountability necessary for assurance that our contemporary exegesis, theology, preaching, teaching, worship, spirituality and ethics are indeed Christian. In the process, we see the enormous value of tapping the treasure of tradition to provide insights, accountability, community and improved Christian life and ministry.

How Have We Understood
Tradition Historically?

When the church began, Christians believed that they were the continuation of God's chosen people, the new Israel, grafted into God's mighty plan. Theirs was a great past, a treasured tradition that they would continue into the future. As the church developed, its understanding of the nature and value of the tradition also developed. Today, after twenty centuries of Christian expansion into multiple continents, cultures and contexts, we see the tradition valued quite differently by various groups of Christians.

This can be difficult for Christians to grasp. How did this happen? How do Christians understand the tradition today? This chapter will lead us through many names, documents and developments over the major periods of Christian history. The path may seem unfamiliar at first, but we will soon discover that these real persons and events are markers for us to see important shifts in how Christians understood tradition—shifts that produced the widely diverse church that exists today. We will see not only that they valued the tradition, but also how they understood the tradition, emerging changes in that understanding, and what benefits and liabilities these developments provided. Some of their insights will challenge us to assess our own understandings of tradition.

EARLY CHURCH

In the earliest church Scripture and tradition were thought of as completely compatible, if not identical. At the very least, Scripture and tradition were

> All possible care must be taken, that we hold that faith which has been believed everywhere, always, by all.
>
> **VINCENT OF LÉRINS**

always consistent. At first, "Scripture" was the Old Testament Scriptures, though letters from apostles were also considered to be Scripture shortly after they were written. For example, 2 Peter 3:16 speaks of false teachers distorting Paul's letters, as they distort "the rest of the Scriptures." So Peter considered Paul's letters to be among "the Scriptures." Tradition in the earliest church was the oral transmission and demonstrated practices taught by the apostles and those that they approved. Earlier, 2 Peter 3:2 says that the believers "should remember the words spoken in the past by the holy prophets, and the commandment of the Lord and Savior spoken through your apostles." The Lord's commandments were no doubt passed on orally, at least before they were recorded in the Gospels. These two ways—oral and written—were reliable because they came from one, seamless source. The truth of Christ came to the church through the apostles—their written instructions and their oral instructions.

In the earliest church Scripture and tradition were thought of as completely compatible, if not identical.

The early Christians believed that both the Scriptures and the developing beliefs and practices of the apostolic church were given by the Holy Spirit, who, as the source or guarantor of the truth, provided that truth through the apostles. Their teaching was the "rule of faith" or the "rule of truth." The second-century bishop Irenaeus of Lyons describes the concept in several places, at times using the term itself.[1] This rule of truth was considered the church's norm. F. F. Bruce clarifies, "If at times it is formally distinguished from Scripture in the sense that it is recognized as the interpretation of Scripture, at other times it is materially identical with Scripture in the sense that it sums up what Scripture says."[2]

After the apostles and their disciples died, Christian practice continued to develop. There was less certainty about the necessity or truth of these postapostolic practices. Although some books of the biblical canon were still being considered Scripture in some places and not yet everywhere, those books already accepted as Scripture were regarded as apostolic and were used as the basis to test the emerging beliefs and practices. When the beliefs and practices became nearly universal, they often were accepted alongside the written instructions of the apostolic band as part of the rule of truth.

Emerging teachings and practices were compared to the apostolic teaching. The Scriptures held a special authority because the believers had certainty that they were apostolic and from the Holy Spirit, whereas emerging developments must be tested against the rule of truth. When dispute arose over the meaning of Scripture, Christian practice or doctrine, second-century Christians looked to their local bishop.

In the earliest church the congregations had a plurality of elders, also called "bishops." For any number of possible reasons, eventually one of the elders/bishops would lead the others and be considered *the* bishop, with presbyters (elders) under him. We see the earliest example of this in the bishop Ignatius of Antioch at the end of the first century. In most places it appears that this happened later, but by the end of the second century the concept of one bishop over a city or larger territory permeated the church throughout the Roman Empire. Christians generally believed that their bishop held apostolic authority in the area he pastored, called his "see." Bishops usually appealed to Scripture first, to local or regional practice next, and to other bishops or other regional practices next. Irenaeus, for example, appealed to the writings of the apostles and then to the bishops to whom the apostles committed the churches: "For how should it be if the apostles themselves had not left us writings? Would it not be necessary, to follow the course of the tradition which they handed down to those to whom they did commit the churches?"[3]

When competing teachings arose, they were argued convincingly as true or as false by leading bishops and theologians. Sometimes strong agreement pretty much settled the conflict, but often there was no strong agreement, and it could take decades or longer for the church to come to agreement.[4]

Eventually, bishops of major territorial sees, especially key cities in the empire whose sees were founded by apostles, were regarded as holding a higher level of authority in resolving these differences. One generally regarded as preeminent over a region was called "metropolitan" or "archbishop." Rome, Constantinople, Antioch and Alexandria came to be valued at an even higher level. Their bishops also had the title "patriarch." The bishop of Jerusalem held the title of patriarch as a position of honor, since Jerusalem was the most ancient see. Still others, such as the bishops of Ephesus and Carthage, were not regarded as patriarchs but had preeminence in their regions in much the same way as patriarchs.

Regional bishops, under the presidency of their patriarch or preeminent bishop, met to decide the orthodoxy of particular teachings and practices. At times there were two men claiming to be the bishop of a see, each supported by a group of believers within the see, so it was difficult to determine the true bishop.

After Emperor Constantine declared his vision from Christ in 312 and legalized Christianity in the Roman Empire, he encountered major disputes in important sees, now also called "dioceses." With the Eastern bishops planning a great council of bishops at Ancyra, he decided to convert their council into a huge council to include all prelates (bishops and other key church leaders), which would meet instead at his Nicaea residence in 325. This began a long-standing tradition of Roman emperors calling councils of bishops to settle disputes that might threaten Christian unity. At these supposedly empire-wide councils, the prelates appealed to Scripture first, and then to tradition, to establish which of the competing teachings was orthodox, or at least to squelch the teachings that the majority deemed false. Imperial interference could also sway the majority.

When some councils were later accepted universally, they were called "ecumenical." Although Nicaea 325 and Ephesus 431 were primarily regional councils, the emperor invited all bishops and other prelates, and they were later called ecumenical. But other councils to which the emperor invited all bishops and prelates were not later considered ecumenical: several church-wide councils were convened by imperial invitation between Nicaea 325 and Constantinople 381, including the fourth century's largest council, the dual council held at Seleucia and Rimini in 359. These were disregarded because Constantinople 381 and later Chalcedon 451 considered their decisions to be incorrect or inappropriate. Ephesus 431, which accomplished virtually nothing, was regarded as ecumenical primarily because Chalcedon 451 referred to it with authority.

Eventually, however, there was fairly universal acceptance of the teachings of these early ecumenical councils, and the concept of the ecumenical council took on additional authority. The council appealed to Scripture, and then to (1) widespread or universal faith and practice, or (2) widespread or universal teachings from the fathers (key Christian leaders who had written in the past). Of course, as with all conclusions in all times, these decisions were made within the construct of the council members' philosophical worldview assumptions.

Through all of this time churches continued to worship, develop liturgy, pray, celebrate the Eucharist, and practice their Christianity in similar (sometimes identical, sometimes varied) ways from location to location. Songs were written, local baptismal confessions were recited, and territorial practices were employed.

So by the end of the early period, we see a major development in how Christians understood the tradition. The search for truth followed a fairly established line of authority: they appealed first to Scripture, then to the local bishop, then to the regional metropolitan or archbishop, then to either the real or functional patriarch or the regional synod under his direction, then to other patriarchs or to an ecumenical council. These leaders were to guarantee the truth in the church. They often were regarded as the seat of authority for determining what the Scripture taught or what should be regarded as apostolic on that basis. In their deliberations they considered the counsel of trusted exegetes and theologians. This practice continued into the Middle Ages.

What about the concept of *sola scriptura* ("Scripture alone") in the early church period? Generally speaking, the idea of considering Scripture alone in isolation from the faith and practices of the church would not have come to mind. The early Christians believed that their faith and practice, like the New Testament Scriptures, traced back to the apostles. In the fifth century, however, one key leader, the bishop Vincent of Lérins, emphasized the priority and sufficiency of Scripture, but not in isolation from the history of the church.

Vincent believed that everything that the church needed was contained in Scripture. Yet in the face of false teachers also using Scripture, Vincent also believed that the church's interpretation was necessary to understand the Scripture properly: "Since the canon of Scripture is complete, and sufficient of itself for everything, and more than sufficient, what need is there to join with it the authority of the Church's interpretation? For this reason,—

because, owing to the depth of Holy Scripture, all do not accept it in one and the same sense, but one understands its words in one way, another in another; so that it seems to be capable of as many interpretations as there are interpreters."[5] In the same document he says that because of "various erroneous opinions" about Scripture, "it is therefore necessary that the interpretation of divine Scripture should be ruled according to the one standard of the Church's belief, especially in those articles on which the foundations of all Catholic doctrine rest."[6]

Vincent's principle was that the truth would be consistent with what had been believed in the church everywhere, always, and by everyone. His principle became so important for understanding Scripture that we call it the "Vincentian Canon."

> Moreover, in the Catholic Church itself, all possible care must be taken, that we hold that faith which has been believed everywhere, always, by all. For that is truly and in the strictest sense "Catholic," which, as the name itself and the reason of the thing declare, comprehends all universally. This rule we shall observe if we follow universality, antiquity, consent. We shall follow universality if we confess that one faith to be true, which the whole Church throughout the world confesses; antiquity, if we in no wise depart from those interpretations which it is manifest were notoriously held by our holy ancestors and fathers; consent, in like manner, if in antiquity itself we adhere to the consentient definitions and determinations of all, or at the least of almost all priests and doctors.[7]

Vincent's principle, then, does not speak of two sources of tradition. Gabriel Moran explains, "This is what Vincent meant by tradition: the Church's understanding by which Scripture is clarified and explained."[8] In Vincent's view, Scripture is perfect and all-sufficient, but many heresies have arisen using those Scriptures, so we need to know the proper understanding by appealing to the church's historic, universal faith. As George Tavard puts it, "Tradition provides the form in which Scripture is received by post-apostolic Christians."[9]

With few exceptions, Christians in the early period saw Scripture and apostolic tradition as one great rule of truth. By the end of the early period it had become evident that there could be contradictory or competing traditions, sometimes with each position supported by widespread acceptance and long-standing practice.[10] This caused a number of problems. Yet most

Christians, supported by evidence or despite evidence, continued to believe that these disputes would be settled, through the guidance of the Holy Spirit in the life of the church, by careful appeal to the single source, which was Scripture *and* tradition. Scripture was sufficient, they believed, but only when interpreted properly. Proper interpretation would always be consistent with what the church has taught everywhere, always, and by all. D. H. Williams points out, "From the days of the patristic church and for most of the Middle Ages, the Tradition and Scripture formed not two but one mutually inclusive authority. Doctrinal historians have referred to this symbiotic-like relationship between Scripture and the Tradition as 'co-inherence' (or 'co-incidence'), since the content of the church's confessional tradition co-inhered with the content of Scripture."[11]

MIDDLE AGES

By the dawn of the Middle Ages, the bishop of Rome was almost universally believed to have the primacy of honor, but in the West he was increasingly coming to be regarded as having ecclesial jurisdiction over other bishops as well. This was not immediate or sudden, but a gradual process over many years and through many events. Eventually the bishop of Rome, the pope, became the West's ultimate keeper of the Tradition and the ultimate interpreter of Scripture.

> *For our faith rests upon the revelation made to the apostles and prophets, who wrote the canonical books, and not on the revelations (if any such there are) made to other doctors.*
>
> **THOMAS AQUINAS**

Many factors led to this rise. Rome was the most important city in the empire, or at least in the West, and so people already had a tendency to look to Rome for leadership. The pope was believed to occupy the see of Peter, Jesus' closest apostle, or the see of Peter and Paul, the two greatest apostles. Hundreds of faithful Christians had given their lives as martyrs at Rome, so there was a sense of divine presence, or locus of divinity. In addition, medieval Christians believed that in Matthew 16:16-19 Jesus had promised to build his church upon Peter and to give Peter the keys to the kingdom of heaven. In their thinking, the kingdom was the church, and the keys were the authority to rule the church. In theological disputes and political crises people appealed to popes for support, enhancing papal authority, and several popes declared that the see of Rome was the head of the world.

Papal ascent was aided by, though not caused by, the use of the Pseudo-Isidorean Decretals, a collection of documents supposedly tracing to the collection of seventh-century archbishop Isidore of Seville, though actually they were collected or composed later. These included a number of spurious documents. Among them was the *Donation of Constantine*, forged in the eighth century, which claims to be a letter from emperor Constantine to Sylvester I, the bishop of Rome, granting him ecclesial dominion over all the West and political control over all of Italy (and, by extension, over all of the West).

So now the West had an additional layer of appeal. Popes made decisions on truth and published them with the expectation that at least the Western bishops would accept their declarations on the basis that the preeminent apostle, Peter, was resident in his successors. Sometimes the bishops obeyed, and sometimes they did not.

The Middle Ages saw a continuation of two traditions regarding the relationship of Scripture and tradition. One emphasized the sufficiency of Scripture as the final authority in the church and the source of all other traditions. The other emphasized both the written apostolic message (Scripture) and unwritten components of the apostolic message, considering both equally authoritative. By this time, there were many traditions that could not be traced to oral tradition passed down from the apostles. But all postapostolic developments were theoretically considered to fall into this category.

The Great Schism in 1054 officially divided the East and the West, when papal legates excommunicated the patriarch of Constantinople, who shortly thereafter excommunicated the pope. In territories with representatives of both regions, especially in the East, there might be competing bishops, one Eastern Orthodox and the other Roman Catholic. The Orthodox recognized the pope's primacy of honor, but not his jurisdictional preeminence.

Many medieval theologians continued to teach that Christian truth must be derived from Scripture read through the eyes of the church. Some called for a return to the meaning of Scripture by abandoning proof texting and twisted applications. John Scotus Eriugena, for example, in the ninth century taught, "In everything the authority of sacred Scripture is to be followed." Eriugena opposed proof texting to support a particular matter of speculative theology, expecting that the meaning of the Scriptures themselves should take precedence.[12] Another example is Rupert of Deutz, who in the early twelfth century taught, "Whatever may be arrived at, or concluded from arguments, outside of that Holy Scripture . . . does in no way belong to the praise and confession of almighty God," and "Whatever may be arrived at outside of the rule of the Holy Scriptures, nobody can lawfully demand from a Catholic."[13]

Other medieval theologians clearly accepted the extension of the canon of truth beyond Scripture. In the twelfth century Hugh of St. Victor said,

> All divine Scripture is contained in the two Testaments, the Old and the New. Each Testament is divided into three parts. The Old contains the Law, the Prophets, the Historians. The New contains the Gospel, the Apostles, the Fathers. . . . In the last category (*i.e.* the Fathers) the first place belongs to the Decretals which are called canonical, that is regular. Then there come the writings of the holy Fathers, of Jerome, Augustine, Ambrose, Gregory, Isidore, Origen, Bede and the other Doctors; these are innumerable. Patristic writings, however, are not counted in the text of the divine Scriptures.[14]

Here Hugh includes the Fathers in the body of Scripture, but not in the text (or canon) of Scripture. It appears that the ancient appeal to the Scriptures through the tradition in Hugh's time had taken a carefully nuanced shift to include both the text of Scripture and the writings of highly regarded doctors of the church. Hugh's own words confirm this: "Do not attempt to learn by yourself, lest, believing yourself introduced to knowledge, you be rather blinded. That introduction is to be sought for from men of doctrine and wisdom who may bring you in and open to you as you need it, with the authorities of the holy Fathers and the testimonies of the Scriptures."[15]

We see here the developing belief that the Scripture extends to items outside of itself, though the canon of Scripture does not. The canon of Scripture is closed, but the teaching of Scripture includes writings outside of the canon of Scripture, which therefore share the inspirational power of Scripture. Hugh includes these noncanonical writings as "divine Scripture." So the scholastics through the fourteenth century saw the Scriptures as the source of revelation, but they also considered the fathers as part of the living interpretation of Scripture.[16]

In the thirteenth century Thomas Aquinas made extensive use of the church fathers, but he revealed his own view of the authority and role of the fathers when he said,

> Nevertheless sacred doctrine makes use of these authorities as extrinsic and probable arguments, but properly uses the authority of canonical Scriptures as a necessary demonstration and the authority of the doctors of the Church as one that may properly be used, yet merely as probable. For our faith rests upon the revelation made to the apostles and prophets, who wrote the canonical books, and not on the revelations (if any such there are) made to other doctors.[17]

Aquinas was positive about the fathers, but with cautions, since the fathers sometimes spoke before heresies emerged and before technical language about those heresies was developed.[18]

In the fourteenth century it became more common to separate the teaching of the church from the words of Scripture. A stream of this teaching of separation had already established itself at the end of the thirteenth century. The degree or expression of this separation varied among theologians, but the assumption of a separation was clear. For example, Henry of Ghent suggested that one who puts faith in the Scripture and observes the church contradicting Scripture must choose to believe Scripture. This growing line of thought indicated that some held, at least theoretically, that the church could be wrong and a smaller group within the church could be right.[19] Others responded that the church and Scripture cannot be in disagreement, since the Holy Spirit is their common source. One example, Gerald of Bologna, taught that individuals can teach falsely, but the true church cannot. Still others in the fourteenth century wrote about a clear dichotomy between Scripture and the church. For example, Peter Aureolis, around 1315, quoting Godfrey of Fontanis, says that what the pope means in his decretals is of less authority than Scripture.[20]

Eventually two alternatives surfaced. One position taught that the church is in every way subservient to Scripture: Scripture and its meaning are the church's source. The other position taught that the Scripture thoroughly depends on the church's authority: the church is the Scripture's source. Some tried to integrate these. Marsilius of Padua in 1324, for example, taught

Christians to believe the Scripture, the councils and the fathers but to judge the fathers by their compatibility with Scripture.[21]

The primary conflict came with regard to demands and expectations of the pope. William of Ockham taught that Scripture and the doctrine of the universal church could not err and must be used to evaluate decrees of the pope. In other words, the pope and his advisors could be wrong. Guido Terreni of Perpignan (d. 1342) countered by defining heresy as any teaching that contradicted either Scripture or conciliar decisions approved by the pope. He said that the church selected the canonical Scripture and the canonical councils, so both depend upon the church's authority. Heinrich Totting of Oyta (d. 1397) went so far as to consider the pope the judge of any postapostolic teachings.[22] This is a noteworthy shift in understanding about the tradition.

In the fifteenth century the Great Papal Schism resulted in two, and at one point three, men claiming to be pope, with regional loyalty to each and regions sometimes switching loyalty. Theologians of what came to be known as the conciliar movement responded that the ecumenical council stood over the pope, and early fifteenth century councils both decreed and tried to implement this teaching. Popes generally resisted, though sometimes they submitted. Multiple popes remained, and no pope affirmed that the ecumenical council stood above the pope.

As more and more economic, nepotistic, nationalistic and worldly concerns seemed to dominate power and authority in the church, teachings and practices were introduced or maintained that seemed far distant from the teaching of Scripture and often appeared to be in direct opposition to Scripture. The power of the bishops, integral to the entire medieval system and maintained by the princes, kept this system in place for many years.

These developments in the late fourteenth and the fifteenth centuries contributed to a fairly broad call for reform in the church. But the power structure, the economic system, the social system and the absence of effective communication, among other factors, made effective reform nearly impossible. Since many bishops seemed to be primarily interested in maintaining their power and wealth, and since episcopal decisions often were based not on Scripture but rather on powerful self-interest, many Christians developed deep distrust of their local bishops and the hierarchy, collectively called the "magisterium."

Still, many believed in the supreme authority of the pope. Several late medieval teachers even taught that the pope could reverse a decree of Christ because he was acting as Christ's vicar. Johannes Andreae (d. 1348), the greatest canon lawyer of his generation, said, "The Pope . . . holds the power of God on earth: he is the vicar of him to whom the earth and the fullness of the universe belong." Panormitanus affirmed, "The pope can do whatever God can do," and "Whatever is done by the authority of the Pope is done by the authority of God."[23]

In other words, by the fifteenth century most Catholics believed that God had given the pope absolute authority over church and state. This exalting of the pope above both Scripture and tradition was a clear departure from the traditional position. George Tavard calls this "a quasi-divinization of the Pope and an 'apostolization' of a fictitious oral tradition."[24]

Reform-minded leaders looked to the Scriptures to correct what they saw as a major problem. Jean Gerson, the leading theologian of the conciliar movement, affirmed six degrees or levels of catholic truths, all belonging in different ways to sacred Scripture: (1) actual words of Scripture, (2) apostolic traditions recognized by the church, (3) postapostolic revelations, binding on those to whom revealed, (4) conclusions drawn from the above, including sacred canons, (5) conclusions only probable or containing a non-revealed premise, (6) pious truths promoting piety rather than absolute truth.[25] For Gerson, the role of tradition and ecclesiastical authority is "correlative to and ancillary to the bible as their task is to expound the bible."[26]

John Wycliffe earlier countered with the doctrine of *sola scriptura*, taught openly in *On the Truth of Sacred Scripture* in 1378. Wycliffe said, "Without a doubt, everyone ought to remain staunchly Christian in these matters, yielding to Holy Scripture, which is the Catholic faith."[27] For Wycliffe, the Scriptures have unique authority because they are the Word of God and thus reflect the divine mind.[28] Wycliffe believed that the institutional church of his day was not the primitive church, the true church, but rather an imposter laden with avarice, ignorance and abuse of power.

John Huss, who was highly influenced by the writings of Wycliffe, also asserted the primacy of Scripture over the primacy of the pope. But Huss recognized the need for proper understanding of Scripture and asserted as late as 1414 that the law of Christ includes more than the letter of Scripture because the spirit of Scripture is found in the fathers. "With God's help, we do not intend to explain Scripture otherwise than the Holy Spirit requires and than it is explained by the holy doctors to whom the Holy Spirit gave understanding."[29]

By the end of the medieval period, therefore, widely held belief about Scripture and tradition had shifted. Some still contended for ancient and early medieval belief that apostolic truth is understood through Scripture as understood properly through the church—through tradition. In the minds of many, however, Scripture and tradition were separate categories. Some held that since the church wrote and chose the Scriptures, the church stood above the Scriptures, or at least that the pope's supreme authority stood above everything else, including the Scriptures. Others held that the Scriptures were God's Word, and the church was responsible for interpreting and carrying out God's word properly. Traditions should be consistent with what Scripture teaches or allows. Everyone recognized that church leaders often abused their authority, even if they had canonical authority to do so. Nearly everyone called for reform in the church's leaders and in its members. This situation, as we will see, gave rise to the Reformation, whereby a large portion of the Western Church not only questioned but also openly rejected certain elements of the tradition.

REFORMATION PERIOD

By the beginning of the sixteenth century many leaders saw important discrepancies between Scripture and both teachings and practices of the church. They demanded change. Humanist and reform-minded thinkers called for a return to the church's source, though they

> *The Reformers opposed the authority of tradition and of the church, but only insofar as this authority usurped the authority of Scripture.*
>
> **MOISÉS SILVA**

often differed on the value of particular resources in determining the source. Some challenged the magisterium to return to Scripture and the early church. Others appealed to the doctrine of *sola scriptura*. When they did turn to the tradition, they did not see this as a shift from *sola scriptura*, because they appealed to tradition to prove that earlier Christian leaders had come to the same conclusions about the teachings of Scripture. Here we will consider a representative group of those sixteenth-century Reformers.

Desiderius Erasmus, a humanist who always remained Catholic, acknowl-edged the coherence of the church and Scripture. His own study and his pro-duction of the first critical Greek New Testament show his commitment to Scripture. Erasmus also cited the church fathers, so much so that Jan den Boeft says, "Without exaggeration it can be said that the writings—and for that matter the personalities—of the Church Fathers accompanied and even guided Erasmus' career."[30] So Erasmus, who nearly always cites the early church fathers, returns to the source—for him the early church—emphasizing as one the Scriptures and the early church's understanding of those Scriptures.

Martin Luther, most famous for the doctrine of justification by faith alone but also committed to *sola scriptura*, often cited the church fathers, espe-cially to disprove the right of the pope to dominate the church. Here he cited Scripture, but he also cited the Council of Nicaea, Jerome, Chrysostom, Au-gustine and even Gregory the Great. Yet Luther discounted the opinions of the fathers when they appeared to disagree with Scripture. This willingness to cite and to correct the early church shows his appreciation for the fathers and his rejection of the notion of a pristine early church.[31] He praised or criticized the fathers depending upon how their teachings matched his own understanding of Scripture and his own theological paradigm. We should note that Luther included the Apostles' Creed in his *Large Catechism* and *Small Catechism*. But he included the Apostles' Creed because he believed that it accurately reflects Scripture. For Luther, all church teaching must conform to Scripture, as least as he understood Scripture in accord with the doctrine of justification by faith alone.[32]

The Lutherans in 1580 gathered key documents that supported their un-derstanding of Luther's theology, with few exceptions, into the *Book of Concord*. While affirming the Scriptures, it was by no means only Scripture, but Scripture plus the Apostles' Creed, the Athanasian Creed, the Nicene Creed and several documents by Luther, Melanchthon and the leaders who produced the collection. Many of these documents make reference to the early church fathers. Yet they believed that they were still affirming *sola scriptura*, for they believed that these additional creeds were accurate expla-nations of the one reliable source of revelation: Scripture.

Although John Calvin considered the Scriptures to be the inspired Word of God, he also read and quoted the early church fathers extensively. In the

1536 edition of the *Institutes* he spoke of "the tyranny of human tradition,"[33] but he also spoke positively about early church creeds. In his *Reply to Cardinal Sadoleto* in 1539 he said, "Our agreement with antiquity is far closer than yours, but that all we have attempted has been to renew that ancient form of the church."[34] F. F. Bruce asserts, "Calvin himself was no mean patristic scholar and adduces patristic evidence freely and copiously in support of his arguments."[35]

The mainline Reformers, therefore, did not reject the tradition, but rather the abuse of tradition that exalted the papacy and the magisterium above the Scripture or threatened the doctrine of justification by faith as they understood it. In fact, they often appealed to the tradition to justify their own reading of Scripture. Moisés Silva points out, "It would not have occurred to them to interpret the Scripture as autonomous individuals. On the contrary, they were most forceful in their interpretations when they were convinced that they were giving expression to the truth *given to the church*."[36]

Among the Radical Reformers, Anabaptist leaders such as Conrad Grebel, Balthasar Hübmaier and Menno Simons openly appealed for a church separate from state control, influence and interference. They held Scripture as the authority, but they also turned to the early church fathers to substantiate their understanding of Scripture. Although Anabaptists did not see the church fathers as a continuation of God's revelation, they valued teachings of the church fathers as the historical, ancient understanding of the truth of Scripture.

Both mainline and Anabaptist Reformers, then, asserted the doctrine of *sola scriptura* either explicitly or implicitly. At the same time, they cited the early church fathers to support their own understandings of Scripture or to disagree with those same fathers when they believed that the Scriptures taught otherwise. They rebuked the magisterium when they believed that the hierarchy was ignoring or contradicting Scripture. As they articulated their theology, they quoted the fathers to evidence their own understanding or to counter abuses that they perceived in others. In other words, both mainline and Anabaptist Reformers believed that they were placing Scripture above all else, including the tradition, the magisterium and the pope. Timothy George says it well: "Overwhelmingly, however, the Reformers saw themselves as part of the ongoing Catholic tradition, indeed as the legitimate bearers of it. This was seen in numerous ways; here I shall mention only three:

1) their sense of continuity with the church of the preceding centuries; 2) their embrace of the ecumenical orthodoxy of the early church; 3) their desire to read the Bible in dialogue with the exegetical tradition of the church."[37]

We must note that some Radical Reformers took a more extreme or radical view of *sola scriptura*. Many denied the historic, orthodox teachings of the church, such as the Trinity, the dual natures of Christ, and the personality of the Holy Spirit. This nonorthodox wing of the Reformation resulted in a number groups and positions too extensive to delineate here.[38] Their efforts, however, demonstrate the point that autonomous or parochial reading of the Scriptures without accountability can produce dangerous teachings. Once again we see the ever-present need for each generation of contemporary Christians to include the community of the faithful, both past and present, as they seek to determine the meaning of the Scriptures.

Roman Catholics who countered the Reformers took several positions. Some, like Sylvester Prierias, strongly affirmed the pope's authority over Scripture and demanded that one affirm this in order to be considered orthodox. Others, like Johann von Eck, affirmed conciliar and papal authority but linked them to Scripture and subjected them to the authority of Scripture. But Eck expected equal obedience to the both the Scripture and the non-apostolic writings authenticated by the church. According to George Tavard, "Eck had started with the superiority of Scripture over the Church. He ends at the opposite pole: superiority of the Church over Scripture." Johann Cochläus, the most prolific writer against Luther, placed the church over the Scriptures, since the church determines what is Scripture.[39]

The Roman Catholic Church responded to the Protestant doctrine of *sola scriptura* by making a dual appeal to Scripture and tradition, seen clearly at the Council of Trent. Whether Trent saw these as two sources or simply as two means has been recently argued. Interestingly, the original draft said, "The truth of God is contained partly in written books and partly in unwritten traditions." After some discussion, the final decree omitted the "partly" language. Some contemporary Roman Catholics argue that the prelates intentionally avoided defining Scripture and tradition as separate sources.[40] That may have been the intent of the few who pushed for the revised language. But others say that Trent carefully defined oral tradition as a separate source from Scripture, since the prelates overwhelmingly held to this position and exegetes of the council later affirmed this position. They contend that only their position allows Catholic doctrines not addressed in Scripture—such as Mariology, sacramentology, canonicity—and that the church established these doctrines on the basis of extrabiblical tradition.[41] For this reason, and because there is no doubt that the post-Tridentine theologians stressed the equality of tradition and Scripture as opposed to the Reformers, the two-source position dominated Roman Catholic understanding for four centuries.[42]

As later Reformers developed their theology of Scripture, they described the tradition as arising from human—meaning fallen and faulty—authority. Not only was tradition not binding on Christians, but also tradition itself was suspect. They affirmed the Scriptures as apostolic and inspired. Tradition, on the other hand, was nonapostolic and either entirely human or so fraught with human self-centeredness and sin as to make the divine portion indistinguishable from the human, at least with enough certainty to be trustworthy.

The Reformation brought another significant shift in understanding. Whereas Christians historically had looked to the pope and to the bishops for proper understanding of Scripture and tradition, now many Christians considered the pope and the bishops to be the antithesis of Christian truth, some even identifying the pope as the antichrist. The notion of one church in one world, still held by East and West even after their separation in 1054, gave way to a variety of denominational commitments, depending for authority upon leading theologians and the support of their political princes. Protestants still appealed to the tradition, but many viewed the tradition with a strong sense of suspicion.

SINCE THE REFORMATION

After a century of religious wars and persecution, the Enlightenment exalted the individual and personal autonomous reason above any competing source of truth, repudiating earlier sources of authority. All assertions of truth must be substantiated from reasoned evidence considered by the rationalists to be unbiased and objective. Beliefs unsustainable from rational proof or investigation were to be rejected. Any form of tradition besides

> *The most severe attack on the concept of tradition . . . was launched in the Enlightenment.*
>
> **STANLEY GRENZ AND JOHN FRANKE**

scientific, autonomous proof was not only suspect, but almost certainly false and by its very nature hostile to real truth. The religious experiences and thinking of historical figures were therefore not as important as contemporary experience.

This is paradigmatic of what came to be known as "modernity," to be sure. It developed first in European universities and spread almost immediately to the United States. Soon scholars in Christian circles adopted Enlightenment assumptions and used Enlightenment methods. For many, this theology took the form of classic theological liberalism. Classic theological liberals became committed to philosophical idealism, rejecting any appeal to the "supernatural" or "metaphysical" as unrepeatable and therefore unprovable. So ideas about the supernatural were unreliable and therefore irrelevant.

This was a new brand of distaste for Christian tradition. No longer was tradition suspect because it did not match the Scriptures. Now, tradition and the Scriptures were equally suspect, even dangerous, for neither could be empirically verified. Both claimed to derive inspired truth from a source other than independent human reason.

Suddenly everything traditional was up for grabs. Historic doctrines of Christianity, including the unique deity of Jesus and the vicarious atonement, were dismissed as meeting the needs of an earlier time. Ideas about "supernatural" revelation or any other aspect of the supernatural working within the tradition were discredited. Accounts of supernatural events from Scripture were regarded as religious myth designed primarily to teach an important lesson. Furthermore, the religious experiences of historical figures were not as important as contemporary experience. The rise of evolutionary theory in the nineteenth century gave modernists further reason to believe that their superior development and thinking were "correcting" the fallacies or the naiveté of past generations.

Although the study of tradition and the Scriptures was not rejected, any a priori notion of divine inspiration or the supernatural was openly rejected. Enlightenment liberals purposed to liberate historical study of the Bible and early Christianity from ecclesiastical dogma. According to Grenz and Franke, this "provided a powerful acid that effectively dissolved the role of tradition in theology in Protestant circles and increasingly among Roman Catholic modernists as well."[43] The study of Scripture and Christian history simply as academic exercise began to dominate the universities. Many considered the church unnecessary to the study of either.

By the nineteenth century these Enlightenment or modernist assumptions about truth so permeated studies of the Bible and religion that the church life and personal commitment of the scholar in the university was considered irrelevant to his or her ability to exegete Scripture and explain religion. In many Western universities the history and tradition of the church, including the Scriptures, became simply objects of study rather than aids to spiritual insight and understanding.

This severance of Scripture and tradition from religious studies can have extreme consequences. Even avowed atheists, for example, have been promoted to positions of biblical and theological scholarship in European and American universities. Yet this severance is exactly what many continue to recommend. Several years ago at the American Society of Church History meeting it was suggested that Christians be excluded from the study of Christian history because they cannot be objective. The implicit, though unstated, assumption was that non-Christians could be objective.

Nineteenth-century American liberal theologians stressed divine immanence, helping to spark transcendentalism, an important part the American liberal theological tradition. They affirmed a mystical spiritual union between the divine and humanity, inherent in every human person. God created human beings with everything that they needed already innate. The human spiritual task was for each person to think or meditate in order to experience the already immanent deity and the already innate spirituality. By the late nineteenth century some suggested that the social mission of the church was to build God's "kingdom"—God's rule on earth through benevolent human leaders and government.

Although Enlightenment thinking revolutionized the approach to truth in the West, strong streams of faith and learning remained or arose that did not reject tradition. Seventeenth- and eighteenth-century Roman Catholic theologians followed the Tridentine understanding of two sources of revelation for the church: Scripture and tradition. Some nineteenth-century Roman Catholic theologians began to emphasize the tradition as a set of ideas contained in early patristic writings.

Many Protestant theologians continued to focus on the doctrine of *sola scriptura*, though all the while appealing to the writings of the early church fathers and subsequent theologians to substantiate their doctrinal positions. For some, this was more intentional than for others. In the eighteenth century, for example, John Wesley proposed what Albert C. Outler later called the "Wesleyan quadrilateral."[44] Wesley appealed to Scripture, tradition, reason and experience. The United Methodist Church's *Book of Discipline* explains, "Wesley believed that the living core of the Christian faith was revealed in Scripture, illumined by tradition, vivified in personal experience, and confirmed by reason. Scripture [however] is primary, revealing the Word of God 'so far as it is necessary for our salvation.'"[45] Hundreds of other Protestant scholars affirmed *sola scriptura* while also standing firmly on traditional language and practice to affirm their positions.

In response to the Third World Conference on Faith and Order in 1952, a theological commission on "Tradition and Traditions" was set up. They submitted their final report at the Fourth World Conference on Faith and Order in 1963 at Montreal, which issued the document *Scripture, Tradition and Traditions*.[46] The document gave working definitions for "tradition," "traditions," and "the Tradition." The first, "tradition," is the general category and includes both the process of transmission (*traditio*) and what is transmitted (*res traditia*). This first category includes two terms that I used above: "tradition" (the general category) and "traditioning" (the process of transmission). The second term from Montreal, "traditions," includes various patterns of beliefs and practices by which congregations, denominations, and wider groups of churches acquired their distinctive qualities and characteristics. The third Montreal term, "the Tradition," is the history by which God's people live. It includes Israel's history, centers on Christ's history, and continues in the church's history. Its norm is Scripture. Although broader than my use of "Tradition" or "tradition" described above, this targets the same concept of the universal, authoritative norm for the church.

At Vatican II the ecumenical council's Roman Catholic leaders described a close connection between Scripture and tradition, "flowing from the same divine wellspring" and merging "into a unity." Scripture and tradition are "one sacred deposit of the word of God."[47]

The declarations by the Fourth World Conference on Faith and Order, on the one hand, and by Vatican II, on the other, both in the early 1960s, sparked much discussion about potential islands of convergence. Since then we have seen fresh interest among Roman Catholics in studying Scripture, and among Protestants in studying the tradition.

RECENT INTEREST IN CHRISTIAN TRADITION AMONG BIBLE-FOCUSED BELIEVERS

Since the 1970s there have been significant signs of interest in the value of Christian history, or tradition, among Bible-focused Christians. In 1978 the first edition of Richard Foster's *Celebration of Discipline: The Path to Spiritual Growth* stirred a love of the ancient spiritual disciplines among believers young and old.[48] About the same time, Robert Webber's *Common Roots: A Call to Evangelical Maturity* challenged evangelicals to study the second through the fifth centuries, particularly the second century, to gain insights that they needed to recover.[49] Peter Gillquist and former evangelicals began talks to unite with the Antiochene Church, an ancient Eastern Orthodox communion. Forty-five evangelical academics penned "The Chicago Call: An Appeal to Evangelicals," confessing that they had "often lost the fullness of our Christian heritage, too readily assuming that the Scripture and the Spirit make us independent of the past." They affirmed, "We dare not move beyond the biblical limits of the gospel; but we cannot be fully evangelical without recognizing our need to learn from other times and movements concerning the whole meaning of the gospel."[50]

> The challenge for us is to return to the Christian tradition. For here is a faith that, like a tapestry, weaves everything in and out of the main thread, Christ.
>
> **ROBERT WEBBER**

The 1980s brought further indicators of change. Ken Curtis began the magazine *Christian History*, with each issue focusing on an historical personality or theme with a popular audience in mind. Renamed *Christian History and Biography* in 2003, this periodical reaches over forty thousand readers, mostly evangelicals. Thomas Oden began challenging liberals and evangelicals to spark deep renewal by returning to the classical tradition of

Christianity, meaning to the early church fathers. In 1988 Richard Foster founded Renovaré, a renewal ministry that examines the church's rich heritage in order to develop spirituality among Bible-focused Christians. This spurred what Chris Armstrong describes as an evangelical identity crisis, citing Richard Lovelace's challenge to evangelicals to "research into the historical roots of evangelicalism," but including in those evangelical roots the great leaders of the early and medieval church.[51]

In his 1990 autobiographical essay in the *Christian Century* Thomas Oden announced to both liberals and conservatives his shift from liberalism to a new agenda, affirming, "No political project is more urgent for society than the recovery of classic Christian consciousness through the direct address of the texts of Scripture and Tradition."[52] The same year, in *After Modernity . . . What? Agenda for Theology*, Oden declared, "The agenda for theology at the end of the twentieth century . . . is to begin to prepare the postmodern Christian community for its third millennium by returning again to the careful study and respectful following of the central tradition of classical Christian exegesis."[53]

The last decade shows a swelling emphasis. D. H. Williams, professor at Baylor University, has written several books calling for evangelicals and free-church Christians to study the tradition, particularly the patristic, early church tradition, as part of their own heritage. Robert Webber's *Ancient-Future Faith* and its sequels sparked further study. Thomas Oden founded the Ancient Christian Commentary on Scripture, a multivolume series providing verse-by-verse commentary on each book of Scripture from the early church fathers.[54]

Today many Bible-focused Christians find themselves drawn to the traditions and practices of the early Christians. As they observe differences among believers from nearly every Christian heritage who affirm the inspiration of Scripture, they are asking where they can turn to find answers to their questions. In the past Protestants have consulted with their trusted exegetes, but a growing number see the shortcomings of studying only those who already agree with them theologically and culturally. The consensus of the faithful—the *consensus fidelium*—seems to be the best alternative. But who should be included in the consensus? More and more Bible-focused Christians are expanding that consensus to include Christians from other contemporary cultures and from centuries past. These Bible-focused Christians are not questioning the reliability or divine inspiration of Scripture; rather, they are questioning their own finite ability to understand what God has revealed without the help of the other Christians.

As these Bible-focused Christians read the great teachers of the church's past, they see gaps in their own theology being filled, augmented or explained. Hungry to experience God through the historic paths of spiritual formation, they are choosing to sit at the feet of the great spiritual masters across the centuries.

Many young believers enjoy what is often called "contemporary worship" but fear that they are getting little more than a disguised version of their culture in Christian language, so they begin to con-

> Hungry to experience God, many Christians are choosing to sit at the feet of the great spiritual masters across the centuries.

sider alternatives. They enjoy raising their hands, singing songs of adoration to God, and seeing PowerPoint and video clips, but they are no longer impressed. They are not sure what is missing, but they want something more mysterious, deeper, more foundational to who they are. They long for an encounter with the mysterious God, who cannot be defined in consumer-oriented techniques and self-improvement language. Many hope to add historical or liturgical elements to their worship, sensing community with other contemporary Christians but also with historic Christians.

In my own experience of preaching and teaching I find Bible-focused Christians hungry for doctrinal instruction. They have tired of self-help sermons that focus on getting out of debt, communicating better with family members, and feeling better about themselves. A few are seeking logical proofs and information, but most are not. Instead, they want deeper doctrinal explanations that help them know God better and relate God to others.

Some are curious about the spiritual and doctrinal foundations of their own church; they appreciate pastors' opinions, key passages and doctrines of their faith group, and recently popular methods, but they feel instinctively that there must be more. They want to identify with believers and worshipers across the planet and across the centuries.

No doubt other magnets are also drawing Bible-focused Christians of nearly every age to want more than they already experience in church. This is not a rejection of what they already experience, for they have found joy in knowing and worshiping Christ. But they are yearning for more. They are not fully satisfied; they want the rest of the story. As Augustine prayed, "Our hearts are restless until they find rest in you,"[55] so their hearts are still restless, and they long to know more deeply the transcendent, mysterious, eternal God, whom they instinctively recognize is their friend, but far greater than a friend.

At the same time, many Bible-focused believers continue to see the tradition of the church as a threat to authentic Christianity. They know the many abuses of the truth that have occurred in the church's history, especially those that led to the Protestant Reformation. They fear that historical theology, the church's tradition, stands opposed to the authority of Scripture. Their love for God and Scripture rejects anything that might stray from God's divine Word.

How Do We Understand the Tradition Today?

Stefan came with his college roommate to worship with our church. He loved the sense of community among our young adults, and after a few weeks he began asking questions. He had grown up in a Greek Orthodox church. He wanted to know why our church's vocabulary, leadership and emphases were very different. As fellow collegians tried to help, their explanations seemed to miss his intent. Our associate minister, however, was able to bridge the gap. How? Because he knew how Stefan's church approached and valued the tradition—because he knew Christian history—he could "translate" our church life into concepts and vocabulary that Stefan already knew.

We have just come through twenty centuries on the well-traveled path of how believers have understood the Christian tradition. We have come to the present, where the church holds a variety of perspectives. We have seen that all Christians embrace tradition, though at differing levels. Some elements of tradition, such as the core canon of Scripture and the orthodox doctrines of God and Christ, are common to nearly all Christians. Most appeal to denominational distinctives that arose in a particular time and place. Tradition is inevitable, for everyone appeals to tradition. In that sense, contemporary Christians embody the Christian tradition.

Yet, the way faith groups value the tradition and how they approach the tradition vary significantly. Some faith groups have been quite intentional about their commitment to tradition. They appeal to carefully crafted doctrinal statements that explain their official positions. Other faith groups,

cautious or even suspicious of the tradition, embrace tradition less intentionally. Some have official doctrinal statements that clarify their positions.
Others avoid official documents altogether, often turning to descriptions
written by respected leaders to understand their perspectives.

FAITH GROUPS AFFIRMING APOSTOLIC SUCCESSION

Some churches believe that the apostles, through the laying on of hands,
passed on their apostolic authority to bishops, who in turn passed it on to
the next generation of bishops, all the way until today. This is called "apostolic succession," the teaching that today's living bishops stand in the place
and authority of the apostles. We first look at how the largest representatives of this position—Eastern Orthodox, Roman Catholics, Anglicans—
understand Christian tradition.

Eastern Orthodox

Eastern Orthodox Christians understand the Tradition of the church to
be one, seamless whole. Scripture is not a separate source from Tradition.
Scripture is part of Tradition, within the Tradition. All of God's revelation
is word, or *logos*, from God. This reve-
lation has been given to the church by
the Holy Spirit through various means:
the life and ministry of Jesus, the
apostles in writing (Scripture), the
apostles orally, and the universal life
and practices of church.

> Loyalty to tradition means
> not only concord with the
> past but in a certain sense
> freedom from the past. . . .
> Tradition is the constant
> abiding of the Spirit. . . .
> Tradition is a charismatic,
> not an historical principle.
>
> **GEORGES FLOROVSKY**

The fact that most Eastern Orthodox
scholars describe the Tradition as one
body of teaching, not separating
Scripture and tradition, is evident from
the statements of leading Orthodox
teachers. Vladimir Lossky writes, "Whether it be the Scriptures, preaching,
or the 'apostles' traditions guarded in silence,' the same word λόγος or λόγια
can be applied equally to all that constitutes expression of the revealed
Truth."[1] Timothy Ware agrees: "But in reality there is only one source, since
Scripture exists *within* Tradition."[2]

Occasionally an Eastern Orthodox scholar describes Scripture and tradition as separate sources. Even then it seems that this use of terminology is decided by context or by audience. The inherent nature of the unity of the Tradition, sourced from the Holy Spirit, is assumed. Constantine Callinicos is one exception, though his language could be accommodation to a Western audience: "As however those things which God revealed to man were promulgated either from mouth to mouth, or by the written word, we say, therefore that Christianity has two sources: the oral Divine Revelation or Holy Tradition, and the written Divine Revelation or Holy Scripture."[3]

Although Eastern Orthodox scholars agree about what the content of the Tradition includes, the way they describe the Tradition differs. Lossky, for example, is careful to frame Tradition not as content, but rather as the life of the Holy Spirit in the church: "[Tradition] is not the content of revelation, but the light that reveals it; it is not the word, but the living breath which makes the words heard at the same time as the silence from which it came; it is not the Truth, but a communication of the Spirit of Truth, outside which the Truth cannot be received."[4]

Others do speak of Tradition primarily as content. For example, Timothy Ware is specific in describing the Tradition's content:

> Christian Tradition . . . is the faith and practice which Jesus Christ imparted to the Apostles, and which since the Apostles' time has been handed down from generation to generation in the Church. But to an Orthodox Christian, Tradition means something more concrete and specific than this. It means the books of the Bible; it means the Creed; it means the decrees of the Ecumenical Councils and the writings of the Fathers; it means the Canons, the Service Books, the Holy Icons—in fact, the whole system of doctrine, Church government, worship, spirituality and art which Orthodoxy has articulated over the ages.[5]

John Meyendorff affirms the totality of Scripture as foundational for the Tradition:

> These are the basic elements of the Orthodox conception of Scripture and Tradition. Scripture includes the *totality* of the apostolic witness and nothing can be added by way of completing our knowledge of the person of Jesus, his work, and the salvation which he brought us; but this written witness regarding Christ was not launched in a void . . . but was given to a

community which had been founded by these apostles and which had received the same Spirit. This community is the Church, which has received
the Scriptures and acknowledges in it the Truth, fixed in its limits for all
time, and interprets this corpus of writings with the help of the Spirit. This
interpretation and its acknowledgement are what is known as Tradition.[6]

Likely Ware, Lossky and Meyendorff would affirm one another's statements, so the noteworthy differences in expression are not contradictory.

The particular elements of the Tradition are not valued with the same
weight. All come from the Holy Spirit, but some take precedence over the
others when interpreting the Tradition. "A unique pre-eminence belongs to
the Bible, to the Creed, and to the doctrinal definitions of the Ecumenical
Councils. These the Orthodox accept as absolute and unchanging—they
cannot be cancelled or revised. The other parts of the Tradition do not have
quite the same authority."[7]

So Eastern Orthodox Christians see the Scripture as being primary, but
not exclusive. They believe that the truth of the Holy Spirit finds expanded
expression in oral tradition, especially the councils and the fathers, for several
reasons, among them: (1) the church and the gospel existed before the
Scripture, so even Scripture is the product of oral tradition; (2) since there is
no purely objective view, oral tradition is for hermeneutics both inevitable
and necessary; (3) liturgical precedent demonstrates the need for noncanonical tradition; (4) the theological methods of the church fathers support
the need for oral tradition.[8] At the same time, this also means that only the
church can properly understand the truth of the Scripture, for "the Scriptures
are not archives of the truth but its living body," and "the Scriptures can be
possessed only within the church, which is the unique body of Christ."[9]

Decisions by later councils—councils that come after the seven ecumenical councils—can have ecumenical authority, if they are accepted by
the rest of the church.[10] Eastern Orthodoxy lists the thirteen doctrinal statements since the seventh ecumenical council in 787 that they accept as having
ecumenical authority.[11] In practice, "later councils" are those held by the
Eastern Orthodox. This excludes or ignores Roman Catholic ecumenical
councils after 1054, since they were conducted without Eastern Orthodox
bishops by Roman Catholic bishops who were excommunicated from Constantinople. It also excludes Roman Catholic councils where Orthodox

bishops attended and contributed but did not vote (such as Basel-Ferrara-Florence [1431–1439] and Vatican II [1962–1965]).

The teachings of the fathers can also have ecumenical authority, but again, only as those teachings are accepted universally among the Eastern Orthodox. The fathers are valuable not because they provide propositional statements, but because they provide ecumenical community. "The Orthodox must not simply know and quote the Fathers; they must enter more deeply into the inner spirit of the Fathers and acquire a 'Patristic mind,' and must treat the Fathers not merely as relics from the past, but as living witnesses and contemporaries."[12]

The liturgy, for the Eastern Orthodox, is divine in origin and content. Only four liturgies can be used.[13] These are considered among of the doctrines of the church, though in a category whose teachings are not formally defined, yet are held universally and binding upon all. "This inner Tradition 'handed down to us in a mystery' is preserved above all in the Church worship."[14] For the Orthodox, this includes not only the words of the service, but also the gestures and actions (baptism, anointing with oil, sign of the cross, etc.).

Canon law—applying ecumenical teaching to practical life situations—is part of the Tradition, but only in a relative and not an unalterable sense.[15]

Icons are also part of the Tradition. For the Eastern Orthodox, icons are two-dimensional paintings that represent realities far greater than the actual icons; they not simply religious pictures designed to arouse memories or emotions in the beholder. An icon is "one of the ways whereby God is revealed to us."[16]

While Protestants often contrast themselves with Eastern Orthodox and Roman Catholics grouped together, Eastern Orthodox contrast themselves with Roman Catholics and Protestants grouped together. Aleksei Khomyakov sees Protestants as crypto-Catholics operating within the same Western paradigm but heading in different directions.[17] This is explained by Meyendorff, who says, "Ultimately, the conflict between East and West resides in two conflicting spiritual perceptions of tradition."[18] The assumption is that Roman Catholics and Protestants seek authority from outside the church to ground their faith and practice. Meyendorff says that Eastern Orthodoxy makes its unique contribution by insisting upon the auxiliary character of authority, since "it is not authority which makes the Church to be the Church, but the Spirit alone, acting in the Church as body, realizing the sacramental presence of Christ Himself among men and in men."[19]

Eastern Orthodox, therefore, believe that the West has created an artificial antagonism or irreconcilable separation between Scripture and tradition, which in turn inserts a hermeneutical divide between Scripture and the church, with Scripture standing above the church.[20] In contrast, the Orthodox believe that "the Church . . . stands mystically first and is fuller than Scripture."[21] So for the Orthodox, Tradition does not add to the message, but rather Tradition *is* the message. The contents of the Tradition other than Scripture are not some kind of additional revelation, but rather are "expressions of the same faith in different forms."[22]

Roman Catholics

For nearly four centuries after the Council of Trent (1545–1563), nearly all scholars understood the Roman Catholic Church to teach that there are two sources of authority in the church: Scripture and tradition. As discussed earlier, the idea that Scripture and tradition were separate became widespread by the end of the Middle Ages. Many in the church were suspicious of the tradition, at least the tradition that seemed to grant unfettered power to the pope. The Reformers responded with *sola scriptura*, denying any authority beyond the Scriptures, including the tradition of the church. The Council of Trent later met to reform the church and to refine and reaffirm the doctrine of the Roman Catholic Church.

> *Sacred tradition, sacred Scripture, and the teaching authority of the Church, in accord with God's most wise design, are so linked and joined together that one cannot stand without the others, and that all together and each in its own way under the action of the one Holy Spirit contribute effectively to the salvation of souls.*
>
> **DEI VERBUM, VATICAN II**

The prelates at Trent believed that *sola scriptura* opposed the teachings of the church throughout the centuries. They said that the marked diversity in doctrines among the Protestants gave further evidence that the church must provide proper interpretation of the Scripture. They also believed that the Holy Spirit worked through the life of the church. In *Decree Concerning the Canonical Scriptures* they taught,

> These truths and rules are contained in the written books and in the unwritten traditions, which, received by the Apostles from the mouth of Christ Himself, or from the Apostles themselves, the Holy Ghost dictating, have come down to us, transmitted as it were from hand to hand. Following, then, the examples of the orthodox Fathers, it receives and venerates with a feeling of piety and reverence all the books both of the Old and New Testaments, since one God is the author of both; also the traditions, whether they relate to faith or to morals, as having been dictated either orally by Christ or by the Holy Ghost, and preserved in the Catholic Church in unbroken succession.[23]

God is the source of Scripture, but God is also the source of the church's traditions, for they were delivered to the church by Jesus Christ or by the Holy Spirit. Yves Congar summarizes, "It is this conviction, this doctrine—that the Holy Spirit dwells in the Church, that he is at work in the most decisive acts of its life—that the Council of Trent continually refers to as a guide in establishing the authority of traditions. Although the Council . . . makes no distinction between *tradition* and *traditions*, its position can be expressed as follows: the traditions are guaranteed by Tradition, whose principle is the Holy Spirit."[24]

Little changed in the Roman Catholic understanding of tradition and Scripture for the next three centuries. In fact, Vatican I (1869–1870) simply affirmed the decision at Trent by quoting that decision. In the twentieth century, however, scholars began to disagree over the implications of Trent's declaration.

In the decades preceding Vatican II (1962–1965) Roman Catholic theologians described their understanding of the relationship of Scripture and tradition in a range of expression. Some, like Ludwig Ott and Henry Denzinger, argued for tradition and Scripture as two sources of revelation. Others, like John Henry Newman, Joseph Ratzinger, Yves Congar and Louis Bouyer, understood tradition as the interpretation of the revealed truths of Scripture, though they also believed this interpretation to be guided by the Holy Spirit and therefore infallible.[25] Avery Dulles states, "The relationship, therefore, is not linear but rather circular. Revelation gives rise to tradition and Scripture, but Scripture and tradition, in turn, transmit revelation and make it resound in the minds and hearts of believers today."[26] So when the prelates met for Vatican II, they were ready to clarify the church's teaching on Scripture and tradition.

After much deliberation, Vatican II declared the church's teaching in *Dogmatic Constitution on Divine Revelation*, commonly referred to by its Latin name, *Dei Verbum*. Chapter 2, "The Transmission of Divine Revelation," teaches that God revealed and guaranteed the transmission of truth, through the apostles and through the bishops as their successors. God preserves this truth through inspired books and through a line of preachers. The Holy Spirit develops tradition, and the church fathers' words bear witness to tradition's living presence. There is "a close connection and communication between sacred tradition and sacred Scripture." Both flow "from the same divine wellspring" and "merge into a unity." Scripture is God's word in writing, inspired by the Holy Spirit, entrusted to the apostles' successors to preserve, explain and disseminate.

The relationship between Scripture and tradition is explained further. "Consequently it is not from sacred Scripture alone that the Church draws her certainty about everything which has been revealed." Both "are to be accepted and venerated with the same sense of devotion and reverence." Authentic interpretation, written or handed on, "has been entrusted exclusively to the living teaching office of the Church." The teaching is encapsulated in one very clear statement: "Sacred tradition and sacred Scripture form one sacred deposit of the word of God, which is committed to the Church."[27]

Dei Verbum is therefore a bonding of the two preconciliar perspectives. While affirming God as the single source of the divinely revealed word, it describes Scripture and tradition as two means God uses to mediate this revelation. Furthermore, God has overseen the process of tradition to guarantee the truth in full integrity throughout history, whether through prophets, apostles or bishops in apostolic succession. So Scripture and tradition cannot be in conflict, for they are the same word of God. They are to be equally valued because they spring from one source and merge as a single deposit of God's word. Furthermore, authentic interpretation of this word of God is entrusted exclusively to the living teaching office of the church. This means that tradition, Scripture and the church's teaching authority are so linked that one cannot stand without the others. Together they are the Tradition.

More recently, the *Catechism of the Catholic Church* simply affirms the teachings of Vatican II by quoting *Dei Verbum*, with occasional clarifications.[28] The catechism carefully differentiates between Tradition and traditions: "Tradition is to be distinguished from the various theological, disciplinary, liturgical, or devotional traditions, born in the local churches over time. These are the particular forms, adapted to different places and times, in which the great Tradition is expressed. In the light of Tradition, these traditions can be retained, modified or even abandoned under the guidance of the Church's magisterium."[29] Note that later the catechism uses "magisterium" for *Dei Verbum*'s "the teaching office of the Church."[30]

Before and after Vatican II a deep trend toward the Bible has made profound impact on Roman Catholic theology. All Roman Catholics, lay and clergy alike, are encouraged to study the Scriptures, for they are one very important means for the word of God. Tradition is the other means. Both are properly understood, however, only through the teaching office of the church. This leaves only one vehicle for understanding divine revelation: the church's traditions as understood through the magisterium.[31]

Anglicans

Anglicans, including Episcopalians, see themselves as the "middle way" (*via media*) between Roman Catholics and Protestants. Anglicanism resembles Roman Catholicism in that it affirms apostolic succession, places a strong emphasis on hierarchy, and holds sacraments in high regard. Anglicanism resembles Protestantism in its appeal to Scripture as the highest earthly authority and the judge of tradition, expecting faith and practice to be allowable from Scripture.

> *[The Anglican] conception of authority is not single-stranded but the three-fold cord, not easily broken, of Scripture and tradition and reason.*
>
> **J. A. T. ROBINSON**

The Church of England separated from the Roman Catholic Church in 1534 when Parliament declared the Act of Supremacy, recognizing the English monarch, then Henry VIII, as the earthly leader of the Church in England. This was repealed in 1553 when Roman Catholic monarch Mary became queen. In 1559, the year after Elizabeth I became queen, Parliament issued another Act of Supremacy reasserting the English monarch's earthly leadership the Church of England. In 1563 Parliament declared the *Thirty-Nine Articles of Religion* to be the official doctrine of the Church of England.

Today the Church of England defines its system of belief in the *Canons of the Church of England*. These canons affirm that both the *Thirty-Nine Articles of Religion* and the *Book of Common Prayer* are "agreeable to the Word of God" and may be correctly followed. Furthermore, the "ordinal" (directions for consecrating clergy) and the Anglican form of church government "are not repugnant to the word of God." Finally, "The doctrine of the Church of England is grounded in the Holy Scriptures, and in such teachings of the ancient Fathers and Councils of the Church as are agreeable to the said Scriptures."[32]

These documents—the *Canons of the Church of England*, the *Thirty-Nine Articles of Religion*, the *Book of Common Prayer*—form the official basis of doctrine and practice for the Church of England. With slight modifications, the Anglican family of churches throughout the world affirms these documents.

Anglicans, therefore, believe that "infallibility always resides in the Word of God itself," and "there are no official church authorities nor official church pronouncements that as such can claim infallible and absolute authority."[33] So the Scriptures are foundational, the first line of appeal. At the same time, Anglicans also affirm tradition, which "is grounded in and nourished by the Scriptures."[34] This tradition includes decrees of councils of the undivided church, as well as hymns, devotional books, lives of saints, writings of theologians, accounts of martyrdom, and so forth. "When Anglicanism appeals to tradition it does not mean that the latter is a separate source placed alongside or above Scripture. However, when there is question of the well-considered judgment regarding the intention of Scripture in respect to the forms which church life gradually accepted, especially during the first centuries, then tradition alone can make plain how God's word has functioned from the beginning in the practice of the Church."[35]

The Church of England's historic position on tradition, particularly Scripture and tradition, is based on articles 6 and 20 of the *Thirty-Nine Articles*. Article 6 affirms, "Holy Scripture containeth all things necessary to salvation: so that whatsoever is not read thererin, nor may be proved thereby, is not to be required of any man, that it should be believed as an article of the Faith, or be thought requisite or necessary to salvation." Article 20 teaches, "The Church hath power to decree Rites or Ceremonies, and authority in Controversies of Faith: And yet it is not lawful for the Church to ordain any thing that is contrary to God's word written, neither may it so expound one place of Scripture, that it be repugnant to another. Wherefore, although the Church be a witness and a keeper of holy Writ, yet, as it ought not to decree anything against the same, so besides the same ought it not to enforce any thing to be believed for necessity of Salvation."[36]

Anglicans also believe in the teaching value of human reason, including theology, philosophy, the modern sciences and other post-Reformation discoveries. These truths, reflected upon in light of the Scriptures and tradition, form an important part of the Anglican system. It has been said that Anglicanism "lives by an accumulation of inheritances."[37]

The Anglican understanding of Scripture and tradition, therefore, is much like the Reformation understanding in that Scripture is paramount, and tradition helps to verify Scripture and explains church practice not contrary to Scripture. While most groups employ reason to inform their understanding of Scripture, Anglicans are explicit about their intent to do so. For example, F. F. Bruce explains, "This collocation of reason alongside Scripture and 'the voice of the Church' (which is at least one phase of tradition) has characterized Anglicanism in all its comprehensiveness."[38] J. A. T. Robinson provides a powerful picture when he adds that the Anglican "conception of authority is not single-stranded but the three-fold cord, not easily broken, of Scripture and tradition and reason."[39]

FAITH GROUPS NOT AFFIRMING APOSTOLIC SUCCESSION

Most of the hundreds of global Christian faith groups do not believe that today's bishops stand in the place and authority of the apostles. They do not find Jesus or the apostles making such a promise in Scripture, and they see contradictions between the teachings of the apostles evident in Scripture and the teachings of subsequent bishops, whether individually, regionally or ecumenically. They find no justification in Scripture or even in the early tradition for many of the teachings developed later by the Roman Catholic or the Eastern Orthodox Churches.

Many of these Christians still desire to be apostolic, but they do so by focusing on the Scriptures—books of the Bible that they confidently believe were written or approved by the apostles. Extrabiblical teachings from the early period might possibly be apostolic and are held in high regard, but they are not afforded equal authority with the Scriptures because they cannot be affirmed as essential directives from the apostles. These Christians believe that with the passing of time church leaders developed many traditions that may have served the churches well in particular times and places but are by no means commandments of God incumbent upon the contemporary church.

Still others reject the traditional belief that the Scriptures are uniquely inspired by God. We include them in the discussion only briefly, since our focus is on challenging those who believe the Bible to see why church history matters. These more liberal Protestants would consider our discussion interesting, but they reject as highly doubtful our premise that the whole of Scripture is inspired by God, authoritative and foundational for the Church today.

Bible-focused Protestants

Protestantism began in the sixteenth century as a response to widespread discontent with the morality, power and doctrine of the Roman Catholic Church. Earlier we saw the late medieval rise of nearly unfettered authority of the pope and magisterium. At the dawn of the Reformation, practices and relationships that opposed Scripture and church teaching could be allowed in specific cases, often attached to payment or power. Indulgences, an official means of removing some punishment for sin, became an important means of raising funds for church projects. Many believed that if they performed enough good works, they could qualify themselves for salvation.

> Orthodox Protestant belief about Scripture can be summarized in three main points: Scripture is inspired, infallible, and sufficient.
>
> **PETER KREEFT**

Luther, Zwingli, Calvin and many others objected. Soon they led movements that resulted in excommunication by the Roman Catholic Church. These Reformers believed that they were leading the true church away from the false teachings of Rome. We have already seen that the Reformers did not reject tradition, but they rejected the notion that tradition itself could overturn Scripture. Although they were not always consistent in their application of the principle, they committed themselves to *sola scriptura*, which maintains that the revelation of God comes to us through Scripture alone.

In the centuries since the Reformers, many groups have emerged from families of churches that began in the Reformation period. As a result, the term *Protestant* can have several meanings. Generally speaking, it refers to any group emerging since the Reformation that is not Roman Catholic or Eastern Orthodox. Some include Anglicans among Protestants, while others do not. Usually only groups who hold to orthodox doctrines of God and Christ are included. Note that most of these groups are content with being labeled as Protestant, though some groups or individuals object. This first section will examine classical Protestants, here called "Bible-focused Protestants."

To understand how Bible-focused Protestants understand tradition, we must first explain their commitment to Scripture—*sola scriptura*—and what they mean when they say "Scripture alone." They believe that the Bible is direct revelation from God, so the Bible has divine authority. They believe that the Scriptures are enough—sufficient—for Christian instruction and truth. They affirm the Bible as the final written authority from God, and that God made the Bible understandable both to informed clergy and to lay readers. Bible-focused Protestants claim that the most reliable interpreter of Scripture is Scripture itself, meaning that clear texts are determinative for understanding the meaning of less clear texts. Finally, Bible-focused Protestants believe that the Scriptures are infallible, though Christians must meet the challenge of understanding the Scriptures correctly.

Roman Catholic professor Peter Kreeft has insightfully described how Protestants "experience" the Bible. First, the Bible is sacred, and God speaks through Scripture to humankind and to individuals. Second, the Bible is sacramental, meaning that it effects what it signifies, but by the power of the reader's faith. Third, Scripture is truth—both logical correctness and spiritual nourishment. Fourth, Scripture is certain and sure—an anchor in a day of relativism. Fifth and most important, Scripture is where we meet Christ.[40] His description demonstrates how Bible-centered the "Bible-focused Protestants" really are. From the Scriptures they experience God, truth, faith, assurance and salvation in Christ.

Since Roman Catholics also affirm the Scriptures as direct revelation from God, it is important to explain the difference in how Protestants and Catholics affirm Scriptures. Norman Geisler and Ralph MacKenzie here differentiate between *sola scriptura* in the material sense—all the content of saving revelation is in Scripture—and *sola scriptura* in the formal sense. Here is the distinction: "What Protestants affirm and Catholics reject is *sola scriptura* in the formal sense that the Bible alone is sufficiently clear that no infallible teaching magisterium of the church is necessary to interpret it."[41]

So when most Bible-focused Protestants come to tradition, they already assume that everything necessary for salvation has been revealed in and can be understood from the Scriptures. As a result, they have often minimized the importance of Christian history. Many embrace tradition, but with caution. Church councils, doctrinal expressions and ecclesiastical practices are important for the church, maybe even authoritative in a derivative sense, when they are consistent with Scripture. But tradition is neither absolute nor revealed. D. H. Williams explains, "In the Protestant mind, the difference between Scripture and tradition is that the revelation of Scripture has ceased completely, and there, the Bible is absolutely unique as canon, whereas tradition is not inspired and has not ceased, making it (perhaps) authoritative but not canonical."[42]

Many Bible-focused Protestants maintain an abiding distrust of tradition. This is especially true of free-church faith groups. For them, it was tradition, particularly Roman Catholic tradition, that the Reformers abandoned in order to embrace *sola scriptura*. They suspect that tradition by its very nature tends to corrupt the truth of Scripture. Stephen Holmes observes, "One characteristic position found regularly in . . . Evangelicalism, the charismatic movement, Separatism, Anabaptism . . . today, is an impatience with what tends to get called 'tradition.' God has given us his truth in the Bible; our job is to live it and proclaim it; what other people may or may not have thought about it in the past is of no interest to us; that they were generally wrong is evident from the poor state of the 'traditional' churches."[43]

Bible-focused Protestants have several reasons for rejecting the teaching that tradition is infallible (that it should be capital T in that sense). They reject the argument that tradition is really the oral teaching of the apostles kept by the church through the centuries, for often the doctrines are taught or declared only centuries after the apostles. Medieval examples include indulgences, required clerical celibacy, papal supremacy, purgatory and prayers to saints. More recent examples include Mary's immaculate conception (1854), papal infallibility (1870) and Mary's bodily assumption (1950). In the intervening centuries leading church fathers, ostensibly passing on the oral teaching of the apostles, often contradict one another.[44] In other words, there is no "unanimous consent of the fathers."

These Protestants believe that the appeal to tradition is not consistent, that sometimes the Roman Catholic Church even declares dogma that runs counter to the majority of earlier tradition, such as the expansion of the biblical canon to include apocryphal books at Trent and the declaration of papal infallibility at Vatican I—both apparent reversals of the church's historic teaching. They contend that other traditions cannot be demonstrated from Scripture when interpreted by Scripture, such as transubstantiation and the seven sacraments.

Some Protestants are also so repulsed by developments leading to the Reformation that they tend to consider tradition itself to have been the root problem. They believe that the Roman Catholic Church wandered from its foundation by exalting tradition while ignoring the Scriptures, leading people away from salvation by grace through faith.

How do Bible-focused Protestants actually approach the tradition? Many have tried to exclude or ignore Christian history as a resource for considering what they should believe. They deny that the tradition is revelation, and on this basis they pay little or no attention to the history of the church. They accuse Roman Catholics and Orthodox of having ignored the Scriptures while exalting the tradition, yet they stand at the opposite pole, exalting recent study of the Scriptures while ignoring the tradition. Particularly troubling is that Bible-focused Protestants often have paid little attention to historic interpretations of the Scriptures themselves—Scriptures that they believe are transcultural and transtemporal. We might even say that Protestants have a "tradition" of ignoring the tradition, even the tradition having to do with Scripture.

At the same time, most Bible-focused Protestants have no problem using technical theological expressions and vocabulary developed as part of the

tradition, particularly in their teachings about the triune God, the human
and divine natures of Christ, and the canon of Scripture, among others. They
avail themselves of the tradition whether they know it or not. To their credit,
they believe those traditional theological paradigms because they believe
that the Bible teaches them. They reject early doctrines and practices that
they believe contradict Scripture.

Whether intentionally or accidentally, therefore, all Bible-focused Protestants build on Christian tradition. This is inevitable, since the major doctrines of Christianity will be discussed in every age and every culture. But it
is also true that everyone follows some particular set or family of traditions.
Each faith group has its own distinctive traditional foci, often tracing to the
founding stimuli of their own denomination or family of denominations.

Bottom line: Bible-focused Protestants still fall far short of giving sufficient attention to the tradition. Hearing Christians from across the centuries
is indispensable as we seek to know God and to follow the Scriptures. This
participation in the community of the faithful throughout the centuries demands that we study the history of the church. From the university classroom
to the pastoral study to the worship pew, Bible-focused Protestants could
benefit from a more focused, intentional study of Christian history.

Liberal Protestants

Theological liberals, as we have seen, tend to place confidence only in what
they believe can be demonstrated objectively, scientifically or rationally.
Scripture and tradition, once obstacles to critical
thinking, do not reveal God, truth or God's
will, at least as these have been historically understood. Scripture and tradition are records
of past human efforts to understand the spiritual yearnings already inherent within each
human person. Neither Scripture nor tradition is supernatural, metaphysical or a divinely given deposit of truth. Peter Kreeft says,
"Modernists reduce the Bible to a human book.
This low view of Scripture they (naturally) call
'higher criticism.'"[45]

> *The abiding and eternal in Jesus is absolutely independent of historical knowledge and can only be understood by contact with His spirit which is still at work in the world.*
>
> **ALBERT SCHWEITZER**

Many contemporaries believe that the cultural distance between our time and earlier periods of Christian development is too remote for direct meaningful connection. D. H. Williams offers three examples. Patristics scholar Frances Young argues against orthodoxy on the basis that doctrines develop in particular conditions and often are decided on the basis of politics, philosophical presuppositions and random historical events. John Hick sees orthodoxy as a myth that inhibits the freedom of modern scholarship. Maurice Wiles dismisses any standard Christian doctrine because Christianity evolves like a stream that wanders without discernible control.[46]

Liberal Protestants reject this direct meaningful connection. Christianity's earlier conclusions, whether about Scripture or doctrine or Christian practice, may have worked then but are in no way incumbent upon us. So there is no discernible body of Christian orthodoxy from either Scripture or tradition.

What theological liberals do find in common with historic Christians is the human experience of story, struggle and the desire to know. Although a biblical or historical account may not be verifiable by modernist standards, theological liberals believe the story itself may nonetheless have theological value. We must differentiate between the Bible as story and the Bible as event. Whether the biblical story was an actual event is irrelevant. The understood intent of the story is itself the central truth of the biblical passage or historical account. Real connection with the past—continuity with earlier believers—is not that we understand the same absolute truths revealed to earlier generations, but rather that we tell and experience the same stories, though in very different cultures those stories may result in varied conclusions or existential responses.

Liberal Protestants openly and intentionally embrace the current cultural norms and philosophical presuppositions, assuming that current thinking is superior to previous thinking, that humanity continues to advance with the coming of each new corrective. Strangely enough, while denying traditional Christian orthodoxy, they have, in a way remarkably similar to the theological bigotry that they hope to reject, erected a new "orthodoxy" of politically correct principles and positions that often drive them to condemn the thinking of others.

This stereotype of the modern Christian liberal is, of course, precisely that—a stereotype. Each theological liberal has a personal set of commit-

ments, sometimes stepping outside the boundaries here described. Consider
that many contemporary Christians are conservative or traditional in some
areas but liberal in other areas. Each person fits somewhere between traditional and liberal on the theological spectrum. For example, some affirm
biblical inspiration but interpret the Bible using liberal presuppositions and
methods. But the stereotype is helpful for the purposes of this chapter in
that it characterizes how liberal theologians approach the tradition today.
Very few would describe themselves as Bible-focused, to be sure. Most dis-
allow any notion of particular, divinely guided revelation in either Scripture
or tradition. Others affirm "divine inspiration" or "biblical authority" or
"tradition," but they do not mean what Christians have traditionally affirmed
by those words.

CONCLUSION

Through twenty centuries the church has looked to the past to understand the
present and to plan for the future. As we can see, believers have understood
the tradition variously depending on their time, location and faith group.

Some look to the tradition to discern the Holy Spirit's ongoing revelation.
They must examine Christian history to see what the Holy Spirit has revealed to the church through "ecumenical" decisions, practices and declarations, whether from common church practice, conciliar declarations, magisterium deliberations or papal decrees.

Others believe that the Holy Spirit works in the church, but that there is
no revelation beyond the Scriptures. They examine the past to confirm or
alter their own conclusions from Scripture. They seek the help of earlier
exegetes and theologians to confirm or alter their own biblical understanding. They appeal to the teachings and practices of earlier Christians to
lend credibility to their contemporary conclusions or practices. Sometimes
when they begin, they are hostile to tradition. They study the past to see
where the church went wrong, especially in Roman Catholic or Reformation
developments they consider antibiblical. They tend to find affirmation of
distinctive practices or emphases that their faith group initiated in light of
the need for reform, though in the process they often broaden their own
positions. They may prefer the ancient rites and ceremonies but see in them
no inherent authority or revelation.

A variety of believers stand somewhere between. While they affirm that foundational revelation has ceased, they look to the Holy Spirit for enlightenment for specific events or persons or life situations. They confirm their own existential experience in the experience of Christian ancestors.

No doubt, contemporary Christians can learn from each other through cross-reading and dialogue. Despite our differences of theological viewpoint, we can consider one another's positions, embrace what we see as true, and reject what we see as false. But those are only a few pieces of a much larger puzzle. We must also hear the voices of the past, listening to their positions and allowing them to help us discover unconsidered precepts, realize ancient spirituality, and experience traditional practices.

> Whether we affirm the canon of Scripture, trinitarian explanations and vocabulary, christological explanations or even denominational distinctives, we embrace tradition.

Every Christian follows tradition. Whether we affirm the canon of Scripture, trinitarian explanations and vocabulary, christological explanations or even denominational distinctives, we embrace tradition. This is true whether we call it "tradition" or prefer softer terms such as "precedent," "custom" or "common practice."

This leads us once again to the focus of this book: every Christian of every faith group can learn from the church's great tradition. Whether Roman Catholic, Orthodox, Anglican, conservative Protestant, evangelical, fundamentalist and/or charismatic, the great work of God through the church's centuries is indispensable in clarifying the truth. No less than other believers, Bible-focused Christians, who love and concentrate on the Scriptures, must be informed by great Christians across the centuries. This is true whether those Bible-focused Christians are in faith groups that emerged in ancient, Reformation or more recent times. Otherwise, they limit their ability to understand those Scriptures because they remain uninformed and inadequately shaped by the biblical and theological positions of God-lovers and Scripture-lovers of the past.

Part Two

Expanding Circles
of Inquiry

INTRODUCTION

Christians need each other. No one comes to faith in Christ without someone sharing the gospel, whether in written, oral or electronic form. No one grows in the faith without the help of others—pastors, church members, friends, Bible translators, publishers. We need each other in order to understand who we are in our relationship with God and where we stand in our relationship to other believers. More than that, we need each other to make informed decisions about which beliefs, behaviors and standards we believe are God's will for us and which are not. Part 2 of this book challenges us to embrace all Christians, living and departed, as we come to those convictions and make those decisions.

Our working model is expanding, concentric circles of inquiry (fig. 1). We move through these concentric circles from the innermost circles to circles increasingly less familiar. This means that we begin with people and ideas that are closest and most intimate to us, and we move increasingly into those with whom we are still related yet less familiar and intimate. For Christian living and inquiry, this means that we move from our closest Christian friends, to our congregation, to our faith group, to our denominational families, to our theological point of view, to those of very different points of view, to those of divergent cultures, to those throughout Christian history.

These circles include Christians from across cultures, across the continents and across the centuries. We will see that Christians throughout this spectrum, particularly Christians from the past, can have tremendous impact on our faith.

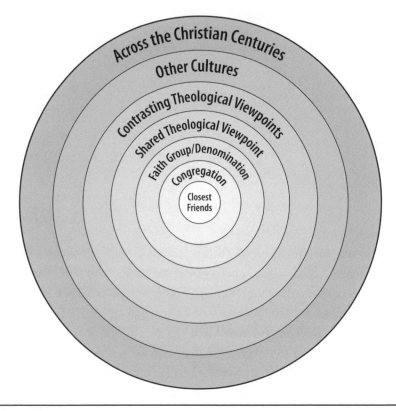

Figure 1. Circles of inquiry

Each chapter in part 2 considers a key aspect of Christianity through these expanding circles of inquiry. First, we consider our personal identity in God, asking life's fundamental questions. Key personal experiences involving believers closest to us bring moments of discovery, where we alter or expand our prior self-understanding. Our investigation broadens through the circles of inquiry to include believers from throughout Christian history.

Second, we examine how Christian history expands how we interact with other Christians—how we practice Christian community. For both identity and community, we follow parallel processes, expanding our inquiry so that we move from more intimate circles through wider circles. Christians want to belong. They want to belong to something greater than themselves or their immediate friends. Here the challenge in our inquiry is to embrace Christians from across all cultures, continents and centuries—to embrace all the Christians.

Third, we consider how the same expanding circles are also expanding circles of accountability. As we look to historic Christians, we evaluate them, and they evaluate us. Their understandings and practices come under our scrutiny, and we subject our understandings and practices to theirs. We receive historic brothers and sisters openly, yet judiciously. In this process we seek global, cultural, historic agreement—what Christians for many years have called *consensus fidelium* ("consensus of the faithful"). We will discover that many times we find this consensus, but that many times we do not.

Fourth, we see how expanding circles of inquiry broaden our horizons and fill gaps in theology that we may or may not have known were gaps. We discover that Christians in all places and all times have wrestled with issues of the faith, sometimes just like our struggles and sometimes different. As they believed the truth and lived lives surrendered to God, they emphasized some of the same and some very different elements of faith and practice. Again, we do not always find *consensus fidelium*. In the process we see how their search can help our own, and how their answers can either clarify our answers or confuse us.

These four elements are very closely related. Identity and community are inseparable, for both the foundations of identity and the context of identity are necessarily communal. Real community must have real accountability, for accountability provides both affirmation and correction. Without accountability, relationships are shallow at best. Together, community and accountability help us reassess our self-understanding in Christ and expose us to additional viewpoints. These alternative perspectives broaden our horizons and fill gaps in our theology.

Always running in the background are the subthemes of certainty and authenticity. As inquisitive beings, we always contemplate how our study can help us have confidence that our beliefs and practices are consistent with God's will. This is also true when we study Christian history. We will see that when we believe that we have discovered a *consensus fidelium*, our confidence is strong. We will also explore how to have peace when *consensus fidelium* escapes us—when we are faced with Christians who today and across the centuries hold quite diverse understandings and practices. We will explore how Christian history shows us variations and paradoxes and can encourage us to embrace those paradoxes, not because we give up on discovering the truth, but because we come to believe that in those very paradoxes we have discovered truth. Confidence emerges in part because we know that our inquiry has been broad, honest, fair and faithful—in other words, authentic.

4

WHO AM I? CHRISTIAN HISTORY
AND CHRISTIAN IDENTITY

Once hesitant to trust anyone over 30,
now I hesitate to trust anyone under 300.

THOMAS ODEN,
"THEN AND NOW: THE RECOVERY OF PATRISTIC WISDOM"

In the 1970s a wise rabbi told a brilliant social idealist that he would remain uneducated until he read early and medieval Christian writers extensively. Taking the challenge, the young scholar soon found himself asking new questions and offering creative answers, which he shortly recognized as old questions already addressed and often resolved in the past. More study brought more discoveries, and the young man found himself increasingly formed and re-formed by the spiritual wisdom of these historic Christian thinkers. By 1990 he could say, "Now I experience wider cross-cultural freedom of inquiry into and within the variables of Christian orthodoxy mediated through brilliant Christian voices of other times and places."[1] Today he finds answers to contemporary problems in the deep well of Christian tradition—in the consensus of the faithful. The more he consulted earlier Christians, the further he moved from social idealism to tradition-informed orthodoxy. Christian history transformed his Christian identity.

This world-class scholar is Thomas Oden. He is well known for his books and articles challenging serious Christians to study Christian tradition. His conceiving and editing the Ancient Christian Commentary on Scripture series reflects his belief that exegetical methods and conclusions from across the centuries are critical to Christian identity.[2]

Today many Christians find themselves on a similar journey. Disenchanted by their own culture's values, and seeing countless alternatives, they long for direction and affirmation from the broader church. This opens their hearts to consider ideas from other Christians.

Identity Formation

Christianity is a global phenomenon that exists in many cultures. The global community is a mosaic of nations, heritages and people groups who live by a variety of worldviews, religions and belief systems. Christians emerge from, and live among, these contributors to the global mosaic. Christians can be very different from one another, across cultures and across centuries. Yet in every culture the Christians hold core beliefs in common. They believe that there is objective, absolute truth. They submit their lives and hearts to Christ, affirming that their eternal salvation comes through him. They believe that the personal God created the universe, including our world and our very persons. They trust that God is the ultimate source of everything that exists. They ask the fundamental questions that everyone asks, but they find their answers in their faith in the God of Abraham, Isaac and Jacob.

Every culture asks the fundamental human questions: "Who am I?" "Where did we come from?" "How did we get here?" "Where are we headed?" Christian faith necessitates corollary questions. "Who is God?" "What is God's purpose for creation?" "How do we relate to God?" "How has God related to us?" "How does God now relate to us?" "How should we relate to one another?" From these questions arise all of the categories of theology, whether directly or indirectly. Christian theology, whether biblical, historical, philosophical or systematic, seeks to answer these and related questions. Christians, especially Bible-focused Christians, find the answers to those questions in the Scriptures, examined from their own theological perspectives and within the context of their church communities. Christians want to know the meaning of life.

How? We experience that meaning in key life moments when our understanding of Christian identity moves significantly forward. A Bible reading, prayer or reflection touches the core of our being, and suddenly we see some aspect of life from a deeper perspective. We believe that the Holy Spirit works in our hearts to clarify truth and to help us grow.

We remember times when a teacher or preacher challenged us with truth that we had not previously considered or had not valued. Several fragments of our thinking came together to make sense like never before. We realized that we could learn not only from our own spiritual experience, but also from the experiences of others who had grown beyond our spiritual maturity.

Many of us also remember times when personal and interpersonal experiences brought confusion. In our expanded understanding we questioned, altered or even contradicted our earlier understanding. Rather than solving the confusion, further study compounded the difficulties. Sometimes another teaching moment brought resolution. Other times the difficulties remain, while we live with the paradoxes. Yet in every case we invest our time, energy and thought in these opportunities because we want clarification about the fundamental questions of life.

These formative experiences are "Who am I?" moments. We gain a new or different perspective. We reassess our thinking, affirming or revising our understanding. We later point to important breakthroughs as life-changing times in our development. Why? Because at the heart of the Christian experience is the quest to know who God is, who we are, and how we relate to God and to God's entire plan and creation. This is because Christian identity is at the core of Christian thought, worship, investigation and spirituality—indeed, at the core of every Christian experience.

We realize that personal experiences which form self-understanding occur most often in conjunction with others—in the contexts of sharing, worship, preaching, teaching, and study. As we share these opportunities together, learning alongside others, and from others, we experience personal growth. We also stimulate growth in others, as we learn together about our relationship with God.

This starts with those closest to us, often within our own congregation (fig. 2). We expand that circle when we include others with whom we generally agree, especially within our faith group or faith group family.

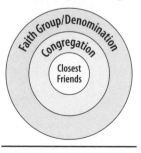

Figure 2

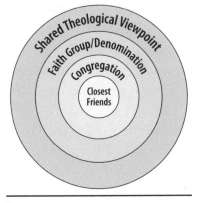

Figure 3

Next we engage key teachers, leaders, organizations, or agencies who share our major theological perspective (fig. 3). For many Bible-focused Christians, though not all, this is the "Bible-believing" community, or the evangelical community.

We extend the circle further when we venture outside our comfort zone to consider leading contemporary thinkers from other major theological streams (fig. 4). Often, they disagree with us. While we sometimes hope to garner information to defend our commitments or to attack theirs, more often we want to be sure that we have not overlooked important factors or to clarify our thinking. When we realize that most of the world's Christians live in cultures very different from our own, we include American, Latino, European, Asian and African Christians.

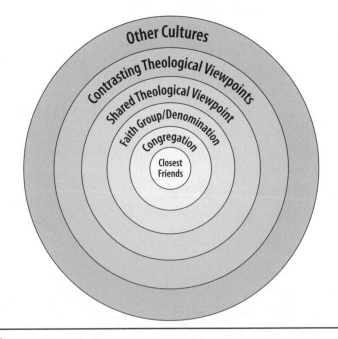

Figure 4

When we stretch ourselves into this great variety of resources, our quest for self-understanding in God becomes transcultural and global. Our search to understand our own Christian identity reaches beyond the levels of immediate security. Yet we grow increasingly confident in knowing that we have considered experiences of Christians across the globe with whom we share Christ and Christian faith. We see how faith interacts with culture, and in the process we see that Christians tend to emphasize parts of their faith that particularly respond to the values and needs of their culture.

When we study historical theology, or Christian history, our expanding circles of membership reach beyond contemporary circles to include Christians across the centuries who addressed the fundamental questions that drive Christian inquiry (fig. 5). When we begin to consider the lives and thinking of significant believers throughout the church's history, we quickly see that the "theological spectrum" is much larger than we had imagined.

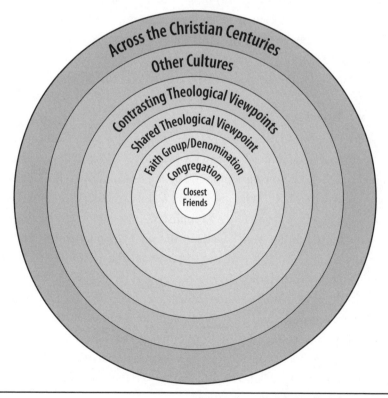

Figure 5

The opportunity to see distinctive emphases and to supplement our personal discoveries by the contributions of others expands exponentially. We discover that believers throughout the church's history have sought answers and provided tools to help others find answers to theological inquiry. Because these historic Christians lived in varied places, multiple cultures and several centuries, our resource base is inherently not only transcultural and global, but also transtemporal.

This raises significant challenges. We must be sensitive to the philosophical, cultural and temporal presuppositions, or worldview, of those we study. Sometimes we find thoughts, ideas and experiences very different from our own. We must carefully avoid embracing or dismissing them too hastily. But we also find important areas of agreement. As we see ourselves in step with Christians from across the centuries, we gain confidence—a higher level of certainty—that we understand the core truths of Christianity. We have a stronger sense of personal and corporate identity because of that confidence in the truth.

Christian identity, then, is much more than independent, personal, felt identity. Christian identity always includes broadening circles of membership—broadening circles of community. Here we participate in the whole church—with Christians across cultures, continents and centuries.

SHARED IDENTITY

How does this work? While my personal relationship with God is foundational for understanding who I am, my identity as a Christian is also determined by other relationships, particularly my relationship to the Christian community as a whole. Who am I? I am a child of God, created in God's image, the object of God's love and ministry, indwelled by the Holy Spirit, redeemed through the work of Christ. But my Christian identity is more than that. I am also a brother or sister of all the redeemed, not only throughout the world today, but also throughout the centuries. When I am in the family of God, with God the Father as my father, then every Christian brother is my brother, and every Christian sister is my sister. Some of those brothers and sisters have died, and the only way that I can know them, and know how they impact my identity, is by learning what others said of them and by encountering what they said and wrote. This means that Christian history is my opportunity to know who I am.

From the church's beginning, history presents believer after believer whose study of Christian history formed, or transformed, how they saw their Christian identity. Who, for example, could question the impact of learning from his predecessors on the identity of Irenaeus and those he taught? Confronted by late second-century Gnostics who said that the church either read the wrong Scriptures or read the Scriptures wrongly, Irenaeus appealed to the rule of truth passed from the apostles.[3] Tertullian appealed to the same rule, which he called the "rule of faith," as he opposed heretics.[4] This meant that living Christians could turn to historic Christians who preserved the apostles' teaching, passed on through key Christian leaders throughout the empire up to their own time.

We see bold fifth-century leaders, such as Ambrose, Augustine, John Chrysostom and Cyril, quoting predecessors as they faced opposition.[5] Great thirteenth-century leaders, such as Francis and Dominic, rejected family privilege, embracing abject poverty, because they realized that Christ, the apostles and spiritual masters became poor on purpose to serve others.[6] Spiritual writers such as John Cassian and Evagrius spent extended time among the desert fathers; their identities were molded as they learned spirituality from great masters who passed on the tradition that they had learned.[7] Benedict learned from Cassian's reports of those conferences and made them standard mealtime reading for monks who followed his Rule.[8] The most important source for Luther and Calvin was the Scriptures, but how much were the great Reformers' identities also formulated by reading church fathers, particularly Augustine?[9] This procession of historic Christian leaders continues to swell as Christians of every century who embark on studying Christian history find themselves joining the march.

IDENTITY CONFIRMATION AND TRANSFORMATION

Each Christian, therefore, owes his or her identity first to God, but also to Christians across cultures, continents and centuries. We can never know our Christian identity fully, but as each of us becomes familiar with more of the persons and forces that formed our identity, we become more aware of who we really are. Former archbishop of Canterbury Rowan Williams says it well: "Who I am as a Christian is something which, in theological terms, I could only answer fully on the impossible supposition that I could see and grasp how all other Christian lives had shaped mine and, more specifically, shaped it towards the likeness of Christ."[10]

Many forces brought me to love Christian history. Probably because my father loved American history, I became interested in history very early, but my interest in Christian history was delayed. In college and in seminary I learned about key persons, places, events and doctrinal developments. I embraced Christians from across the centuries as my brothers and sisters, especially when they agreed with my own inner circles of identity. Later, as I considered Christian history from perspectives other than my own, I was amazed at how I shared the struggles and experiences of historic brothers and sisters, and how their work could inform my life. I became aware of the variety of early Christianity, and how regional, cultural and philosophical values shaped the way early Christians emphasized various aspects of Christianity. I found soul mates among the early Christian ascetics, and there I met my mentor, John Cassian. I embraced a Christology that understands Christ's incarnation to be central to Christian theology. In the process, my sense of identity—who I am—expanded considerably. I have not abandoned my own religious heritage. In fact, I treasure the contributions of its founders more than ever. I still hold their emphases very dear. Yet my understanding of Christian identity, and its corresponding Christian community and accountability, have expanded to places I would never have dreamed were possible.

> Each Christian owes his or her identity first to God, but also to Christians across cultures, continents and centuries.

Many others could share similar stories. D. H. Williams, for example, renowned Baptist scholar and professor of Christian history, remains within his Christian heritage yet challenges free-church Christians to learn from the early church fathers.[11] His readers expand their understanding of Christian identity as he has expanded his.

John Henry Newman is an example of one whose study of Christian history led him to a different faith group. Newman's study of the early church fathers intersected with a series of mentors who helped him resolve his reservations about Roman Catholic doctrines. This was a long process, which he chronicles in his classic work *Apologia pro vita sua*. He became a leader in the Anglo-Catholic Movement, or Oxford Movement—influential

Anglicans whose study of Christian history motivated them to point the Church of England toward worship and teaching more closely resembling Roman Catholicism. Most in the Oxford Movement remained Anglican, but in 1845 Newman became Roman Catholic.[12] Bible-focused Christians are puzzled by Newman's conversion, but they appreciate many contributions from the fruit of his study. Newman's concept of a Christian university, for example, has lasting impact for the Christian identity of educators and students across the globe.[13]

Christian history has confirmed my convictions in many areas, but I have been transformed in several others. Had I allowed my fear of change to prevent me from learning from the Christian centuries, I have no idea what I would have become, for the study of Christian history has both preserved and transformed my identity.

While many Christians carefully reconsider their identity in light of Christian history, most Christians, comfortable in their own context and culture, ignore much of Christian history. Reasons vary widely. Although some make a conscious choice to ignore the tradition, most do so simply by default. Why? Christians tend to look primarily to the tradition of their particular faith group, denomination or denominational family, especially of the formative years or formative movements. This is particularly true of Bible-focused Christians. Others intentionally limit their study of the past because they see significant problems with the tradition—problems that lead them to devalue or ignore the tradition.

A key point of reference for many Protestants, for example, is the late medieval Western development that the pope stands above the tradition. This became justification for abuse of indulgences, which in turn led reformers to reject several doctrines, including papal supremacy. Through several series of events, this produced the Reformation. The Reformers insisted on *sola scriptura*, though we have already seen that they often cited the church fathers as they discussed Scripture. As a result, many Bible-focused Christians today still see the tradition as the primary problem. Their foundational paradigm pursues church history to show how the church failed and to rediscover what the church should be. They see the past as a source of deception, a failure that lost or hid the truth. So rather than considering the tradition as a rich resource for contemporary Christians, they are suspicious of the tradition.

Another common misunderstanding considers the earliest church to be a pristine expression of God's perfect will throughout; only later did the church abandon that perfection. In this scenario, at some identifiable point in history the church began its slide into the "great apostasy." Times suggested range from soon after the death of the last apostle, to just after Constantine's legalization of Christianity in 313, to just after Chalcedon in 451, to the end of the first seven ecumenical councils in 787. After that point, they believe, the church just got worse and worse, piling one unbiblical tradition upon another, until nearly no true Christians existed. Then another point in history came, when God rose up a new movement or set of movements to bring the church back to what is was in its perfect, pristine period. Times of return suggested here range from the beginning of the Reformation to the beginning of one's own faith group, especially if that faith group began after the sixteenth century.

This scenario needs careful scrutiny. On the one hand, nearly all Bible-focused Christians see in the tradition the growth of practices in the church that the early church did not embrace. No doubt, we see Christians throughout history practicing Christianity in the way they understand best and then crystallizing those practices into a theology that they pass on to future generations as essential to the faith. This produces tradition that blesses the church and tradition that causes problems for the church.

On the other hand, the "great apostasy" scenario has several problems. First, the church was never "pristine." The original church was already incomplete and imperfect, though it had the distinct advantage of having apostolic leadership. In fact, many New Testament books were written to correct false teaching, poor leadership and bad practice in the congregations to which they were sent. Second, the "great apostasy" model promotes the notion that those who lived and taught between the beginning of the great apostasy and the beginning of the return can be dismissed as noncredible. Protestants often refer to them as "Catholics" (though in the West there was little alternative until the Reformation); if they were "Catholic," some Protestants propose, they are not worthy of study, for they were part of the "apostate" church. Exceptions are granted, of course, when someone in the "apostate church" period agreed with one or several doctrines highly emphasized by the later group.

Here I propose another scenario. Perhaps Christians in this middle period are Christians in the church, as I am a Christian in the church. They are part of the trunk, from which later branches emerged. This means that they are not part of someone else's group, but rather part of my group, or I am part of their group, or, better said, we are part of the church group. After the splintering of Christianity in the West, we have a more parochial place in the great church. These newer groups are attached to the trunk, but through other branches, so we may not be attached to the same branch. As already discussed, our own expanding circles move from my congregation, to my faith group, to my family of faith groups, to my theological perspective, to those beyond my theological perspective, to global Christians of all groups, to Christians throughout the centuries from various times, cultures and continents. When I overlay that paradigm onto fourth-century Asia Minor and think about the Cappadocians, for example, they are at least within the circle of my theological perspective, and probably more intimate than that. I cannot simply dismiss them, for I am attached to the trunk.

Although many Bible-focused Christians intentionally or unintentionally ignore historical theology when asking the questions of Christian identity, they depend upon Christian history nonetheless. In fact, even their suspicion of the past is part of a long tradition—an attitude rooted in historical development. We cannot live the Christian life apart from the legacies of those who have gone before us. We can hardly be Bible-focused Christians without depending upon the canon of Scripture, provided by God but preserved and recognized by historical Christians. Key theological teachings, such as the doctrine of God (Trinity) and the doctrine of Christ (two natures, one divine and one human, in one person) are vital to understanding Christian identity and stand at the core of what nearly all who consider themselves to be Bible-focused Christians believe. Churches that embrace creeds, particularly ancient creeds, are already including Christians across the centuries as part of their Christian identity. Worship patterns, both liturgical and nonliturgical, owe their origins to Christians from the past. Regardless of faith group, Bible-focused Christians owe much of their Christian identity and understanding to Christians from across the centuries. We benefit from Christian history sometimes not realizing how dependent we are on historic Christians who paved the way for us.

There are threats. If we think that studying Christian history will simply confirm the positions that we have already taken, we will likely be surprised.

Many of our convictions will be confirmed, but others may be altered or even overturned. And we must recognize that those who study the tradition do often come to different conclusions about where they should land. We have seen historical examples showing some students of history moving from one faith group to another, particularly when they come to appreciate the emphases that make another faith group distinct. Others who study the same tradition wonder how those who made that shift could come to those conclusions. But in the process we often discover a strong consensus on specific Christian teachings about Christian identity across the centuries. Where we find that consensus, particularly where the consensus confirms or enlightens what we understand from the Scriptures, Bible-focused Christians develop tremendous confidence that we know who we are. Where we find differences, we embrace what we believe the Scriptures teach us about our identity while appreciating those who believe the Scriptures teach otherwise.

The search for truth is always risky business, for we must always open our minds and hearts to receive what we learn. We know this as we study the Bible, but encouraged by faith that God works on our hearts and minds, we continue to study the Scriptures even when we know that our study may challenge our convictions and take us beyond our comfort. The same is true when we study Christian history. We constantly compare our discoveries to the findings of Christians across the centuries who come from multiple cultures, varied philosophical presuppositions and profound practices of spirituality. Sometimes what we find there is strange and difficult, even foreign to our contemporary world, but nonetheless we realize that it is part of who we are.[14]

No doubt, then, Christian identity is deeply rooted in Christian community. Central to our Christian identity is our personal relationship with God. But we cannot understand who we are without the help and support of Christians across continents, cultures and centuries. I need them to know who I am and where I came from. I need them to know what forces, people and ideas formed me.

Our desire to understand Christian identity, therefore, calls us to consider the faith of a variety of Christians—across continents, cultures, centuries. As we move through expanding circles of inquiry, we see ourselves from a fuller perspective. Our spiritual identity is simultaneously formed, confirmed and transformed.

5

A GREAT CLOUD OF WITNESSES

Christian Community Across the Centuries

Therefore, since we are surrounded by so great a cloud of witnesses,
let us also lay aside every weight and the sin that clings so closely,
and let us run with perseverance the race that is set before us.

HEBREWS 12:1 NRSV

The Christian believer approaching the Christian past
does so first in the consciousness that he or she is engaging with
fellow participants in prayer and eucharist, fellow readers of
the same scriptures; people in whom the same activity
is going on, the activity of sanctifying grace.

ROWAN WILLIAMS, *WHY STUDY THE PAST?*

Christian identity and Christian community are inseparably related. We might say they are two ways of looking at the same reality, or two aspects of one reality. We understand who we are in the context of where we live, to

whom we are related, and how we interact with others. We are naturally
connected, and then we choose to connect, with those who share common
geography, values, and interests. Last chapter we talked about expanding
circles of identity. In this chapter, we consider the same circles, but as expanding circles of community. We include all of the Christians, past and
present, as part of our own Christian community. This means we explore
the importance of historical theology for Christian community.

THE HUMAN DESIRE FOR COMMUNITY

Human beings are created by God with innate desire for interpersonal relationships. We know this instinctively, but we also observe it everywhere.
Every culture places a high value on community. They craft careful rules for
deciding who is and who is not part of the community. They make exclusive
commitments to people who are in the community. An unspoken loyalty
exists between members, so that they support, encourage and defend one
another. When two strangers discover that they both are part of a community that they hold dear, they may very well extend trust simply because
they sense a "brotherhood" or "sisterhood."

Examples are everywhere. Two sorority sisters from different universities
meet, and there is an instant bond. Members of the same service organi-
zation, such as the Lions or the Kiwanis, quickly support one another.
Members of political parties, such as Democrats and Republicans, support
fellow members with whom they might even fundamentally disagree.

Recently, Bible-focused Christians have expressed a desire for experiencing community at a deeper level. Books, articles and courses emphasizing Christian community abound.[1] Yet many Christians feel isolated.
Why? Our rapidly changing world, with ever-increasing means of communication, makes contact with others easier than ever, but it also lends itself
to more shallow or utilitarian relationships. Add a strong dose of individualism, and contemporary Bible-focused Christians have all the ingredients
necessary to find themselves in a loss of real Christian community.

Even conversion among Bible-focused Christians is understood to be
individual: one individual has a "personal experience," connecting the
person directly with God. Subsequent fellowship in the church is treated as
an optional by-product of this personal conversion—helpful, but not nec-

essary. The real goal is to sustain, repeat, maximize or supplement this individual experience. Again, there is loss of community.[2]

This self-focused living threatens the very nature of Christian community. N. T. Wright says, "We have been so soaked in the individualism of modern Western culture that we feel threatened by the idea of our primary identity being that of the family we belong to—especially when the family . . . is so large, stretching across space and time."[3] Leaders are tempted to market a self-centered Christian "product," so that sermons, lessons and literature offer self-improvement—better finances, better marriage, better self-image. Worship focuses on the individual worshiper's felt experience; singing, praying and preaching reinforce what God has done for *me*. When people ask for deeper relationships, they hear a barrage of talk declaring community where no deep community exists. This itself is evidence, both existentially and analytically, of a lack of real community.[4]

What is missing? Christians sense a need to know what others in the church think and how their decisions affect the kingdom. Something inside drives us to know and to feel the unity, support, common purpose and accountability of belonging to God's grand fellowship of the redeemed. Deep inside we crave this fellowship, especially with those in our closest circles. But we also know intuitively that the community of inquiry must be larger than those who are mostly like us. So we want and need conversation partners from throughout the Christian community.

The good news is that Christians have considerable basis for authentic community. We call each other "brother" and "sister" because we share the same Father and see ourselves in the same family. The covenant with Christ is also a covenant with the faithful, with the church. We can choose to live as believers who enjoy God's gift of community. How?

When we meet someone who claims Christ, we evaluate that person's actions and beliefs by the standards that we believe determine who is genuinely a member of the Christian community. This includes, for example, tenets of orthodoxy, acts of service, and personal or corporate morality. But until there is reason to doubt, we tend to accept and support each other as Christian brothers and sisters. The more convinced we become, the more intimate the relationship, and the greater our expressions of unity and community. In other words, the level of expressing our bond is directly proportional to the degree of intimacy that confidence in our relationship implies.

The same is true throughout our expanding circles, which here I call "expanding circles of community." We find it easiest to affirm those in our congregation, especially when we see their lives, hear their faith, and watch their service. We next extend that community to those within our denominational or faith group families. Next are teachers, leaders, organizations and agencies that share our major theological perspectives—say, the international evangelical community. For many, this is as far as Christian community extends, at least in practice.

Once again, some include contemporary thinkers outside our major theological perspectives, embracing believers from cultures different from our own, including American, Latino, European, Asian and African. This deepens confidence that we are part of the transcultural and global community of faith.

However, the full Christian community includes all who surrendered their hearts and lives to Jesus Christ regardless not only of culture, ethnicity and gender, but also of century. The great throng of believers before the throne pictured in Revelation 7, from every nation, tribe, people and language, is a mass of believers from across the centuries. They are my brothers and sisters even now. We might say that they have taken their seats among the great cloud of witnesses mentioned in Hebrews 12:1, joining those in the Hebrews 11 gallery of pre-Christian believers. They are "absent from the body" but "present with the Lord" (2 Cor 5:8 KJV). They "cheer us on," so to speak, but their writings also teach us, and at times even correct us. We will see more on this accountability in the next chapter.

While I am here on earth, I have no way to meet these departed brothers and sisters. But some wrote treatises, sermons, commentaries and letters, leaving a literary legacy of their theological, behavioral and moral commitments. Many left records of their theological searches and the solutions to which they came. They are part of *my* Christian community—some day, yes, but now as well.

The only way to broaden our experience of this Christianity community is to study Christian history—to know these brothers and sisters from across the centuries, with very diverse cultural and philosophical presuppositions, by studying their texts and their contexts. When we do, we accrue multiple perspectives, helpful criteria for understanding Scripture, and needed reflections on theology.

This provides us with tremendous opportunity. We can stand against individualism and relativism. We can find truth-based challenges for commitment, and we can integrate historical truth in everyday living. Bible-focused Christians hunger for that kind of community challenge. Broken, mobile families do not provide it. Impersonal churches, where anonymity often trumps intimacy, do not answer the need. Relativistic, politically correct, me-obsessed culture does not help. But community with the historic Christian family can bring increased confidence and stability, reinforcing and enhancing a personal faith that can be lived and experienced.

How Historic Christian Community Helps

Here we are not simply asking what the church did in a particular time, or even what the church believed the Scriptures say about a particular subject in a particular time. The thoughts and actions of any time, past or present, are equally subject to cultural influence. Instead, contemporary Christians must ask if there is a preponderant majority consensus by believers throughout the centuries on what the Scriptures say about the matter under consideration. For Bible-focused Christians, this means asking if there is a consensus across the centuries about what God has revealed about the issue. We will see more on this consensus in the next chapter.

Community also provides models for living. We look to mature, godly believers to see how we can become more mature and godly ourselves. The contemporary church has many examples, but the historic church includes hundreds of great examples—seasoned mentors from other times and cultures. Stanley Hauerwas observes, "By attending to what they did in the past we hope to know better how to live now."[5] They teach us how to grow spiritually in the disciplined, ascetic walk. We see how to work with others to help them become what God called them to be.

Decades ago I became familiar with John Cassian, whom I mentioned earlier. Cassian was a fifth-century ascetic. He and his friend Germanus committed their lives first to monasticism, and then to learning from reputed monastic leaders, particularly the anchorites of the Egyptian desert, who generally lived alone but taught inquiring disciples. These "desert fathers" taught Cassian and Germanus deep spiritual insights from the corporate wisdom learned and passed down by many who struggled to reject spiritual vices while embracing the path toward becoming like God. I always felt drawn to disciplined spirituality, and I had read several contemporary authors pointing in that direction. Cassian's report of conferences with these desert fathers introduced me to experienced mentors who could help me on that path. Today much of my personal prayer, daily spiritual routine and devotional method has grown out of my relationship with desert spirituality through John Cassian. Their discoveries, learned because of God's grace, and their realization that any move along the path toward God comes from God's assisting grace, set both boundaries and direction in my daily spiritual exercises. I share this with others who are walking on the same path, learning from community both ancient and contemporary.

Had I not met John Cassian through the pages of history, I trust that God would have worked in my life through other means. I have embraced several mentors in my Christian walk, both living and departed, sometimes many centuries departed. I have no idea how much more I will be challenged as I continue to learn from the historic Christian community. But I am sure of this: without the community of Christians across the centuries I would have missed many resources for becoming what God wants me to become.

My own students often are astounded to learn that past believers confronted the same teachings that today find their way to our front doors or, through television and other media, into our homes. They are grateful to understand the excellent arguments and the technical vocabulary that historic Christians articulated. They see the importance of key Christian doctrines that they previously had heard but not seriously considered deeply— often major teachings, such as Trinity, Christology, incarnation. Studying Arianism sharpens trinitarian theology, but it also equips them to meet modern-day Arians (e.g., Jehovah's Witnesses) who come to their homes. Understanding Sabellianism readies them to face today's modalists, who think that Father, Son and Spirit are the same person (e.g., United Pentecostals). Familiarity with Gnosticism prepares them to answer questions about many varieties of New Age religion popular today.

Refuting reemerging false teaching is only one benefit of community with the historic church. Students find themselves reinforcing, adjusting or changing their convictions as they see past believers appeal to Scripture, reason clearly, and live exemplary lives. They connect with heroes of the past, no longer thinking of them as distant ecclesial cousins, but rather knowing them as real brothers and sisters, part of their own Christian community.

In other words, when we are confronted with difficult choices, the whole Christian community, both historic and contemporary, stands ready to help. Often we find Christians in fairly universal agreement—a compelling consensus. But often there is no clear Christian consensus. Some decisions cause anxiety and debate among Christians in every age. We will explore further our response to consensus or the lack of consensus in the next chapter on accountability. Here I simply introduce the historic Christian community as an important place to turn to inform our own decisions and behaviors. Why? Because we share with them the same Father, the same Lord, the same Spirit, the same church.

What is God's will, for example, in regard to Christians serving in government, in the military, or in war? Bible-focused believers in every age have turned to Scripture to answer that question, yet their sincere conclusions cover a wide spectrum. Some argue for nonengagement (e.g., Amish, Mennonites, many individuals), while others think the opposite (e.g., Christian politicians and soldiers). Many are unsure exactly what to think, holding different positions in particular circumstances. Who should be considered in the searcher's inquiry? No doubt we should turn to believers beyond our own time and culture, including historic Christians. We can hope for general agreement, but for this particular question, once again, we find that some argued for nonengagement, while others thought the opposite. We also find others who began as pacifists but modified their positions in the face of great evil (e.g., Dietrich Bonhoeffer, H. Richard Niebuhr, Reinhold Niebuhr).

Or how should Christians respond when persecuted or oppressed? Christians in our world are being martyred daily, as they have been in every period of the church's history. What happens when some Christians compromise their faith under persecution? Contemporary answers vary widely, from ignoring the problem, to overlooking the problem, to confronting the problem directly. Once again, historic answers similarly vary. Yet we gain tremendous insight from early Christians who defended the faith against false accusations (e.g., the third-century apologists), faced torture and death (e.g., Polycarp, Ignatius, many under the emperors Decius and Diocletian), faced decisions about those who compromised (e.g., Cyprian). Once empowered, we see medieval church leaders becoming the persecutors (e.g., the Inquisition, the Albigensian Crusade). Reformers often were persecuted (e.g., Roman Catholics against Luther, Calvin, Zwingli, Anabaptists), but they also persecuted others (Luther, Calvin, Zwingli against Anabaptists). Since the Reformation we have seen Christians face Nazism (e.g., Pope Pius XII's accommodation, many Christian resisters), atheistic communism (e.g., many compliant, but outstanding resisters, such as Karol Wojtyla, who became Pope John Paul II) and the more radical Muslim governments (in several countries).

So how does studying the historic Christian community help us even where there is no clear answer to our questions? Several ways. Studying issues biblically and historically prevents hasty judgment, offers well-reasoned arguments for each direction, and softens harsh judgment toward others. Whether we find clear answers or not, we can make informed, careful decisions in light of broader contexts and options, because we have consulted with our Christian brothers and sisters across the centuries.

As we teach Christian history, we hope to develop this desire and ability. How? Assignments can encourage us to make those connections. Readings, examinations and research papers will always be foundational, for we become familiar with important persons, movements, documents, doctrines and ministries. But we can supplement traditional assignments with other options. We might ask students to worship with a faith group that emerged in the era being studied and/or to interview a minister about the group's heritage. Or they might reflect or journal on the teachings of a spiritual master whose writings they read. They could make a dramatic presentation focused on a key character or event from the course. Or they might debate two sides of a historic issue, maybe even taking the side of opposing historic figures. We can choose from any number of creative ways to pursue this sense of authentic Christian community.

When we do pursue intentional encounter with Christians across the centuries, we understand and experience greater Christian community. We lead more effectively in our inner circles of community, appreciate larger circles of community, and enjoy a much larger and much richer Christian community than we ever imagined. As a result, we may experience greater intimacy, first with those in our closest circles, but also with those in wider and wider circles of community.

Christian community, however, always involves accountability. I have hinted at this in the examples. To this we turn next.

6

ACCOUNTABILITY PARTNERS

Sharing Accountability with Historic Christians

*We cannot be in the Church without taking as much
responsibility for the theology of the past
as for the theology of our present.*

KARL BARTH, *PROTESTANT THEOLOGY IN THE
NINETEENTH CENTURY*

I was delighted to get a call from Jim.[1] Jim had come to Christ as teenager. I had baptized, mentored and supported him. He even lived with
me for six months after high school while waiting for his next assignment. After warm greetings, Jim got to the purpose of his call. He had
joined a church that rejected the Trinity; they believed that the three
persons of God are really one person. He said that the church's credibility was verified by signs and wonders. Because he loved me, he wanted
me to come to the truth and to experience what he had experienced.

With pain in my heart, I told Jim that it was impossible for me to
adopt his position. Father, Son and Spirit are three persons. The Son is
eternally begotten of the Father; on earth he prayed to the Father and
depended on the Father. The Spirit is "another" advocate, proceeds
from the Father, and glorifies the Son. The Father speaks to the Son.
Otherwise, many passages of Scripture would make no sense. Who
could imagine words of Scripture actually meaning "Myself, myself,
why have I forsaken me?" Or "I will send another advocate—well, ac-

tually I will send myself, not another." Or "I am my beloved me, in me I am well pleased." Or "This is my beloved me; listen to me." These are absurd images—Jesus speaking to another or about another but actually referring to himself, or the Father doing likewise.

Jim was surprised to hear that Christians have rejected this teaching from its earliest days. He had never heard of Sabellians, nor had he considered that signs and wonders have occurred not only among orthodox believers, but also among others.

Jim and his pastor loved the Scriptures. But their understanding of Scripture did not extend beyond their closest circles of Christian community, their own denomination. They had a very small circle of accountability. If Jim or his pastor had known the historic understanding of Scripture in the Christian tradition, they might have avoided a dangerous heresy.

ACCOUNTABILITY IN COMMUNITY

Christian community, by its very nature, embraces Christian accountability. Because we hope to be more than a collection of individuals, we share with one another our thoughts, beliefs and actions. We are also ready to correct and advise, while likewise we accept correction and advice. This accountability is essential to our life and growth, and it flows out of our commitment to one another. The level of intimacy and commitment within a community is directly proportional to the level of accountability that the community practices.

The Scriptures contain numerous references directing Christians to confess their sins to one another, call one another to account, confront one another, and exercise redemptive community discipline to help one another. For example, Ephesians teaches that part of being "filled with the Spirit" is that we "be subject to one another out of reverence for Christ" (Eph 5:18-21 NRSV). And James instructs us to "confess your sins to one another, and pray for one another" and says that "whoever brings back a sinner from wandering will save the sinner's soul from death" (Jas 5:16, 20 NRSV).

> Christian community, by its very nature, embraces Christian accountability.

Today many who call for community are unwilling to submit their lives to one another for reflection and evaluation. They want the joys of interpersonal relationships without the responsibility of commitment and submission. If others confront them, they may respond, "That's none of your business," or "What gives you the right to judge me?" This is the major reason that many believers today in groups designed to build community find themselves dissatisfied. There is little or no real accountability in those relationships. When we treat personal lives as being autonomous, we prohibit intimacy because we refuse to submit to one another.

On the other hand, Christians have always recognized the need for accountability. Ascetical circles consistently assigned younger ascetics to be mentored by those more advanced, stressing accountability in every aspect of life. Early Christians in both East and West insisted on accountability to their statements of faith and to their leaders. Roman Catholics and Orthodox continued this after their separation. The sixteenth-century Reformation produced Protestant groups doing the same. Emerging free-church groups, especially among Anabaptists, developed congregational practices to bring accountability. Many of the failures that we see in Christian history occurred when accountability was lost or diminished. Public moral failures among Christian leaders since the 1980s have removed any doubt.

Christians who want to obey Christ have learned that having someone with whom they share intimate details of life can help significantly in the struggle against temptation and sin. Not only the encounter, but also just the reminder, can interrupt the temptation and give the moment of reflection that one needs to make the right decision. Each time we make the right decision, making the right decision the next time becomes a little easier. The opposite is also true. So there is little doubt that we need personal accountability.

But accountability is much more than personal. Groups within churches are accountable to their leadership. Congregations are accountable to one another within their faith groups, sometimes through a hierarchy, sometimes through voluntary associations, sometimes through peer evaluation. Some accountability occurs in dialogues between faith groups. Further accountability could be helpful between Christians of varying cultures in a world where communication shrinks the distance between us. This transcultural Christian accountability might help us see areas of need that we might not notice otherwise.

How Do We Practice Accountability Across Centuries?

The 1980s brought a different way of thinking among emerging generations. Rather than assume that propositional information, reasoned carefully through Enlightenment standards, would give them the objective truth, they began to evaluate truth by how well experiences explained the meaning of life. Bombarded by information, especially through the media, they instinctively became aware that communicators always "spin" information to persuade others. Truth—the standards by which they would live—seemed relative to one's life situation. Some asserted that there is no absolute truth— an oxymoron, to be sure, since the statement itself asserts an absolute truth!

Christian believers, of course, would not assert that there is no absolute truth. In fact, Christians strongly contend precisely the opposite. Christians believe in God, and they believe that God sees all truth, knows all truth, experiences all truth, defines all truth. God is the absolute standard, the absolute truth. But Christians have also experienced the barrage of information, and they also know instinctively that the way communicators see the truth, and their own perception of the truth, may not be exactly what the truth is. They believe that the infinite God always sees the truth fully, but they also realize that as finite creatures, we have a limited understanding of truth. So the truth itself is absolute, but our access to that truth is relative, being influenced by our geography, our life circumstances, our current knowledge, our cultural and philosophical presuppositions, and our previous experiences.

This means that Western Christians today live in a less certain world. This does not mean that earlier Christians knew the truth much better than we do; rather, many of them had far greater confidence that their knowledge of the truth could be objective. Post-Enlightenment Christians tended to believe that using scientific, "objective" methods to examine propositions might very well produce "control" of that absolute truth. But today Western culture tends to reject that kind of mastery because contemporary thinkers realize that no one can be entirely objective—although, as we noted earlier, we believe that we can be "objective enough" for particular purposes.

Contemporary Christians want to be more certain about what they believe. They may be comfortable with knowing that they cannot "control" the truth absolutely, but nevertheless they want to "know" that they believe what is really true; they want to be certain enough about the truth that they can commit their hearts and lives to the One who at the same time is the truth and provides truth.

Contemporary Christians want to be certain enough about the truth that they can commit their hearts and lives to the One who at the same time is the truth and provides truth.

What does this have to do with accountability? Bible-focused Christians study the Scriptures to know this truth. But many times when they reach a personal conclusion, they have relatively limited confidence that they are correct. They realize that their own search was filtered through their own life situation and experiences. Their conclusions are bolstered when they agree with people from their church, their denomination or faith group, and their major theological perspective. Still, they may wonder if the common philosophical, cultural and theological perspectives of these limited accountability partners have caused them to overlook important considerations.

Here is where Christian history can help. Expanding circles of inquiry, already discussed as expanding circles of identity and community, are also expanding circles of accountability.

We believe that God's Spirit has worked in believers throughout the centuries. For Bible-focused Christians throughout the centuries, the Scriptures were at the core of understanding God's will. They searched the Scriptures to discover God's will, though their search was necessarily limited by the context of their worldviews, cultural parameters and finite understandings. Today we find ourselves limited by the same factors. Like them, we tend to consult our closer circles of inquiry—the default setting. Like them, we are limited to the context of our worldviews, cultural parameters and limited understandings.

In a very real sense, we can be accountability partners with them. Although we cannot exchange with them the existential details of our lives, we nevertheless can practice accountability with them—mutual accountability—in several ways. As we grow familiar with their lives and teachings, we can learn from their successes and avoid their mistakes. We have all heard it said, "Those who ignore history are likely to repeat its mistakes." This is true, but it is also true that those who ignore history are likely to pass over its successes or to spend countless hours reinventing arguments, methods and strategic actions that have been modeled for us time and again. At the same time, we can evaluate their arguments, methods and behaviors by the discoveries that we have made since their time. We can do this in several areas.

First, we compare our worldviews and our philosophical assumptions with theirs. Scholars have always done this, finding inadequacies in the philosophical presuppositions of their forebears and making adjustments in their thinking. This is accountability, but only in one direction. We must also evaluate our worldviews and philosophical assumptions by comparing them to theirs in order to discover shortfalls and find weaknesses in our own thinking. We can find problems in their assumptions and learn to evaluate our own presuppositions. As Clark Pinnock says, "The distilled wisdom of tradition offers a social check upon one's own biases."[2]

Shifts in philosophical thinking have always affected the presuppositions that Christians bring to theology. Christians believe that God has revealed what we need to know of infinite truth, though our finite minds perceive this truth with the parameters of our philosophical presuppositions. Each philosophy is a finite effort to understand infinite truth. Each time a new paradigm surfaces, Christians must rethink how they understand truth, and reality, within the parameters of that emerging paradigm. For example, when the thirteenth century moved from Neoplatonic to Aristotelian understandings of reality, within a generation the shift was widespread. Thomas Aquinas, in his *Summa theologiae*, utilized the principles of Aristotle's *Metaphysics* to reason for Christian faith and tradition. Lines of reasoning changed, but the truth about which they reasoned did not change; they critiqued Neoplatonism, but if doctrinal explorations differed from the tradition, they allowed the earlier Christians to hold them accountable as well.

The late twentieth century brought a similar paradigm shift. The scientific theory, coupled with the Lockean notion that the human mind is a *tabula rasa* ("blank slate") on which information is "written," encouraged thinkers from the eighteenth century onwards to believe that they could come to an objective knowledge of absolute truth if they applied mind and method to the task. Although thinkers such as Immanuel Kant and others objected, this "modern" method dominated academics well into the twentieth century. As described earlier, by the 1980s younger "postmodern" Christians were less certain, accessing "truth" in additional ways.

My point here is not to argue for or against the validity of any one shift, but rather to show how later Christians can share accountability with earlier Christians. We see weaknesses of prior methods yet appreciate the positives that earlier thinking produced for us. We allow them to spark us to reconsider our own assumptions, methods and conclusions. Is one philosophical perspective better than the other? Not necessarily. We need each other: our correctives can improve their legacy, and their cautions can safeguard ours.

We can do this because we believe that truth remains truth, though the patterns of thinking, paths of inquiry, and demonstrations of truth may change. We present truth as a gift to one another and to future generations. We package that gift in the philosophical presuppositions and commitments of our own time. We can enjoy mutual accountability across the centuries because we believe that although the packaging changes, the gift itself—the truth of God—does not. For Bible-focused Christians, this means that the truth taught by Scripture does not change, but the way we come to understand that truth, and the way we package it for others, do change.

We also practice accountability with past Christians when we decide whether we think that their teachings were correct. Living Christians have always evaluated their predecessors by comparing their own positions with prior positions. This is both appropriate and necessary. Otherwise, we will indeed repeat their mistakes, reinvent their problems, and even take on their heresies. In order to do such evaluation, we consult Scripture, but we do so mindful of the conclusions by others about Scripture throughout the centuries.

Examples where we hold past Christians accountable for their teaching abound. On the positive side, most of what we believe to be true has been discussed in great depth by earlier Christians, and we profit from their thinking. Christians today appreciate the church's historic exploration and articulation of teachings about the Trinity, the incarnation and natures of Christ, the Holy Spirit, the inspiration and canon of the Bible, God's plan for redemption, Christ's second coming, and much, much more. We conclude what we believe from Scripture, but we utilize their vocabulary, reasoning and emphases to clarify, correct and sharpen our own. On the negative side, it is easy to target aberrant teachings of the past among the Christian community. The Reformers, for example, rejected the erroneous notion that Christians could buy indulgences for themselves and their loved ones in order to escape centuries of purgatory. The notion of purchasing indulgences was a departure from the Scriptures and the tradition. Today nearly all Christians evaluate that teaching as wrong.

We can extend this accountability when we also allow their teachings to evaluate ours. Once again, it is we who are doing the evaluating, but this time we use their understandings to assess ours. In other words, we must hold our teachings accountable to theirs. Why? Because we share Christian identity in Christian community. Earlier Christians also loved God and learned from the Scriptures with a sincere heart. We cannot assume that current theological tendencies, built on our own cultural presuppositions and methods, are superior to earlier thinking. When we weigh our own teachings on the scales of those who have gone before us, we decide whether to maintain, alter or transform our own conclusions. As Grant Osborne recently affirmed, "Church history helps us to avoid the facile assumption that the current community understanding is inviolate . . . by enabling theologians to view the larger picture."[3]

> John shared openly with his university class that he had struggled to understand both Trinity and Christology, particularly how Jesus could be both human and divine. His questions to his church leaders and circle of Christian friends had brought no resolution. However, he then affirmed, "Through interaction with the works of past Christians I was able to form a Christian identity that was orthodox, and I was held accountable for the ideas that I was building."

A recent case study of past Christians holding contemporary Christian teachings accountable may be found in theological reflection on open theism. Proponents argue for "the openness of God"—the idea that God does not foreknow human decisions, at least most of them, and adjusts the divine response and plan according to what God sees us decide.[4] Christians have historically believed that God knows all things, including what each human being will decide. My purpose here is not to debate the issue, but rather to see how contemporary Christians might hold themselves accountable to Christian of the past. One of the chief considerations against open theism is that Christians throughout the centuries have taught

otherwise. We must either embrace the historic position or explain convincingly why they were mistaken. In either case, we as contemporary Christians
are subjecting our teachings to twenty centuries of Christian accountability.

Another way we practice accountability with earlier Christians is when
we assess their actions in light of Scripture, once again as understood by us
and by the church over the centuries. Human nature calls us to see our
identity and our behavior as consistent. This allows us to model our behavior
after those who share our Christian identity and those who have made what
we believe to be excellent choices.

When we believe that they acted improperly, we can avoid similar choices.
Hardly any Christian today would endorse the military conquering of pagan
peoples in order to subject them to institutional Christianity, whether by
Roman legions, Frankish kings, Spanish conquistadors, Russian tsars or
anyone else. Few Bible-focused Christians see the Crusades or the medieval
and Reformation treatment of Jews as appropriate Christian conduct. At the
same time, we should consider how biblical scholars understood the Scriptures in those times.

But when we believe that they acted properly, their decisions for action
become models for us as we face similar decisions, as we will see. We capitalize on the successes of evangelists and missionaries by learning their motives and methods. We are inspired by early church evangelism during persecution, early medieval monks from Ireland and Britain, Anabaptist
preachers, Second Great Awakening evangelists, Dwight L. Moody, Billy
Sunday, Billy Graham and many others.

At the same time, we allow them to assess our own actions, for accountability goes in both directions. We allow their examples to critique, inform
and sometimes transform our understanding of our mission, ministry
methods and challenges. Christians today continue to learn about mercy
ministry and social justice from great Christians of the past. We admire the
Franciscans and Dominicans, the Waldensians, the Wesleys and many
others who lived the simple life to serve others, and who sometimes adopted
radical, countercultural rejection of materialism for the sake of evangelism
and spiritual maturation. No doubt, Mother Teresa will continue to inspire
Christians to self-denying service among those whom the world finds least
desirable. Once again, we do the assessment, but we measure our own be-

havior by the inspirational standards that these past Christians set for us.

Mutual accountability is built on the foundation that believers throughout the ages are one people of God. We benefit from knowing mature, surrendered disciples of Christ who loved God and believed the Bible in other times. Partnering with them, we include in our thinking diverse cultures, multiple paradigms, wide-ranging time periods and various pieties. In this way, corporate resourcing and discovery provide accountability across the centuries. This is true when we find consensus and when we do not. In either case, the value of studying Christian history is no less clear. Even when our study reveals multiple perspectives, we understand our positions better, argue for them with more clarity, and leave a stronger legacy for those who follow. This accountability is transcultural and transtemporal.

Neglecting this accountability can have negative consequences, with us simply reinforcing our own particular perspectives. At one end, we see churches evaluating themselves by their own standards, with no consideration of what Christians in the rest of the world or throughout the centuries would think of their actions, expenditures and emphases. At the other end, we see leaders following narrow theologies and leading their followers into dangerous doctrines, even heresy. In the extreme, cult leaders who live their untested convictions might even lead followers to their deaths, as in the cases of Jim Jones and David Koresh.

Historic Examples

Thus far, I have argued for transcultural, transtemporal accountability by showing that our shared accountability with Christians through the centuries greatly benefits us, and I have proposed in more general categories how this occurs. We turn now to more specific examples. How might we approach studying particular events, persons and developments in the church's history in a way that holds us mutually accountable?

We often assess current events or peers by imagining ourselves as each of the individuals we evaluate. Of course, the more we know about social, economic, political, religious, philosophical and relational factors involved, the better we understand the situation. We realize that later we may learn more that could change our assessment. We avoid projecting our perspectives and personalities onto others.

The same is true when assessing historical events and persons. When we envision ourselves as the people we study, we ask ourselves, "What would I have done it that situation?" Of course, we never know for certain what we would have done. So we ask a series of related questions. "What should I have done in that situation?" "What should they have done?" "How would I have thought or acted if I were the leader in that conflict? The follower? The bishop? The professor? The nonbeliever?"

Consider, for example, the Council of Nicaea in 325. A number of key characters converged to determine the church's position on Arianism. When they arrived, they held several theological positions. The challenge here is to envision myself as each category of person present: the emperor Constantine, the emperor's chaplain Hosius, Arius and other Arians, Eusebius of Caesarea and other semi-Arians, Sabellians, conservatives, previous confessors who suffered under imperial persecution, and so on. The more we know about their social, economic, political, religious, philosophical and relational factors, the more likely we are to understand them. "What would I have done if I were Constantine? Hosius? Arius? Others?" "What should I have done?" "What should they have done?"

We may come to realize that assessments of historical characters or events may change from one period to another. For example, with few exceptions, most in the early church considered Constantine a sincere Christian hero who authentically came to Christ and changed the Roman world for Christ. Later historians suggested that Constantine may have simply used Christianity for his own purposes. The past century has seen most scholars doubting Constantine, with notable exceptions defending him.[5] We may never reach historical consensus on Constantine, but in the process of studying Constantine, Christians practice Christian accountability, which is always tied to identity and community. We sharpen our identity and formulate clearer understanding of who we are and how we should behave.

Because we want to be mutually accountable with Christians of the past, we also consider current events and characters from the point of view of trusted historical characters. We ask questions such as "How would Augustine have countered that problem?" "What sermons and passages would John Chrysostom use in my situation?" "How would Francis of Assisi respond to current social problems, such as homelessness, in my urban center?"

In the process of these analyses, several important things happen. We become aware of perspectives that otherwise we would not have considered. We avoid simplistic answers because we see the complexities of the events, teachings, methods or characters. We begin to identify with those who participated in the event, even when they disagree. We come to understand why sincere believers who love God contend for incompatible views or are on opposite sides of conflict. When we face similar events and decisions, we are equipped to consider a more complete view because of our sensitivity to others. We will still have strong convictions about right and wrong, orthodoxy and heresy, morality and immorality. No doubt we will tend to give greater credence to our presuppositions. But as we connect with the hearts and minds of those whom we study, we reconsider our assumptions, contemplate other points of view, become more fair-minded, and develop more sensitivity.

Again, we must be cautious. We find things in our heritage that embarrass us. Christians do not always make the right decisions or have the right motives. We discover self-serving acts by our Christian ancestors that we could never approve. Some are so appalling that we can hardly believe that anyone who claims to love Christ could ever do such a thing. Still, knowing this helps us understand who we are as our values are reinforced by rejecting what we see as unspiritual or even evil.

In addition, we see that through the ages many teachings, often contradictory, have been suggested. We might be tempted to see twenty centuries of Christianity as a veritable smorgasbord of options from which we may choose whatever we like. This predictable tendency brings very little accountability beyond our closest relational circles. But even if we ignore the tradition, that danger is already before us. Students of Scriptures who ignore much of the tradition already tend to consult their closest relational circles and to cite passages that lend support to their positions while glossing over passages that do not.

One safeguard is to consider the positions of teachers throughout history. I have already alluded to this in the two previous chapters. The ideal is to find convergence across the centuries—*consensus fidelium*, the consensus of the faithful. We hope to discover what has been taught "everywhere, always, and by all" by steadfast believers.[6] The consensus is never complete. And many times we simply do not find the consensus we seek. Yet we benefit from the study nonetheless. When we do find a strong consensus, the preponderance of voices from across times and cultures speaking the same conclusions is powerful, and we grow more certain. When we cannot find a satisfactory consensus, we hesitate to speak on the subject with such certainty.

CIRCLES OF AUTHENTICITY

This brings us full circle as regards the value of Christian history for understanding what it means to be a Christian. Christian identity, community and accountability are thoroughly interrelated. Community and identity are interdependent: my identity emerges from my community, and my community is formed of those who share identity. Who I am is inseparable from the communities that produced me and the communities to which I now belong. I can understand my identity only in the context of these communities. In addition, accountability is essential to personal identity and authentic community. At the personal level, to remain who I am and to formulate who I will become, I reach for the ideals that my identity implies. At the community level, people hold one another accountable by comparing themselves to the standards of identity that have been adopted by the community.

Christian identity, community and accountability that include the entire Christian community are transcultural and transtemporal. We are searching for the *consensus fidelium* across the ages. We want to be certain enough to affirm what we believe. The broader the transtemporal consensus, the more universal the witness that we are correct, and the more confidence we have to make those assertions. The expanding circles of inquiry—circles of identity, community, accountability—become for us expanding circles of certainty.

This is because these expanding circles of certainty give us confidence not only in what we believe, but also in our commitment to what we believe. In a culture of limited certainty, where we find ourselves constantly bombarded with absolute assertions made by those whom we suspect may be trying to manipulate, we want to know what we can believe and what we can reject. We want the confidence that *consensus fidelium* helps to provide. We want confidence that our identity is not an illusion, but rather an authentic reality. Being a part of the broad Christian community, including those across the ages, strengthens our resolve that we stand in the truth, that our faith is authentic. Examining the lives, practices and teachings of those who have gone before us while we allow them to examine us gives us confidence that their lives and our lives are authentically Christian.

So the expanding circles of inquiry become more than expanding circles of identity, community and accountability—and more than expanding circles of certainty. They are also expanding circles of authenticity. This expanded authenticity provides a stronger foundation for confidence that we understand the faith, for commitment to practice that faith, and for hunger to become what Christian faith calls us to become, because it has been believed and tested across cultures, continents and centuries.

> The expanding circles of *inquiry* are also expanding circles of *authenticity*.

MENTORS AND FRIENDS

*Historic Christians Broaden Our Horizons
and Fill Gaps in Our Understanding*

*The Church is the community of all
true believers for all time.*

WAYNE GRUDEM, *BIBLE DOCTRINE:
ESSENTIAL TEACHINGS OF THE CHRISTIAN FAITH*

Since the 1990s a renaissance of emphasis on the tradition has been sweeping across the Bible-focused world. There are many examples. We noted Thomas Oden earlier. There are many others—too many to cite here. But consider some important indicators. The Ancient-Future series by Robert Webber challenged Bible-focused Christians to consider the past to inform the future.[1] D. H. Williams wrote or edited several books calling for free-church Christians to study the tradition, particularly the patristic, early church tradition.[2] The 2007 Wheaton Theology Conference, "The Ancient Faith for the Church's Future," in its call for papers said, "One of the most promising developments among evangelical Protestants is the recent 'discovery' of the rich biblical, spiritual, and theological treasures to be found within the early church."[3] The Ressourcement series and the five-volume Ancient Christian Doctrine series, edited by Thomas Oden, are other examples among many.

Beyond scholarly circles, Bible-focused Christians of many stripes hunger for connection with the past, driven, as I have asserted, by the need for clearer Christian identity, broader Christian community and more authentic Christian accountability. As we encounter great teachers of the past, we are drawn to fresh discoveries that fill, augment or explain truths not typically covered in our closer circles. Many free-church Christians, for example, love the freedom in their worship, but they sometimes find in consumerist, individualist, market-focused worship little more than a thick layer of the very culture that leaves them full of things, yet feeling empty. They suspect that they are really getting a disguised version of their culture, camouflaged in Christian language. They long to experience the mysterious God, whose majesty and presence cannot be reduced to words. They are excited to hear about earlier Christians who did. They are attracted to more contemplative liturgy and to celebrate events highlighted in the historic Christian calendar.

NEW HORIZONS AND FILLING GAPS

Because we live within the limits of time, space and culture, we naturally develop distinct understandings of Christian truth and experience, sharing most intimately with our closest circles of identity, community and accountability. That commonness helps provide Christian intimacy—an important expression of Christian community. But it also tends to develop parochial understandings of Christianity. Unless our identity, community and accountability expand beyond our own place and time, we remain acquainted only with the things with which we are already familiar.

As we move through expanding circles of inquiry, however—circles of identity, community, accountability—we discover whole new vistas. They were always there, but we did not see them. We broaden our horizons because believers of other times and other cultures show us zones of life and theology to which they were driven by their own life concerns. We learn that Christians across the centuries considered teachings to be central that we did not previously see or consider important. We discover areas of theology, ministry and spirituality that we earlier ignored. In some cases, we realize that our prior prejudices devalued teachings and practices that could meaningfully benefit our Christian walk.

As we embrace emphases that were not so evident to us before, we see the great benefit of these additional, and often traditional, theological orientations, doctrinal truths and spiritual behaviors. We are able to fill gaps in our theology—to remove former blind spots with truths that might transform some, or even much, of our theological understanding. Many of us, for example, share the common experience of finding "true Christians" beyond the circles that we once considered orthodox. Some of us once thought of our own faith group as the only true church, or at least the best church. Historical examples abound, including Roman Catholics, Orthodox and Protestants of many persuasions, especially those who emphasized revival or renewal. This was modeled for me when I was a teenager, so I held a similar view well into college. Most friends from other Bible-focused heritages seemed to suppose the same. We might attend each other's churches, but only if we carefully filtered everything we heard. Because we were unsure of one another's Christian identity, we had doubts about embracing each other in authentic Christian community. When we considered past Christians, we focused on those who agreed with us, most often the founders of our own faith group heritage, but sometimes other historic Christians where they affirmed our featured doctrines.

In college church history courses I was introduced to the thoughts, teachings and examples of believers from the past. These believers showed me points of view that I had not considered. My friends at other schools later related similar experiences. Then in seminary we were challenged to consider authors and perspectives far beyond our commitments, and soon I found myself accepting ideas I believed were consistent with Scripture. My PhD program exploded many of my prejudices, as I worked to be faithful yet fair in my theological analyses. Studying historical theology at a Roman Catholic university in the Jesuit tradition, I found myself reading and considering authors whom I never would have chosen before. The openness of the faculty was impressive and refreshing.

EXAMPLES OF EXPANDED PERSPECTIVES

Each of us who has moved through these expanding circles of inquiry could share his or her own story. I am grateful for each of those expanding circles, from the most intimate, where I learned to value truth and commitment, to the most historic, where my horizons were stretched and my life is still being changed. Many students and friends have shared their personal stories of discovery that changed their lives. To clarify how Christian history broadens our horizons and fill gaps in our theology, I will share some of those stories here.

The first example has been very helpful both to me and to my students. Many students bring to their study of early Christianity a presupposition that the early church was the same everywhere, that early Christians shared the same theological perspectives, emphases and approaches to their understanding of the faith wherever they lived. Learning that Western or Latin Christians approached Christianity with a legal mindset, framing their descriptions of salvation, Jesus, and so forth in legal terms, images and vocabulary, affirms their own "Western" thinking. For example, Western emphasis on terms such as "justification" and "redemption" for salvation, and images such as "judge," "advocate" and "sacrificial lamb" for Jesus, are quite familiar. When students find that Eastern or Greek Christians approached Christianity with a philosophical mindset, however, they are surprised to find very different vocabulary and images emphasized. These students are familiar with terms such as "incarnation," but they see the incarnation primarily as something that was necessary for Jesus to get to the greatest salvation event: the cross. They are generally unaware of the Greek theology positing that God the Son lifted human nature to a higher level by taking on human nature. They are intrigued that Greek Christians thought of Jesus (and think of Jesus) primarily as "Logos" or "teacher." They find it strange to consider the Son's incarnation as the greatest salvation event, with the cross as one very important piece of the incarnational plan. Students are also puzzled at first to find that early Syriac Christians highlighted a different set of values, emphasizing growth to become like God in everything but the divine nature, and seeing Jesus primarily as a model to be imitated, especially in his intentional poverty, celibacy and homeless itinerary.

Students realize that most Western churches (Roman Catholic, Protestant and their heirs) still have these early Western emphases, and that the Eastern churches (various Orthodox churches and others) still have the early Eastern emphases. Some are relieved when they find convergence—for example, Western Christians using ideas and vocabulary of Eastern Christians. But they are intrigued that in many cases the Western centers of focus are important subpoints in Eastern Christian theology, which targets other centers of focus, and vice versa (e.g., the cross versus the incarnation, cited above). They discover that both Western and Eastern heirs have incorporated important elements of the monastic life from early ascetics of the Syriac traditions. Soon these students are reading the Scriptures with more powerful lenses, still seeing their prior emphases but now also noticing the accents that historic and contemporary Christians of other heritages and cultures have always seen. These accents inform every part of their theology, broadening perspectives and filling holes.

This may raise alarm in some readers. The point here is not to convince everyone to explain the differences in the same way, but rather to show how the study of Christian history broadens horizons and fills gaps in theology. No doubt professors and their students will explain these characteristics variously, or they may even dispute the premises. But students and professors alike can appreciate invaluable discovery through the study of early Christians and contemporary heirs.

The second example addresses recent shifts in thinking in our culture mentioned earlier. Many students were trained in Enlightenment-directed methodology, expecting a clear, "objective" answer to their questions, especially their theological questions. But as they study issues of theology, either historically or systematically, they find themselves having difficulty being certain on many issues. Their love for the wonder of God makes determinative explanations of complex or eternal truths seem arrogant. Some truths, they believe, defy explanation.

When they discover the apophatic understanding of the Eastern Christians, from the early period through the Orthodox Churches today, they receive "permission" to maintain the wonder that they already embrace. Apophatic theology uses the tools of reason to move as far down the path of understanding as possible, all the way to the threshold of the eternal. At that point, when reason has taken us to its limits, we realize that fuller truth lies beyond our finite capacity to grasp. For the apophatic thinker, it is there that we have the best human understanding—knowing what can be known yet knowing that we cannot know further. There the "mysteries" of God dwell, beyond our finite, rational understanding.

This is especially clear for students who approach the doctrine of God—of the Trinity. They have little difficulty affirming one God in three persons. They understand that the Father is not the Son or the Holy Spirit. They affirm that the one divine nature, one Being, is unique to the three divine persons. From great theologians such as Augustine, the Cappadocians and the Councils of Nicea 325 and Constantinople 381 they can articulate the doctrine of God. But although they hunger for more clarity, they know that this teaching goes beyond their limited human capacity—their finitude. Here there is mystery, "otherness." Many explain that they experience a deep sense of intimacy with the God who is also distant and "other." While they find intimacy in their experience of divine immanence, at the same time they find comfort in the transcendence, or "unknowableness," of God.

I have discovered that my own study, particularly with infinite truths, almost always surfaces realities that seem to be in tension. It seems that every major theological or foundational issue is characterized by paradox. As a result of apophatic theology, I have come to expect and even to embrace some degree of paradox. The apophatic emphasis gives me confidence that when I have studied an issue thoroughly but have not resolved it, I may be closer to the truth than I would otherwise think. My students often share the same experience. Their existential experience is affirmed, challenged or altered as they study historical developments among early Eastern theologians, particularly those who embraced the apophatic. Students grow content with theological paradoxes where both sides seem supported by Scripture, and they find wonder in those doctrines.

What kind of doctrines? There are many. But consider major doctrines held by orthodox Christians throughout the centuries. How can God be one being yet three persons? How can the Son of God, creator and sustainer, become a human being, be nursed as a baby, live perfectly as a model for humanity, then sacrifice his life in torturous execution, only to be resurrected and live for eternity as the divine-human redeemer? How can the Holy Spirit be everywhere always, yet live especially in believers but not in unbelievers, or dwell in the community of the faithful but not outside? How can God know all things yet not determine all things in advance? How can God be sovereign yet allow human choice?

The next example, related to the last, might raise some eyebrows because it considers an issue that has been controversial throughout the Christian centuries. Once again, the purpose here is not to promote a particular point of view, but rather to demonstrate how Christian history—historical theology—benefits the students and expands horizons. Here I share my own experience, and the experience of many students, about the theology of grace.

Western churches generally frame the discussion of grace theology in Augustinian, or Calvinist, terms. We tend to present two alternatives. On one hand is "determinism," or "Augustinianism," or "Calvinism." This position teaches that humankind since the fall is totally depraved, deserving eternal punishment, but that God in divine sovereignty before creating the world mercifully chose to grant divine grace to some (the "elect"), who receive this unconditional and irresistible grace at some point of divine calling and are further gifted to persevere in the faith. On the other hand is "Arminianism," which for Westerners generally means nondeterminism—supporters using the term to point out their rejection of determinism, and determinists using the term to point to the Arminians' departure from what they believe is a core canon of truth.

Many of my students come to seminary conflicted about this issue. Some have only recently realized the differences. Others are strongly rooted in one position. Some grew up in "Arminian" free churches and have grown impressed with the "Reformed theology" of churches they now attend. Others grew up in determinist churches but find real Christians in the "Arminian" free churches that they attend. Still others tend to dismiss those with whom they disagree as simply wrong, or even heretical.

When I began my doctoral studies, I had already concluded that there were scriptural problems with both extremes. I had grown up in a free church that seemed to teach that fallen humankind has fairly uninhibited ability to make choices for God by a thoroughly free will (historically called "Pelagianism," and what I today call "autonomous-free-willism"). In college I discovered many passages of Scripture that taken alone support this, but many others that taken alone support determinism. It seemed to me that believers on both sides quoted the passages that support their own positions and either ignored opposing passages or interpreted them in a way that contradicted their intended meaning. Bible-focused Christians, I thought, should find this problematic. The result: I concluded that I was not smart enough to understand the complexities of grace theology, and that those whom I was reading on both sides apparently were not either, or at least were unable to articulate their positions in a convincing way.

When I read John Cassian, I discovered an alternative position that seemed to embrace all of those passages with little hesitation. This position is often called "synergism," or "semi-Pelagianism," or "semi-Augustinianism." Here fallen humankind is weakened and hindered, having added the pull toward evil to the pull toward good. A person cannot make any move toward God without divine assistance, which God gives to each individual in a way and at a time that is in the person's best interest. Nothing good can occur without the divine power making it possible, yet sometimes God waits to see a tiny spark of good will before flooding with powerful grace, and other times God turns a will toward the good so that it has the option of choosing God. This sovereign supervision of God is seen as the ultimate grace. I was surprised to learn that in contrast with the "Calvinism versus Arminianism" discussion in the West, synergism has been the historic position of Eastern Orthodox Christians throughout the centuries.[4]

As I studied the issue throughout the church's history, I discovered that many godly scholars embraced each of the major positions, particularly determinism and synergism.[5] Study pushed me to reconsider each of the major positions in new light. I became acquainted with alternative positions while coming to understand the traditional Western positions much better.

My own experience is that most students of theology have embraced whatever position their mentors taught them, often without a fair consideration of other positions. The result is that conversations with others focus on knocking down "straw men"—repeating favorite verses and recounting familiar prescriptions without understanding the actual faith of those whom they hope to convince. Studying the issue historically not only provides better understanding, but also motivates us to think more fairly about alternative positions, to study pertinent Scriptures more broadly, and to appreciate fellow travelers on the path to God with affection. Students come with varied positions, and they leave with varied positions, but the process of historical study expands their thinking, clarifies alternatives, and broadens their horizons.

Once again, the goal here is not to persuade readers to adopt a particular position. Probably most readers already find themselves firmly in one camp, with emotional commitments running high. I have many Christian friends who are committed across the three major positions and, quite honestly, to variants within each of the three. I hope instead to show here that the one who studies the grace issue, or any other issue, in light of Christian history expands horizons, fills gaps in theology, and sharpens focus. One who neglects this study limits this potential and runs a higher risk of maintaining conviction based on prejudice.

I have chosen these few examples because my students have consistently shared their similar experiences with me through the past quarter century. They are not definitive, to be sure, for the expanding circles of inquiry grow increasingly broader. Undoubtedly, readers face many areas where studying Christian history will expand horizons, fill theological gaps, and transform understandings.

AUTHENTICITY AND CERTAINTY

In the preceding chapter we discovered that when we find the *consensus fidelium* across the centuries, our expanding circles of inquiry become for us expanding circles of certainty about those conclusions. Here we see that expanding circles of inquiry, when we find no *consensus fidelium*, still increase certainty while giving us permission to limit our sureness about specific conclusions. In other words, when sincere students of Scripture across the centuries consistently come to differing answers, and especially when we see the same differences recur again and again, we can more safely consider the issue "unsettled."

Notice that the issue is not "unsettled" because we ourselves are unsettled. Our foundation in Christ remains firm—strong enough that we are comfortable when we find areas of inquiry that we cannot resolve, that remain unsettled, especially in light of continued nonresolution throughout the centuries. Rather, we grow increasingly confident that the lack of *consensus fidelium* in the Christian community grants us freedom to differ. We conclude that the issue is not one of Christian orthodoxy, and we embrace openly those who come with varied answers.

So whether we find *consensus fidelium* or not, we can move forward with increased certainty because we have practiced more authentic Christian identity, community and accountability through expanding circles of inquiry. Our confidence grows because our inquiry is increasingly authentic, because we increasingly consult more and more of the whole church, both alive and departed—Christians from across cultures, continents and centuries. Rather than supplying answers where there are no clear answers, we find honest peace in those paradoxes.

When believers and unbelievers see this honesty—this authenticity—they more readily believe our good news about Christ and the genuineness of our ministry. We turn to those areas of ministry in part 3, where we will see how Christian history enhances our understanding of Scripture and helps us to minister more effectively.

Part Three

Tradition Serving
the Church

INTRODUCTION

Why would we spend time studying Christian history when we could be investing in Bible study and serving others in ministry? How does Christian history help us understand the Bible better? How does Christian history make us more effective in ministry? Given the demands of life and ministry, will Christian history have a serious enough impact for us to give time and energy to its ongoing study? Part 3 suggests concrete answers to these questions.

We begin by retracing our steps through the centuries, but this time we are looking to see key developments in methods that Christians have used to interpret the Scriptures—in the history of Christian exegesis—leading to the historical-critical or theological-grammatical method popular today.[1] We may meet some surprises along the way. Watch for ways their methods can enhance or supplement ours. Consider how knowing our Christian past contributes to a better biblical text and to better translation. Note ways the work of earlier Christians can contribute to our understanding of Scripture as we practice biblical accountability with them.

Then consider how Christian history helps ministry. As we look at historic models, methods and resources, focus on the specific ministries where you currently work or where you envision you might someday serve. Think about how the work of predecessors can impact your own strategy and preparation. Imagine how you can avoid their mistakes and capitalize on their successes, not reinventing methods long proven helpful. Take note of resources for now and later.

8

Rightly Dividing
the Word of Truth

Do your best to present yourself to God as one approved
by him, a worker who has no need to be ashamed,
rightly explaining the word of truth.

2 Timothy 2:15 NRSV

We are not just to keep our eyes on the ancient interpreters.
We should sit at their feet and accept their tutelage.

R. R. Reno, "The Bible Inside and Out"

Christian Exegesis Across the Centuries

Early Church

When the church began, it already had a set of Scriptures, which we call the "Old Testament Scriptures." Christians approached the Old Testament as God's authoritative Word, expecting to find Christ revealed throughout. As the New Testament Scriptures were written, the early church used them alongside the Old Testament Scriptures, interpreting the New Testament as the apostles had interpreted the Old Testament. The apostles used methods of interpretation that were already popular in their day, established by those who had gone before them.[1] They based their interpretation on the literal, but they believed that other meanings were there also. This included literal, typological and allegorical applications of Old Testament passages.

Within the New Testament Scriptures we already see these methods being used. Many times the authors refer to the literal meanings of Old Testament passages. They also used typology extensively. Paul, for example, calls Adam "a type of the one who was to come" (Rom 5:14 NRSV). New Testament writers also apply allegory to Old Testament passages, events and characters. In Galatians 4:21-31, for example, Paul uses multiple allegory. First he says that Sarah and Hagar are two covenants. Hagar is Mount Sinai in Arabia, which corresponds to present Jerusalem, meaning the unconverted Jews, who live by the old covenant. By extension, Sarah is Jerusalem from above, meaning the Christians, now free in the new covenant. He applies Isaiah 54:1 to Sarah and the new covenant. There are many other examples.[2] We should not be surprised to learn that other Christians in the early centuries employed these same methods.[3]

Irenaeus (ca. 130–202) used both Old Testament and New Testament Scriptures extensively. At the core of his theology is the unity of God, as opposed to the dualistic Gnostics, who considered the Old Testament god to be a demiurge and the New Testament god to be a god of love. Irenaeus interprets the Scriptures through the paradigm of recapitulation, already present in Romans 5 but carried much further in his most famous work, *Against All Heresies*. Christ gave human history a fresh start on the path to salvation.[4] Irenaeus's assumption of unity between the Old Testament and the New Testament was foundational to early church exegesis. He also insisted one must "diligently read the Scriptures in company with those who are presbyters in the Church, among whom is the apostolic doctrine"[5] This he called the "rule of truth."[6]

Eventually in the early church geographical groupings of scholars approached the Scripture with different emphases. Two are best known. On one hand was the Alexandrian school, which saw the necessity of literal exegesis but emphasized greater value in the "spiritual" meanings of the text—typology and allegory. On the other hand was the Antiochene school, which primarily emphasized the literal meaning, although it did use allegory occasionally.[7]

Most early church fathers believed that the mystery of Scripture included meaning beyond the literal meaning. This is because of several presuppositions about the Scriptures. They assumed that the Bible was fundamentally cryptic. They thought of the Bible as a book of lessons instructing Christians how to live in their own day. They trusted that the Bible contained no contradictions and no mistakes and was harmonious throughout. They appealed to the Bible as given by God, with God speaking directly or through others. In short, they believed that "the Bible is cryptic, relevant, perfect, and divinely granted."[8] They also understood the Old Testament passages to point to Jesus, uncovering hidden references to Christ wherever application could be made.

Origen (185–254) is the best-known representative of the Alexandrian school. His description of proper interpretation can be found in *On First Principles* 4.1-3. He taught that just as the human being is flesh, soul and spirit, so Scripture has flesh, soul and spirit meanings.[9] The flesh (literal meaning) is useful for simple believers, but more mature Christians see the deeper, spiritual meanings.[10] Not all passages have all three meanings—some have only the spiritual—but passages true in their literal meaning far outnumber those with only spiritual meaning.[11] Origen used allegory (spiritual) throughout his works, citing New Testament use of Old Testament passages and the literal meanings of other passages to verify spiritual meanings. For Origen, the literal meaning by itself could lead to misunderstanding; the spiritual meaning is deeper and more instructive.

The desert fathers also sought multiple meanings from Scripture. This is clear from Cassian's report of the teachings of Abba Serenus and Abba Nesteros. Serenus says that some passages "offer intelligibility and meaning at first glance," others need "allegorical interpretation" to avoid "more harm than good," and still others are "properly taken either way—that is, both historically and allegorically."[12] Nesteros begins by describing two kinds of knowledge: practical (learned by correcting behavior and rejecting sin) and theoretical (contemplating divine things and sacred meanings). In order to attain the latter, one must first pursue the former "with all his strength and power," since "the theoretical can never be seized without the practical."[13] The theoretical has two parts: "historical interpretation and spiritual understanding." Spiritual knowledge has three kinds: "tropology, allegory, and anagogy." The four meanings of Jerusalem, he says, demonstrate the four meanings: (1) historical—the city of the Jews; (2) allegorical—the church of Christ; (3) anagogical—the heavenly city of God; (4) tropological—the soul of the human being.[14]

Augustine also distinguishes between literal and allegorical discourse, and he tells how to decide between them: "Accordingly, in regard to figurative expressions, a rule such as the following will be observed, to carefully turn over in our minds and meditate upon what we read till an interpretation be found that tends to establish the reign of love. Now, if when taken literally it at once gives a meaning of this kind, the expression is not to be considered figurative."[15] Augustine cites Tyconius for seven rules of interpretation. In each rule the interpreter must discern what in the passage refers to each alternative: (1) Christ or his body; (2) twofold division of the Lord's body, meaning real or counterfeit Christians; (3) the promises or the law; (4) *species* or *genus* (parts and the whole); (5) times, meaning in synecdoche (i.e., the part for the whole or the whole for the part); (6) recapitulation, or recognizing when the Scripture reiterates what it already said; (7) the devil or his body, meaning Satan himself or his followers.[16]

So by the end of the fifth century, despite the influence of the Antiochene school, which became increasingly more literal in its exegesis, most early Christian writers sought both literal and spiritual meanings. Why? They believed that the Holy Spirit inspired the Scriptures. They believed that almost anyone could figure out literal or historical meanings, but "only a spiritually oriented believer can discern the spiritual depths that exist within the literal text."[17]

At the same time, several checks were in place to safeguard that the interpretations would be true. Writers believed, for example, that the overarching interpretive principle for the Bible is Jesus Christ; all Scripture points to him and must be understand in final reference to him. They also insisted that spiritual meanings from any passage must conform to, and must not contradict, the literal meanings of other passages. Furthermore, every proper interpretation conforms to the rule of faith, or the rule of truth—what the church had believed from the apostles. Most important, the insights into the meanings of Scripture could be trusted only from those who demonstrated spiritual maturity through disciplined spirituality, for God would give proper spiritual understanding only to exemplary spiritual practitioners. So not just any interpretation would do. Proper interpretation pointed to Christ, conformed to the literal meaning of other passages, matched the confessed faith of the Church, and came from those whose spiritual lives reflect deep, recognizable experience of God's presence.

Middle Ages

Because Christian interpreters in the early Middle Ages assumed that the Scriptures are one book, telling one salvation story, given to instruct and empower the church, most agreed on the fourfold interpretive paradigm, while developing more precise definitions for each approach.

This fourfold understanding—any passage might have four senses, teaching four truths—was not applied universally. Teachers found that some passages did not lend themselves to all four interpretations, or at least they often did not comment on all four interpretations. Old Testament passages and New Testament parables or stories were more likely to be interpreted in all four senses. Even when exegetes did not employ all four senses to a passage of Scripture, all four were available for discerning a text's meaning(s) and for applying meaning(s) in a variety of situations. Why? "For the medieval, the literal sense of the text opened out into a christological allegory, which, because Christ is the head of his body, opened out into tropological instruction and, because Christ is the King of a kingdom here yet also coming, into anagogical hope."[18]

In the East exegesis continued to highlight contemplative insight into Scripture and confirm the rule of faith through the four methods transmitted from the desert fathers by Cassian. In the West interpretive method became standardized. The literal sense teaches facts or deeds and can be understood by nearly anyone. The allegorical sense (including typology) teaches what one should believe from the passage. The moral sense helps the listeners to know right behavior and right direction. The anagogical sense helped the believer plan for the eschaton based upon spiritual principles.

Gregory I (pope 590–604), for example, systematically employs the literal, then the typological, then the moral sense in his *Commentary on Job*, which became the exemplar for most medieval exegesis. Although each exegete might have peculiar variations, the fourfold method is included and followed by nearly all of the leading Western exegetes, such as Isidore of Seville (560–636), Bede (672/673–735), Alcuin (740s–804), Abelard (1079–1142), Bernard of Clairvaux (1090–1153), Hugh of St. Victor (ca. 1096–1141), Joachim of Fiore (ca. 1135–1202), Thomas Aquinas (ca. 1225–1274), Bonaventure (1221–1274) and Nicholas of Lyra (ca. 1270–1349).[19]

Proper interpretation, they believed, must always match the faith of the church. Few people had access to serious Bible study, though they might hear Scripture read (in Latin in the West) and briefly interpreted in worship, especially in larger churches. Rather than interpreting the Scriptures themselves, many preachers repeated the teachings of their predecessors. Allegorical interpretation increasingly repeated the allegorical applications of those highly venerated. By the time of John Scotus Eriugena (ca. 815–ca. 877) this became standard.

Two other methods illustrate biblical study in the Middle Ages. First, Eastern writers from the early sixth century, such as Procopius of Gaza (ca. 465–528), developed the *catena* (Latin for "chain") method, which Western writers adopted as well. *Catenae* were lists of quotations from respected church fathers on each passage of Scripture. Second, "glossing," developed in the West from the twelfth century, provided helpful grammar, definitions or catenae between the lines of the biblical text and/or in the columns beside the biblical text. These came to be used in schools of various levels.

Soon there arose a class of professional teachers, giving rise to scholasticism. Groups of students gathered around these professional teachers, who taught in their respective schools. The presence of several of these "scholastics" in the same place led to the establishment of universities, where guilds of teachers, or "masters," taught paying students, called "scholars." The most advanced teachers were doctors of theology.

The professional theologians, or "schoolmen," assumed the fourfold sense and preferred the spiritual senses. But there was still widespread respect for the literal meaning of the passages, leading expert teachers to explore the nature of language, to learn biblical languages, to ask rhetorical questions, and to consider other factors that help primarily with the literal meaning of the text.[20] Hugh of St. Victor, for example, insisted on the primacy of the literal sense, and he pointed his school at Paris in this direction.[21] Others, including Thomas Aquinas and Nicholas of Lyra, followed his lead. Yet "spiritual interpretation" continued as the assumed goal, and Bonaventure explained, "There is allegory when one fact points to another according to what is to be believed; tropology or morality, when a fact points to what is to be done; anagogy or uplifting of the soul, when it points to what is to be hoped for, the eternal felicity of the Saints."[22]

Schoolmen also produced collections of excerpts from church fathers. From these they could glean theological teaching gems. In this way, in twelfth-century Paris, Peter Lombard produced his *Sentences*, which became the primary theological "textbook" of the Middle Ages. Until the doctoral level, students' study of Scripture was limited, for teachers thought that Scripture would be misunderstood unless students had proper theological and philosophical foundations.[23]

In contrast to the universities' limitations on direct study of Scripture, in monasteries the monks practiced biblically based spirituality, meditating on the Scriptures systematically and constantly, memorizing and praying large sections, especially the psalms. Knowing the Bible was living the Bible. Insights from disciplined meditation were highly valued, even when they varied from the customary understanding of a passage.

The Renaissance spirit's desire to return to the source sparked not only a renewed interest in the literal interpretation, but also an interest in textual criticism. What did the source actually say? Lorenzo Valla (1407–1457) took the lead. The most accomplished textual critic of the period was Francisco Ximenes (1436–1517), whose *Complutensian Polyglot* (printed 1514–1517, published 1521–1522) juxtaposed columns of Hebrew-Greek-Latin text for the Old Testament and Greek-Latin for the New Testament. Erasmus (ca. 1466–1536) hurried the 1516 first edition of his New Testament text, *Novum Instrumentum* (later *Novum Testamentum*, the basis for the Textus Receptus),[24] to predate Ximenes. Johannes Reuchlin (1455–1522) helped focus Old Testament exegesis on the Hebrew text.[25]

On the verge of the Reformation, then, theologians generally assumed harmony of all biblical verses without contradiction as well as a potential fourfold meaning for any passage of Scripture. The literal interpretation was widely considered foundational for any other sense. Most were ready to use any of the four senses, or all four, to help believers be formed in true faith, the faith of the church. Even when that faith was not yet fully determined, one could use multiple methods to persuade readers to one position or another. The Renaissance spirit had sparked interest in textual criticism and in original languages. At the same time, teachers such as John Wycliffe (1328–1384) and John Huss (Jan Hus) (ca. 1371–1415) foreshadowed a more exclusively literal approach; they believed that the literal truth of Scripture revealed widespread problems with the church and the tradition.

Reformation Period

The Reformation period brought sweeping changes as the church divided and arising emphases spawned new faith groups, all considering themselves to be true to the faith. Text-critical work and interest in Hebrew and Greek continued to grow, seen in teachers such as Jean Lefèvre (ca. 1455–1536) and Erasmus. Scholars who remained Roman Catholic continued to emphasize allegory and mystery.[26]

Most Protestant Reformers began by using medieval methodology but eventually objected to the allegorical interpretations of both early church and medieval exegetes. They believed that serious students could understand the Scriptures without subjecting the interpretation to papal approval. With few exceptions, they rejected the traditional method of fourfold interpretation, contending only for the literal sense. This brought serious objection to many teachings and practices of the church. They felt compelled to act upon their understanding and to encourage others to act. Their exegetical method had great impact on their doctrine and ecclesiology.

Martin Luther (1484–1546), for example, still employed medieval methods both before and early after his Romans 1:17 "the just shall live by faith" tower experience, though he emphasized the literal meaning. Luther criticized theologians' "license to gloss and draw distinctions" to make Scripture say what they wanted regardless of the literal meaning (1521).[27] By 1540 he says, "When I was young . . . I dealt with allegories, tropologies, analogies and did nothing but clever tricks with them. . . . They're nothing but rubbish. Now I've let them go, and this is my last and best art, to translate the Scriptures in their plain sense. The literal sense does it—in it there's life, comfort, power, instruction, and skill. The other is tomfoolery."[28] Luther's rejection of magisterial control over biblical interpretation is indisputable.

Ulrich Zwingli (1484–1531) emphasized that the Spirit of God empowers Christians to understand the Bible, and he taught that an uneducated peasant who had the Spirit could understand Scripture. Although at times he cites the fathers, he challenges students of Scripture to judge the decisions of popes, fathers and contemporaries by the Scriptures. Scripture could be "rightly understood only by faith." Zwingli continues the medieval fourfold sense of Scripture, though with modifications. For him, the literal sense is already a spiritual sense, given by the Spirit. Moral sense is application of the literal to Christian living. He uses allegory occasionally for illustration, but he is quite critical of its abuse. At the same time, Zwingli consulted early, medieval and contemporary interpreters to help him understand biblical passages.[29]

John Calvin (1509–1564) considered the literal sense of the Scriptures—determining authorial intent—to be the core of interpretation. He vigorously opposed allegorical interpretation.[30] The Scriptures should be taken literally: events happened just as described, and teachings should be obeyed just as understood. The Holy Spirit guaranteed the correctness of every passage. The stated purpose of the *Institutes of the Christian Religion* was to prepare theology students for lifelong learning from the Bible.[31] Calvin often interpreted the Scriptures to prescribe and explain church life—doctrine in practical terms. He detected literary devices in the biblical authors and interpreted texts by rhetoric conventions common to his day.[32]

The Radical Reformers held a variety of views on Scripture, though nearly all believed the Bible to be inspired by God.[33] Some juxtaposed the letter and spirit, like Thomas Müntzer (ca. 1489–1525), whose viewpoint was very apocalyptic, or Sebastian Franck (1499–ca. 1543), who emphasized the mystical, invisible church of the Spirit without external signs (preaching, rites, sacraments, excommunication, etc.). Swiss Anabaptists, such as Conrad Grebel (ca. 1498–1526) and Felix Manz (ca. 1498–1527), took the Scriptures quite literally, seeing in the New Testament a "gathered" and holy church, separate from the world, whose members are accountable to one another. The radicals who rebelled at Münster emphasized Old Testament passages that seem to predict God's rule on earth.[34]

The Roman Catholic Church at the Council of Trent affirmed that divine revelation comes in both Scripture and tradition. Bible scholars maintained the fourfold sense but responded to the Reformers by stronger appeal to literal meaning than previously. Examples include Thomas Cajetan (1469–1534), Alfonso Salmerón (1515–1585) and Juan Maldonado (ca. 1533–1583), among many others. Ascetics and mystics such as Ignatius of Loyola (1491–1556) and Teresa of Ávila (1515–1582) assumed the fourfold sense but emphasized contemplation of passages and images.[35]

What of the classic Protestant principle of *sola scriptura*? The Reformers sought to go to the Scriptures, and nothing else, as the final source of God's will and truth. This is the great Reformation principle of *sola scriptura*— "Scripture alone" or "only Scripture."

At the same time, the Reformers' extensive appeal to the church fathers[36] and acceptance of the decisions of the early ecumenical councils demonstrates that they received tradition when consistent with their understanding of Scripture. They rejected tradition that they thought prescribed ideas or behaviors contrary to Scripture.[37] Furthermore, the Reformers affirmed the church's teaching authority, though not the traditional magisterial seat of that authority. Luther, for example, stamped out false doctrine and doctrinal excesses. Calvin and the ministers determined correct Christian doctrine in Geneva, confirmed by the Geneva council. The Anabaptists excommunicated those holding false doctrines.

Recent scholars have pointed out that for most historic and contemporary Protestants, *sola scriptura* does not mean that the Scriptures are the only source of theological truth. They do not see the Scriptures as sole resource, sole source, sole authority or material sufficiency. Rather, *sola scriptura* means that nothing other than Scripture properly understood is the final authority or norm for Christian belief. The fact that the Reformers not only appealed to ancient creeds but also wrote creeds to which their constituents must adhere demonstrates that for them there are other sources of authority, but only insofar as they reflect accurately the teaching of Scripture.[38]

So the Reformation dismantled the fourfold approach to Scripture. The Reformers maintained great faith in the unity of the Bible and in its inspiration by the Holy Spirit, but their primary approach to Scripture was to use all of the tools at hand to reconstruct the proper text of Scripture, to study Scripture in its original languages, and to discover from the literal meaning the divine intention. Occasional appeals still were made to the apocalyptic, typological and anagogical, but the literal sense had emerged supreme.

Since the Reformation

After the Reformation, Protestants increasingly realized that the meaning of Scriptures was not so simple to ascertain. Their disputations and debates showed that they disagreed about the meaning of Scripture. Still confident that informed study would yield the correct interpretation, they turned to the academy to mediate those differences. Although scholars also differed significantly over the meaning, theology and practical implications of Scripture, the relational link between the academy and interpretation by proper method became firmly established.

Roman Catholic exegesis, restricted by dogma, remained similar to the ancients until the mid-twentieth century, when Roman Catholic scholars moved toward more critical methods. Some still contended for the fourfold meaning of Scripture, most notably Henri de Lubac.[39] Orthodox exegesis continued to highlight contemplative insight into Scripture and to confirm the rule of faith through the methods transmitted by early and medieval fathers. Protestant development, though present other places, was strongest in Germany, at least well into the twentieth century. After World War II the English-speaking world exploded with contributions. Here we examine in broad strokes how some of those changes impacted biblical exegesis.

The Enlightenment's skepticism toward traditional beliefs and dogmas replaced foundational medieval assumptions about God, Scripture and tradition with a more reasonable or "scientific" approach. Human rationality—humankind's highest capacity—could dispel ignorant "superstitions" and lead to positive human behavior, hence progress toward higher ethics and fairer law. All beliefs must be subjected not to authoritative tradition, but instead to reason. The impact reached every area of Western life.

This rationalism, coupled with *sola scriptura*'s liberation from dogma, transformed biblical studies. The Reformers had wanted to discover from the authoritative Scriptures the core of the gospel and to determine whether traditions were biblical or not. But Enlightenment skepticism brought the very authority of Scripture itself under scrutiny. The academy, as keepers of truth, explored new approaches to Bible study, and new methods developed. We call the synthesis of these approaches, among other names, the "historical-critical" method, or the "theological-grammatical" method.

Enlightenment thinkers approached the Scriptures from varied perspectives. Christian believers sought factual revelation so that they could choose what to believe, for faith gave certainty.[40] Others, particularly deists, contended that one need accept only what is evident to one's own reason, for they believed that nothing true in biblical teaching opposes human reason.[41] As reason increasingly gained ascendancy over tradition, many abandoned pre-Enlightenment assumptions as antiquated and thus surpassed by modern, scientific knowledge and methods.

Responses varied. Many adopted these new presuppositions with little question. Others reaffirmed traditional beliefs. But scholars, free to interpret the Bible as their presuppositions directed, asked serious questions about matters that before had been received as elements of faith. They questioned the authorship of Bible books, the authenticity of stories that seemed to contradict modern science, and even the inspiration of Scripture itself. Some questioned whether God had given direct revelation through inspired texts, or whether there ever was a normative Christian faith at all. Others argued in favor of the historic faith of the church, employing the same methods and approaches of those who questioned that faith.

German biblical scholarship in the seventeenth through the nineteenth centuries continued to move biblical studies away from prior assumptions, demanding rational explanations for nearly everything. As newer philosophical perspectives emerged, biblical scholars used them as paradigmatic overlays or as additional elements of biblical criticism. Some continued to believe in supernatural events, but others denied them. Even many who believed in the supernatural often wrote as though they did not, reinforcing a growing assumption that faith is irrelevant to serious biblical studies.

Much study has been done, and much more could be said, on the history of the development of the historical-critical method as the norm for interpreting Scripture. This method effectively devalued any meaning of the text besides the literal meaning, or grammatical meaning, or historical-grammatical meaning. Even the literal meaning was to be understood through the paradigm of specific rules and methods and viewpoints. In addition to lexical, grammatical and syntactical analysis, various methodologies were developed, such as literary, form, redaction, source, rhetorical and motif criticisms, and structuralism and poststructuralism. From this expanded toolbox each exegete (or school of exegetes) assembles a particular combination of methods, choosing which approaches and perspectives to emphasize.

As we reflect on the movement in Bible study since the Reformation, we notice major changes. Rationalist skepticism became the default setting for biblical scholarship. People had always read the Scriptures through their presuppositions and methods, but now, reinterpreting the Scriptures by consciously using a particular set of presuppositions or an emerging philosophy or method became the norm. Furthermore, biblical scholars all but dismissed allegorical interpretation as subjective and misleading. Most of the academy assumed that historical-critical exegesis is the best, and for many the only, method for accurately interpreting the Bible; other exegetical approaches were generally dismissed as naïve, precritical and intellectually unenlightened. Finally, unbelievers and many believers reported their research in ways that seemed to make faith irrelevant to "scientific" exegesis. Those who considered biblical texts as merely human productions used historical-critical tools to show how and why the text was written, while those who believed that God inspired the Scriptures used the same historical-critical tools to find what they thought to be the single, accurate meaning of any biblical text.

The widespread commitment to historical-critical presuppositions and tools, now at least a century old, is itself part of the Christian tradition. The challenge to include Christians from across the centuries in our consideration of biblical texts, therefore, drives us to include these exegetes who use the various historical-critical tools.

Recent Trends in Exegesis

A number of textbooks on biblical interpretive method have continued to emphasize the literal meaning and the historical-critical method almost exclusively. In the methods that they present they make no specific mention of considering Christian history or the history of interpretation of specific passages. Among these are T. Norton Sterrett's *How to Understand Your Bible* (1974); Douglas Stuart's *Old Testament Exegesis* (1984); and Gordon Fee's *New*

> It is sheer delusion to think that we can simply leap over all the centuries and encounter the biblical text directly, with a blank mind.
>
> **MOISÉS SILVA**

Testament Exegesis (1993).[42] Some works, such as A. Berkeley Mickelsen's *Interpreting the Bible* (1963); I. Howard Marshall's *New Testament Interpretation* (1977); Walter Kaiser and Moisés Silva's *Introduction to Biblical Hermeneutics* (1994); William Klein, Craig Blomberg and Robert Hubbard Jr.'s *Introduction to Biblical Interpretation* (2004); J. Scott Duvall and J. Daniel Hays's *Grasping God's Word* (2005); and Andreas Köstenberger and Richard Patterson's *Invitation to Biblical Interpretation* (2011) describe exegetical history without challenging readers to reconsider their own conclusions in light of historic exegetes who used other methods.[43] Superiority of the historical-critical method over previous methods seems to be assumed. Students are challenged first to conclude the meaning of biblical texts from their own application of critical exegetical tools and only then to consult commentaries of others. Some point out that Scripture has figures and symbols and therefore meaning beyond the literal; they approve allegory and typology when these appear in the Bible, but they reserve them only for the inspired biblical authors.[44] When I began teaching, exclusive emphasis on the literal meaning was the norm for Bible-focused Christians.

Why did believers tend to consider the literal meaning of biblical texts to be the only proper truth from Scripture? In short, they were committed to the historical-critical method as "scientific" method; they gathered data from and about the text, proposed interpretations, further researched the proposals, and either accepted them or revised them for additional research. They believed that they could thereby hurdle tradition and have more direct access to truth. In addition, they knew examples of poor allegory, typology, tropology and anagogy, and they tended to consider all who used those methods as one group. Finally, they believed that previous generations were necessarily inferior to ours; human development had yielded a more advanced human race.

Each of these reasons has its own problems. Today many scholars doubt that the "scientific" tools produce objective truth, since everyone is finite and approaches the Scriptures within personal parameters of faith and experience. The hope that historical-critical study will carry us over the tradition to the pristine perspective is itself a tradition, and each of the critical methods employed has its own tradition. Eliminating interpretations on the basis that they do not match the God-given literal or historical-critical interpretations is circular logic—earlier exegetes used the "spiritual" methods for precisely that purpose—to find the deeper meanings revealed by God. Rejecting the fourfold sense because some used it poorly would be the same as rejecting the historical-critical method because some use it poorly. Assuming that previous generations were inferior is what C. S. Lewis confessed as "chronological snobbery," because our time, like every other period, has "its own characteristic illusions" that "lurk in those widespread assumptions which are so ingrained in the age that no one dares to attack or feels it necessary to defend them."[45] Certainly Origen, Gregory of Nazianzus, Augustine and Thomas Aquinas rival the best intellects of the twenty-first century.

Since the 1980s, however, many theologians have questioned whether the historical-critical method alone is adequate. Some textbooks changed direction. The first edition of Grant Osborne's *The Hermeneutical Spiral* (1991), for example, recommends as final exegetical steps the examination of systematic theology and historical theology.[46] But the second edition makes a remarkable shift. Osborne's chart relating exegesis, biblical theology, systematic theology and historical theology shows historical theology as foundational to the other three. Historical theology "plays a critical part in the hermeneutical enterprise, though it is conspicuously absent in most commentaries or works of theology." Church history is important for hermeneutics because we see historic interpretations of passages, follow development of particular doctrines, and trace our confessional tradition's origins and belief structure.[47]

The same emphatic shift can be seen in Moisés Silva's exegetical methodology in his commentary on Galatians. In the first edition, *Explorations in Exegetical Method: Galatians as a Test Case* (1996), he says little about historical theology's impact on exegesis.[48] In the revised edition, *Interpreting Galatians: Explorations in Exegetical Method* (2001), he says that some exegetes study history of interpretation to see earlier opinions about particular texts, but another approach "focuses less on *content* (i.e., the results of exegesis) and more on *principles and methods*. The question then becomes . . . *how* they [historic Christians] reached their conclusions and *how* they justified them."[49] He instructs readers to evaluate their own approach by reflecting on the hermeneutical principles of earlier writers, helping students to decide among possible interpretations but also to consider the strengths and weaknesses of contemporary methods. Silva says that teaching students first to form their own opinions of the text falsely implies that they can come to the text without presuppositions. He points out that "not a few Christians" think that reading commentaries, especially ancient commentaries, is "at best a waste of time, at worst an obstacle to faithful Bible reading."[50] Silva contends that historic interpretation is God's gift to the contemporary church.

Others are also challenging exegetes to integrate Christian history and historic approaches into contemporary exegetical method. David Steinmetz (1980) argues for including "the medieval theory of levels of meaning in the biblical text."[51] Robert Stein (1978) surveys ancient exegetes on the parable of the good Samaritan, though after his survey he uses only modern writers.[52] Christopher Hall (1998) joins the chorus of voices.[53] Ronald Heine (2007) examines early patristic use of Scripture.[54] Particularly impressive is John L. Thompson's *Reading the Bible with the Dead* (2007). He contends that we do not know what Scripture means until we have examined what Scripture has meant, that commitment to biblical authority "will actually drive us *toward* a deeper knowledge of Christian tradition and the history of interpretation, not *away* from it."[55]

Many are also proposing alternatives to the divorce of faith from scholarly exegesis. One approach is what some call "participatory exegesis" or "theological interpretation." In this approach, since the triune God acts in all of Scripture, students concentrate not only on linear-historical tools, but also on doctrines, practices and spirituality. Proponents include, among many others, Matthew Levering, in *Participatory Biblical Exegesis* (2008); Peter Leithart, in *Deep Exegesis* (2009); and J. Todd Billings, in *The Word of God for the People of God* (2010).[56] This approach intentionally integrates elements often kept distinct since the Enlightenment—theory and practice, critical methods and spirituality. They affirm historical-critical method but call for exegetes to employ theology ("participatory tools"—doctrines and practices). This recalls ancient practice and the challenges of Henri de Lubac mentioned above.

The recent interest in historical theology is also clear from the production of major resources that provide exegetical help from Christians across the centuries. Every time an ancient commentary is edited and translated, whether by itself or as part of a multivolume series, that commentary is more widely available. The Ancient Christian Commentary on Scripture series recaptures the use of catenae and glossing to collect comments on passages from historic exegetes. The Church's Bible series, a multivolume commentary, draws extensively on patristic and medieval commentators. The Reformation Commentary on Scripture series gathers commentary from a variety of influential as well as lesser-known voices among the Reformers and their immediate heirs.

At the same time, we see increasing interest in knowing how contemporary Christians of multiple cultures understand the Scriptures. This should come as no surprise, for Christianity is growing exponentially in many parts of Asia and Africa, and the rest of global Christianity far outnumbers Christians in the West. The Asia Bible Commentary is a multivolume series written by authors from various Asian cultures to help Asians interpret the Scriptures in their various contexts. This commentary in English will also help non-Asians to see how contemporaries of other continents and cultures understand and apply Scripture. Similarly, the *Africa Bible Commentary*, a single volume on the whole Bible written in Africa by African scholars, sheds light on Christian emphases and elements of Christianity evident to Africans as they read Scripture.

> Detachment of the Christian past from applying the word of God in the present risks . . . having Scripture explained (or ignored) according to the whims or agenda of whoever is doing the explaining.
>
> **D. H. WILLIAMS**

So we see among Bible-focused Christians a swelling interest in what the Christian community across the globe and across the centuries has taught about Scripture, especially about particular Bible texts. More and more Christians exhibit an inner desire to know who we are in the context of the whole Christian community, sharing accountability that reaches across cultures, continents and centuries.

How Christian History Helps Bible Study

Anyone who uses the Bible—from Bible reader to trained biblical exegete—benefits from knowing church history. Here we consider ways that Christian history helps each of us gain increased knowledge and informed confidence in the text, translation and interpretation of Scripture.

Anyone who uses the Bible— from Bible reader to trained biblical exegete—benefits from knowing church history.

Better Text and Translation

As a college sophomore, I eagerly took Greek. I was excited to read and understand exactly what the apostles and other New Testament authors wrote. Near the end of the first year of Greek, the professor pointed out textual variants at the bottom of the Greek text. My heart sank. In order to read exactly what the apostles wrote, I would need to know much more than Greek language. From that day on, I began reading about New Testament textual criticism. I took three more years of Greek, then a seminary textual-criticism course from an expert textual critic. My MDiv thesis was a critical study of John's Gospel from a tenth-century Gospels codex.[57] My study had produced great confidence in the New Testament text, but by then I realized that although the New Testament texts are reliable, I would never know exactly what the apostolic community wrote. I focused on translating the best critical text and on understanding what the apostolic community meant. Discerning the text would still be foundational, but I also needed exegetical tools, Christian history, systematic theology, community reflection and prayer.

Textual criticism. Textual criticism is the science by which trained scholars compare manuscripts of the Bible, taking into consideration the date, geography, textual genealogy, method of transmission and theological orientation of their producers, in order to determine as best as possible the precise text of the Bible. This can be a very complex process.

Thanks to text-critical experts, we can have strong confidence in the text. With little doubt, the New Testament texts are the most trustworthy of all ancient texts.[58] Very seldom do broadly supported variant readings, at least for the New Testament Scriptures, have significant impact on the meaning of particular passages.[59]

The point here is not to argue how reliable particular texts are, but rather to help us see how Christian history can help us discern and have confidence in the text of Scripture. Consider two examples of disputed texts from Bruce Metzger and Bart Ehrman's *The Text of the New Testament*. Treatment of the passage about the woman caught in adultery shows extensive knowledge of Christian history, referring to Tatian (second century),

Didymus the Blind (fourth century), George of Athos (eleventh century), Euthymius Zigabenus (twelfth century) and numerous text traditions, not to mention a sweeping statement covering the first millennium of Greek fathers. The section on the endings for Mark's Gospel cites several texts but also refers to Justin Martyr (second century), Tatian (second century), Clement of Alexandria (second-third centuries), Origen (third century), Ammonius (third century), Eusebius (third-fourth centuries) and Jerome (fourth-fifth centuries).[60]

Most Bible readers inevitably wonder why the passage about the adulterous woman does not appear in their text, or why the passage does appear but is in brackets, or why Mark's Gospel has multiple endings. For many, the simple note about earlier manuscripts is enough, but others want to know more. If they read a source like the one above and find themselves in unfamiliar territory, they may stop, but if they recognize some of the names, they read further. Christian history empowers them to go deeper.

Biblical exegetes, however, are trained to examine resources further. If they know the persons, events and documents cited, they move more quickly through their investigation. Otherwise, they find themselves pressed to become familiar with the persons, events and documents in order to have confidence in their conclusions.

At an even more advanced level, textual critics must know Christian history extensively—key characters, events, doctrinal developments, monastic establishments, paleography and much more—if they expect to make credible decisions about when and why certain readings appeared.[61]

Translation. Since few Christians can read Hebrew, Greek and Aramaic, most believers access Scripture through translations. This makes accurate translation foundational to the biblical knowledge of nearly all Christians who read, meditate upon, memorize and quote familiar translations. The spectrum of translation theory ranges from very literal word-for-word rendering on one end to conceptual paraphrase on the other. Between those poles are various levels of dynamic equivalence—the principle by which the translator strives to capture the sense of the source language but not necessarily word-for-word correspondence. Generally speaking, if one understands the goal of the translation, nearly any translation that seeks accuracy from original texts can be useful, and published Bible versions are available for each.

Knowing Christian history helps both reader and translator. From Christian history the reader understands the development of translation theory, the history of translation within a particular language, and the presuppositions or methods behind published Bible translations. The translator makes theologically informed renderings that take into account the way earlier Christians who were familiar with the original languages understood those texts.

Sometimes translators bypass earlier theological language—ignore translation history—hoping to be true to the original text or to minimize the risk of theological misunderstanding that previous translations might promote. This is often very helpful, but sometimes a core teaching may be altered or an opportunity lost, particularly when earlier theologians speaking the same language as the text understood the passages in the more traditional way.

Consider three New Testament examples of how knowing Christian history can help with biblical translation, moving from more obvious to more debated. Do not be alarmed by unfamiliar Greek words; they are supplied only to help Greek readers. Note how in each example Christian history helps both Bible readers and biblical exegetes.

First, the Greek word *ekklēsia* was a common first-century word for "assembly." Very early in the church, *ekklēsia* was used to refer to the gathering of Christians in local assemblies, but within a short time *ekklēsia* could also refer to the people of God not gathered or assembled, or the people of God throughout the world. These meanings are already present in the New Testament, and in the early church they are used interchangeably by Greek-speaking believers.

In English we almost always translate *ekklēsia* as "church" or "Church" and use that word to indicate anything from a few Christians, to specific denominations, to global Christians, to all Christians across the centuries. Context and adjectives clarify or differentiate. If we were to translate *ekklēsia* as "assembly" or "gathering," many biblical passages and many subsequent statements about the church would lose their meaning.

We want our translations to be accurate renderings of the original languages. At the same time, we must take into account the theological development of language when we translate. This is what translators do when they render *ekklēsia* as "church" rather than as "assembly" or "gathering." They choose a rendering that communicates the intended meaning of the passage.

Our second example focuses on Philippians 2:7, where translation can have a limiting effect, particularly on Bible readers who have no access to the original language. We focus on the phrase *heauton ekenōsen*. The Greek verb in this phrase, *kenoō*, is the word translated differently. Popular English translations include those listed in table 8.1.

Table 8.1

Translation	Philippians 2:7
KJV (1611)	made himself of no reputation
ASV (1901)	emptied himself
RSV (1952)	emptied himself
NASB (1971)	emptied Himself
NIV (1984)	made himself nothing
NRSV (1989)	emptied himself
ESV (2001)	made himself nothing

Scholarly debate is not widespread for this term, though theological dictionaries give several translation alternatives.[62]

Here is where both curious Bible readers and trained exegetes can turn to historic Christians for help. Comments by early Christian leaders from both East and West, though they express various aspects of the theological implications of the passage, consistently align themselves with "emptied himself" as the translation.[63] Many spoke Greek. The early Christian hymn in Philippians 2:5-11 no doubt needs theological explanation, but "made himself nothing" is more difficult to explain than "emptied himself." Is one of these two more true to the original text? That is the debate.

Our third example has been debated by New Testament scholars for over half a century.[64] Compare popular English translations of the Greek word *monogenēs*, especially when used to describe God the Son in the passages listed in table 8.2.

Table 8.2

Translation	John 1:14: *monogenous [para patros]*	John 1:18: *monogenēs [theos/huios]*	John 3:16: *[ton huion ton] monogenē*	John 3:18: *[tou] monogenous [huiou tou theou]*	1 John 4:9: *[ton huion autou ton] monogenē*
KJV (1611)	only begotten [of the Father]	only begotten [Son]	only begotten [Son]	only begotten [Son of God]	[his] only begotten [Son]
ASV (1901)	only begotten [from the Father]	only begotten [Son]	only begotten [Son]	only begotten [Son of God]	[his] only begotten [Son]
RSV (1952)	only Son [from the Father]	only [Son]	only [Son]	only [Son of God]	[his] only [Son]
NASB (1971)	only begotten [from the Father]	only begotten [God]	only begotten [Son]	only begotten [Son of God]	[His] only begotten [Son]
NIV (1984)	One and Only [... from the Father]	[God the] One and Only	one and only [Son]	[God's] one and only [Son]	[his] one and only [Son]
NRSV (1989)	[a father's] only son	only [Son]	only [Son]	only [Son of God]	[his] only [Son]
ESV (2001)	only Son [from the Father]	only [God]	only [Son]	only [Son of God]	[his] only [Son]

How can Christian history help here? During the Arian crisis in the fourth century, authors focused much of their discussion of the Son on *monogenēs*. Arius and others maintained that since the Son is begotten, and only the Father is unbegotten, "there was [a time] when the Son was not." Trinitarians responded that "begotten" referred not a literal begetting, but rather to the fact that the Son shares the Father's very nature, unique as the Father's Son; later they would teach that the Holy Spirit also shares the same nature, but that the Spirit "proceeds" from the Father and is not "only begotten." Greek speakers, then, such as Arius, Athanasius and the Cappadocians, among many others, assumed that "begotten" was part of the meaning of *monogenēs* and made much of this fact, juxtaposing the Son as begotten with the Father as unbegotten. They understood *monogenēs* as derivative of *gennaō*, meaning "beget." On the Arian side, "only begotten" precluded the Son being fully God. On the orthodox side, "only begotten" showed that the Son is indeed fully God, being the same nature as the Father. This was at the heart of their theological discussion.

How does this shed light on earlier and more recent translations of these key passages? On one side, not including "begotten" in the translation lowers the risk that readers might think that the Father procreated the Son or that the Son had a beginning; in other words, the Son's eternity is not questioned. Expressions such as "only" and "one and only" stress the Son's uniqueness without raising these problematic questions. If arguments for *monogenēs* meaning "only" are correct, this is also more true to the original text. On the other side, to omit "begotten" is to lose powerful historical arguments that were stimulated by a word that no doubt needed explanation. Greek-speaking church fathers who discussed the relationship of Son to Father would disagree with recent *monogenēs* research and find some renderings of *monogenēs* troubling.[65]

The primary point here is that historical theology helps the translator of Scripture make better, more informed choices about how to translate. Bible-focused students who understand Christian history have significant advantage in either translating the Scriptures themselves or in selecting translations to use or recommend.

More Balanced Exegesis

Jason was an outstanding student in Old Testament.[66] He had also excelled in several church history courses that he took as electives. So I accepted the invitation to his thesis presentation, where he shared his work on an important Old Testament passage. He applied the skills of modern critical exegesis and surveyed the work of recent European and American Old Testament scholars holding diverse theological positions. The work was impressive, but he made no reference to exegetes before the twentieth century. Jason later explained that he was interested in their work, but he had followed the practices expected for his field.

Jason's presentation was typical of those trained in college and seminary programs producing Christian leaders. More advanced scholarship often includes the text's historical exegesis, but most pastors, students and even professors believe that the historical-critical analysis of Scripture is sufficient to produce for them the correct meaning of Scripture. But is this true? How could we benefit by going beyond recent methods and commentators?

The positives of the historical-critical method are impressive. Using a variety of lenses—looking at the text from several perspectives—we seek to understand what the text meant for the writer and for the original recipients. We consider identity, time, place, purpose and plan of the author. We establish and translate the text, study grammar and syntax, and explore word meanings. We consider what sources the author may have used, how and in what form the accounts were transmitted before the author wrote, why the author chose to include or omit particulars or stories, and how the reading and preaching of the accounts impact the author's presentation. We consider how the author consciously or subconsciously structured each section. We may include a variety of other perspectives as well.

However, the historical-critical method is not enough to carry the exegetical load. Why? The Bible itself has many examples of meaning beyond the literal. Apparently the New Testament writers, inspired by the Spirit, believed that meanings beyond the literal were necessary for an adequate understanding of several passages they cite. Consider several examples.

Nearly every messianic prophecy had a meaning unclear to both the prophet and the original hearers. Original readers or hearers of Isaiah 7:14, for example, could not envision the virgin Mary giving birth to Jesus as one of the meanings of that text, and certainly not as its primary meaning. Yet Christians since the first century, based on Matthew 1:22-23, believe that Isaiah 7:14 predicts Jesus' virgin birth. Matthew 2–3 includes explanations of Micah 5:2, Hosea 11:1, Jeremiah 31:15 and Isaiah 40:3 that are not clear from historical-critical study apart from their fulfillment in Christ. Matthew 21:5 cites Zechariah 9:9 as a prophecy of Jesus' triumphal entry. Christ's passion narratives cite numerous fulfillments that historical-critical reading of the Old Testament passages could not produce: consider Matthew 27:9-10 from Zechariah 11:12; Matthew 27:46 and Mark 15:34 from Psalm 22:1; John 19:24 from Psalm 22:18; John 19:36 from Psalm 34:2; John 19:37 from Zechariah 12:10.

> The historical-critical method is not enough to carry the exegetical load.

We find many other examples of meaning beyond the literal in the New Testament—additional meanings that the early and medieval exegetes called "spiritual" meaning. The New Testament has many examples of typology. In John 1:29 John the Baptist calls Jesus "the lamb of God who takes away the sin of the world"; the type here is the Old Testament lamb sacrifice for sin. In Hebrews 9 the tabernacle's most holy place is a type for heaven, and animal blood for Christ's blood. In Romans 5:12-21 Paul calls Adam a type (*typos*) for Jesus and elaborates in 1 Corinthians 15:45, where he calls Jesus "the last Adam." New Testament writers also use allegory. Historical-critical analysis of Genesis 16–18 and Genesis 21, for example, would never produce the meaning that Paul explains in Galatians 4:21-31. Jewish scholars still do not see what Paul finds there. Paul says that he is "speaking allegorically" (*allēgoroumena*); one would have to reject the literal meaning of Galatians 4:24 to deny that Galatians 4:21-31 is allegory.[67]

This is not to say that the apostolic writers did whatever they wanted with the text. For the authors of Scripture, divine inspiration revealed the meanings that they found and guaranteed the truth of their writings. Exegetes today do not enjoy that inspirational guarantee. But we also have no inspirational or objective guarantee when we use the "scientific" methods of post-Enlightenment exegesis, for we too are subject to cultural, philosophical, parochial and other biases.

Consider also that the great Christian teachers understood God's will through the Scriptures for centuries before the historical-critical method was developed. Early and medieval exegetes appealed to the literal sense, but they also appealed to the spiritual senses. The Reformers targeted the literal meaning, to be sure, but others in the Reformation period continued to find "spiritual" meaning in the texts. For them, once again, the spiritual meanings were always consistent with literal meanings of other passages. The historical-critical tools are helpful, but they are as intimately connected to our culture as earlier methods were to theirs.

We also realize that believers who come to texts with varied denominational presuppositions employ the same methods to understand the same texts but come to very different conclusions. Even among scholars we find that theological givens tend to dictate how we understand the text—sometimes in the face of what appears to be the text's more likely meaning.[68] Here Christian history can be a preventive or balancing perspective against a priori assumptions as we consider Christian conclusions across the centuries.

The fact that both nonbelievers and believers in the academy use the same historical-critical method but come to very different conclusions shows that we need more than method to find truth. Consider that the biblical studies field includes exegetes ranging from Jesus Seminar founder Robert Funk to evangelical scholar D. A. Carson. Why does one method produce such drastic differences? In every academic field we base proof on presuppositions. When we "prove," we begin with givens, or things we believe, and then we work logically from them. We gather facts, test propositions, and come to conclusions using methods in which we are trained. Then we instinctively tend to interpret within the rubric of our original givens, and as a result our interpretation confirms for us the truth of those givens. Although occasionally the evidence is so compelling that we reconsider our presuppositions, most often we run the risk of processing them through our method to convince ourselves that the presuppositions are true.

Early, medieval, Reformation and later Christian thinkers ran the same risk. They too worked in hermeneutical frameworks, assumed particular worldviews, and found meaning that confirmed their presuppositions. Their approaches are not necessarily better or worse than ours. We need them, and they need us—for identity, community, accountability. But there is a major difference. When we look to contemporaries, we see believers and unbelievers alike in a biblical guild where faith is not considered necessary for interpretive excellence. When we study exegetes of the past, we generally look only to the believers—Christians who considered faith and experience in Christ essential to proper spiritual understanding.

Finally, the contemporary tendency to exalt methodological acumen and insight above one's faith is a major problem. Historic Christians studied Scripture in light of the rule of faith, the faith of the church, perhaps favoring conclusions from more skilled interpreters, but always careful that traditional faith prevailed. Many critical scholars are men and women of faith. But when absence of faith and the historical-critical method become intimately connected in the academy, the historical-critical method not only is insufficient to carry the exegetical load, but also can be used in a way that works against biblical truth.

We have seen that what Christians believed about the nature of Scripture directed the approaches and methods that they used in understanding Scripture. Several traditions of interpretation developed, such as the Alexandrian school, the Antiochene school, the medieval fourfold synthesis, the Reformation school and the historical-critical school. Yes, historical-critical exegesis is one more tradition of exegesis, based on one more set of presuppositions about the text. Believers employed each interpretive tradition to understand God's truth revealed in Scripture. In each age they used methods that they believed were most effective, usually questioned by later exegetes, especially when they did not square with later presuppositions.

Here we see Christian history working in us, expanding our circles of identity, community and accountability. In Christian history we find both new opportunity and new obligation. We evaluate our forebears (their methods and conclusions), and we allow them to evaluate us (our methods and conclusions). Better said, we evaluate our own methods and conclusions using their wisdom and commitments. Recently some have begun to do just that.

In light of the church's exegetical history, how might we as contemporary Christians approach Biblical interpretation? In an attitude of humility, we can do our best to gather the best of the church's contemporary approaches and interpretations—Western, African, Asian and more. We gather historical approaches and interpretations—ancient, medieval, Reformation, post-Reformation, post-Enlightenment, contemporary. Partnering with this great cloud of witnesses on our exegetical quest, we seek to understand the truth of Scripture.

This means that we appreciate the best approaches of the ancient and medieval exegetes, including the fourfold sense of Scripture. Here we see great advantages. We affirm with them that the triune God revealed and works through the Scripture, which is a unified whole, and not merely a collection of pieces that may or may not have much to do with one another. Like them, rather than looking in Scripture for clues in our quest to know what might have "really happened," we approach Scripture as the record of what really happened. With them, we reserve—yes, even expect—a sense of mystery that precludes our having epistemological control over the text. Furthermore, we allow the ancients to teach us their conclusions about individual texts, and we respect their understandings as potentially true when we make our own evaluations of those texts. Yes, we will ask, what is the authorial intent of this passage? But we will also ask, how does this text, or its people, or its events serve as a type for Christ, or for his work, or for his people? What eternal truths in the great salvation plan of God might be present in this account? How does this passage shed light on Christian morality? How does this passage give hope for present and future living, both on earth and in heaven?

We keep in mind the correctives of the Reformation period. We reject interpretations that counter the literal sense of Scripture. We realize that church leaders sometimes operate in their own interest rather than the interest of the fallen and redeemed. We allow the ancient teachings of the church to bring accountability to emerging, mammon-motivated practices. We reconsider traditional practices that encourage sin rather than righteousness.

We also embrace the advantages of the historical-critical method. We investigate the circumstances surrounding the composition of a book or a passage. We seek to understand the literal meaning of the passage, taking into account our best understanding of divine intent through authorial intent. We work to determine the best original text, the proper translation, the meaning of words, the effects of grammar. We ask many questions: When was this written, to whom, and in what historical circumstances? What is the author's—and the Inspirer's—purpose, plan and structure? In what genre is this written, and what are the implications? How did this story get from event to text, and in what form was it transmitted? Why did the author—and the Inspirer—choose to include these events and this information here? Why did other authors leave them out? Why are accounts of the same events sometimes different? What are the implications of the text's structure? How did rhetorical and narrative models impact the composing and hearing of the text?

TOWARD AN EXEGETICAL MODEL

Imagine our own exegetical work as one more contribution to the grand mosaic of understanding among God's people across cultures, continents and centuries. Submitting ourselves in faith to God, we are fellow artisans in the great community of God from eternity to eternity. As we partner with them, continuing God's theme, our tiles add fresh elements and colors that reinforce the rule of faith.

As we contribute, we follow a set of values—healthy, well-rounded values that guide us as we seek to understand that the Bible teaches. When we exegete a particular passage of Scripture, whether verse or chapter or book, we value several elements. These elements need not be followed in any particular order of investigation; where we start and end is undoubtedly left to the Bible student's preference, training and experience. Furthermore, these values are not exhaustive, and so they invite constant review and amendment from the broader Christian community, with whom we share identity and accountability.

Bear in mind that none of us commands all of these insights or approaches at once, and we will not be able to go deeply into all of these approaches every time. As with all skills, we begin with what we know. With practice, we add to our conscious repertoire and become more skilled as we grow. Like the young athlete who hopes one day to compete in the Olympics, we embrace the ideal but realize that at each stage of development we do our best. Each of us is at a different place in that development. Some are Bible readers, while others are expert exegetes, with most of us somewhere between. Our levels of investigation differ depending on our training and experience. Also, competing priorities demand our time and energy. But with each of these tools in our own toolbox, we, as increasingly skilled artisans, select those tools most appropriate for each particular craft, as the task demands and time allows.

Historical-critical (theological-grammatical) tools of exegesis. These methods help us understand the history of the period in which the text emerged, capitalizing on the insightful work of the past one hundred years. We focus on the mechanics of the text and speculate about how and why it came to be produced. We lend credibility to our conclusions, not only under the scrutiny of the academy, but also under the scrutiny of our own training. I cannot imagine teaching in a college or university where the historical-critical method is not an integral part of the curriculum used in the Bible department.

Historic methods of exegesis. Consider including methods employed by exegetes throughout the centuries. Here students with contemporary exegetical training might find themselves experimenting, though we already employ typology, allegory and anagogy in our preaching and teaching more than we like to admit. We might also use additional approaches of a church father. For example, Moisés Silva, in his Galatians commentary, appreciates that John Chrysostom, whose homilies he views as the earliest complete commentary on Galatians, defines by negation (what the passage does not mean), anticipates objections, paraphrases passages and devises mock dialogues with Paul.[69] We proceed with caution, however, remembering ancient exegetes' warnings that only those more advanced in spirituality can discern the "spiritual" meanings.

Understandings and interpretations of contemporaries who share our culture. Study the conclusions of exegetes, theologians and church leaders who share our culture. These are available in commentaries or other articles. How does this differ from using the historical-critical method mentioned above? There we used the tools to evaluate the passage; here we consult others, often more skilled in those tools than we, to survey their conclusions about the text. This can be challenging because many times those who use these methods come to vastly different conclusions, depending on their presuppositions, faith commitments and insights. We can choose our resources depending upon our level of training and experience.

Understandings and interpretations of contemporaries of other cultures. Engage the conclusions of exegetes, theologians and church leaders of other cultures. Currently, resources for this study are limited, but as more non-Western Christians publish theological works, resources will become increasingly available. Consider, for example, the one-volume *Africa Bible Commentary* and the multivolume Asia Bible Commentary series mentioned above. If we know Christians from other cultures, we may ask them to describe what they see in our passage.

Understandings and interpretations of historic Christians. Investigate conclusions of exegetes throughout Christian history. We tried their methods above, but here we look at their conclusions. We must be careful not to dismiss too hastily the explanations of those with whom we disagree or who lived by expectations of another time and culture.[70] Once again we find disagreements and varied conclusions among those we study. But we include those conclusions as we consider what will be our own. Volumes of the Ancient Christian Commentary on Scripture, the Church's Bible and the Reformation Commentary on Scripture can be very helpful.

Ideally, after we have valued the conclusions and methods of ancient, medieval, Reformation, post-Reformation and post-Enlightenment exegesis, and after we have appreciated perspectives about our passage from Christians across cultures, continents and centuries, we are ready to make more informed decisions about what we believe God is teaching through the passage being considered. We can integrate our own findings with those of both historic exegetes and historical-critical exegetes, for both study Scripture in a specific tradition of exegesis.[71]

When we find consensus, our decisions are fairly easy, and we emerge with great confidence that we have discovered the truth. But when we find multiple possibilities, we weigh them carefully. Could some passages have more than one level of meaning? Certainly the apostles thought so. Ancient and medieval exegetes agreed. Quite honestly, many of today's preachers and teachers seem to agree as well (more on that topic in the next chapter).

Best of all, we find great satisfaction—yes, much greater satisfaction—in realizing that the infinite, triune God, surrounded by transcendent mystery, has inspired for us a Scripture that embodies that mystery and transcendence. We still work to be objective enough for our purposes, but we humbly abandon any notion that as finite human beings we can have such control over the truth that we can "scientifically" reach objectivity. This is impossible for anyone but Father, Son and Holy Spirit. We can humbly admit that through all of our study, we are finite and limited, and we need each other in expanding circles of inquiry in our study of Scripture.

> The infinite, triune God, surrounded by transcendent mystery, has inspired for us a Scripture that embodies that mystery and transcendence.

We have confidence, therefore, because our study aimed to include the whole church—past, present, across the globe. Our study crossed cultures, continents and centuries. Our perspective was transcultural, global and transtemporal. We minimized the risk of parochial misunderstandings based only on our most intimate circles. Instead, on the broad foundation of shared identity, community and accountability—with expanded horizons and filled theological gaps—we opened our hearts to ideas that we might never have otherwise considered. And if the conclusions that we reached are consistent with God's intent in all of Scripture or in a particular passage, we discovered the truth that God revealed.

This brings us back to the main question that this book seeks to address: why does church history matter? I have included here the primary reasons offered in part 2. To be sure, none of this is possible unless we study Christian history. Knowing the tradition empowers us to gather the best from across the centuries. When we study historic exegetes and their interpretations, more ancient and more recent, and integrate historic understandings with historical-critical analyses, we remove obstacles to proper interpretation, we expand possibilities for understanding, and we maximize the effectiveness of our study.

9

TRADITION AND MINISTRY

All this is from God, who reconciled us to
himself through Christ, and has given us
the ministry of reconciliation.

2 CORINTHIANS 5:18 NRSV

In her tender, preschool voice, the five-year-old asked two questions. First, "Where did God come from?" The teacher thought for a moment and then answered, "God did *not* come from. It seems like everything comes from something else, doesn't it? But if we keep going back, something had to get it all started. That is God." Her next question was equally challenging. "If God is God, and Jesus is God, how can they both be God?" The teacher explained that the Father is God, that the Son is God, and that the Holy Spirit is God—three persons, but one God. Jesus is God the Son, who became human also, to bring us salvation. That was as deep as they went—pretty deep for a five-year-old.

That day historical theology empowered a youth minister to answer a five-year-old's profound theological questions in her most teachable moment. The first answer came from knowing Anselm and Aquinas as they evidenced God's existence through Aristotelian categories. The second answer drew from the theological and christological controversies of the fourth and fifth centuries.

We study Christian history for ministry. We learn historical theology to serve the church. From eternity to eternity—from before time until time is no more—God has a plan for redemption. We Christians, as Christ's body, incarnate God's plan, both as the redeemed and as ambassadors of redemption, for God is "entrusting the message of reconciliation to us" (2 Cor 5:19 NRSV).

Whether we are already involved in ministry, or may someday be involved in ministry—as small-group leader, teacher, pastor, professor or other ministry—Christian history helps us serve Christ and his church more effectively. How? In this chapter we explore the advantages of knowing Christian history for particular areas of ministry. We see how we partner with Christian servants from the past and how they mentor us. We compare current and historic approaches, affirming or amending our own, learning to differentiate between models grounded primarily on Christian truth and those motivated from cultural or parochial commitments. In the process we discern essential from optional practices. This provides greater confidence that we are serving God and the church with truth and compassion.

Following this chapter are some recommended resources for study in each area of ministry. Those marked with asterisks invite students to a more user-friendly understanding. As we progress, the others can take us deeper. For particular areas of ministry, we might take a course online or at a nearby college or university.

Preaching and Teaching

Preaching and teaching have guided the church from its birth on the day of Pentecost shortly after Christ's ascension. Preachers teach truth, exhort believers to spirituality, and challenge Christians to service. Bible-focused Christians emphasize exposing the truth of the Scriptures to their hearers—expository preaching. So the study of Scripture is essential. But how does the study of Christian history help God's messenger preach and teach truth more effectively? We learn from historic preachers and theologians as our partners and as our mentors.

Many preachers today prepare their

> To become a preacher of the Word . . . is to be made part of the history of a practice and a bearer of its tradition.
>
> **MICHAEL PASQUARELLO III**

sermons with partners, whom they consult through a variety of media. Some form study groups with nearby preachers, individually preparing their own versions of the same sermon but helping one another by sharing research, insights and illustrations. They read from books on preaching or books of sermons. They listen to preachers whom they hold in high regard, in person or from recorded media or online. Some purchase sermons in books or from popular sermon websites—presentation materials included.

Why not broaden our circle of partners to include not only preachers of our day, but also the great preachers of the last two thousand years? Imagine: my sermon study group can include Origen, Augustine, Ambrose, John Chrysostom and Martin Luther! All I have to do is to seek them out and embrace them as members of my circle. We are peers in the divine commission to preach the faith.

The preachers whom we choose to include in our circle of resources are not just any preachers of the past: we choose the *great* preachers of the past. They model preaching for us, and we learn from them. How can they partner with us and mentor us?

> Imagine: my sermon study group can include Origen, Augustine, Ambrose, John Chrysostom and Martin Luther!

We saw in the last chapter how Christian history enhances biblical understanding. Improved biblical understanding, which is foundational to preparation for good preaching, is strong motivation for the conscientious preacher. More inclusive exegesis may result in "the renewal of contemporary preaching in light of the wisdom of ancient Christian preaching."[1] We partner with them and learn from them, and this may include interpretive methods beyond the literal sense.

Teachers of preaching today often object to the spiritual senses, or any meaning beyond the literal, in contemporary preaching. Their caution is well founded because the preacher might use allegory to manipulate a passage to say whatever the preacher can imagine. The safeguard for historic preachers, of course, was the historic truth—the rule of faith—which any meaning, literal or spiritual, must match. But even when professors today instead point only to historic expositors who appealed almost exclusively to literal meanings, their looking to the past is a positive step, for great preachers of history become our partners and models, and we develop discerning criteria for how to choose those partners.

That said, we hear many Bible-focused preachers today use spiritual meanings beyond the literal in their preaching and teaching. Most often the pastor first appeals to the literal sense and then in the application proclaims promises or assurances beyond the literal. Others times the preacher passes over the literal meaning of the text from the start. Consider two examples.

First, a preacher's Christmas sermon focused on Gabriel's appearance to Mary in Luke 1:26-30. The application moved beyond the text: (1) "favored one" and "You have found favor with God" indicated that God holds us in high esteem; (2) "The Lord is with you" assured that each of us can depend on God's personal presence, always and everywhere; (3) "Do not be afraid" affirmed that God's presence and protection removes any need to fear. Understood literally, the favor, the presence and the admonition not to fear are very specific, given to Mary alone. The preacher, in this case without knowing it, used tropological (moral) interpretation. The literal meaning of other passages, and the gospel that we all believe (the rule of truth), gave those assurances. The preacher spoke the truth that morning, but not from the literal meaning of our passage.

In another example, the preacher spoke from Acts 2 on the birth of the church, offering verse-by-verse exposition. The preacher then stopped abruptly and, after a few moments of silence, said, "So what! That was then, and this is now. That was two thousand years ago. What does the birth of the church have to do with me?" The last half of the sermon emphasized that the church's birth is meaningless "unless you experience the birth of the church in you." In private, the preacher described his own application as tropological. No one that morning disputed the truth of the sermon.

When we ignore early and medieval exegesis and preaching while using their methods, we unknowingly partner with them, but they are not our mentors. We borrow their methods, but we lose the wisdom of the great practitioners of those methods. It is not my intent here to persuade modern preachers to use methods that they find intellectually questionable. But since we do in fact use allegory, typology, tropology and anagogy, why not consult the great preachers who did it well? They can provide partnership and accountability, demonstrating excellence and limiting the risk of false application.

Historic preachers can also mentor us on how to preach and teach Christian truth more effectively, especially in the face of heresy. The Arian crisis offers excellent examples of using great preaching to teach effectively. On one side, Arius spread his teaching through popular preaching and by writing lyrics for popular songs.[2] On the other side, the *Five Theological Orations* (Sermons 27-31) and *Against the Arians* (Sermon 23) of Gregory of Nazianzus serve as enduring models of careful theological articulation in preaching.[3] We will see more on this below.

The courage of past preachers stirs us to stand for truth, sometimes in the face of inescapable repercussions. For example, John Chrysostom (ca. 347–407), patriarch of Constantinople, spoke frankly about immoral living by both clergy and laity at the beginning of the fifth century. He decried extravagant, provocative female dress, and Eudoxia, wife of eastern emperor Arcadius, assumed that his denunciations were aimed at her. She conspired to have John deposed and banished at the Synod of the Oak in 403, but John was reinstated when an earthquake the night of his arrest convinced her that God disapproved. Soon John denounced a silver statue of Eudoxia near the cathedral. This time he was banished and eventually marched to death. Preachers today can read his *Homilies on the Statues* to evaluate how and whether to address immoral trends or events.[4]

The persuasive proclamation of historic preachers cautions us be careful, for powerful preaching moves believers to action. On one hand, great revival preaching on the American frontier in the early nineteenth century persuaded Christians to give up whisky; great preachers transformed a drunken wilderness into the Bible Belt. Their powerful effect inspires us. On other hand, Clement II's sermon at the Council of Clermont in 1095 convinced thousands to embark on the First Crusade. Many died, and two peasant armies, convinced of God's protection, were slaughtered.[5] Perhaps the power of his persuasion gives us warning in ours.

When we study historic preachers, we learn at the feet of the church's greatest orators. We see how they applied exegesis in their exposition. We see ways in which they understood passages in light of their own time and culture. We see them seek the literal meaning, and sometimes we see preachers in every century find spiritual senses beyond the literal. We see them addressing emerging trends, rebuking immorality, correcting false teachings, inspiring sacrifice, and sparking social action. Our identity is formed as we partner in community and accountability across the centuries, and we see possibilities that we would not otherwise see.

Becoming increasingly familiar with the history of preaching may surface a deeper affinity for one or more historic preachers. They may become mentors for the contemporary preacher, meaning deeper investigation into their lives, reading more of their sermons or their books about preaching. The personal bond could be life–changing.

Consulting great historic preachers may shed light on a biblical text, and we may want to use their applications. Where helpful, we can include what they say so that hearers can share the same blessings and challenges. In the process, we collect potential illustrations not only for this sermon, but also for future sermons. Many recall hearing about Polycarp's courage during execution, Luther's resolve at the Diet of Worms, Anabaptists' willingness to suffer oppression, or the heroic sacrifices of our particular faith group's founders. Preachers continually listen for potential examples; when they study Christian history, they gather illustrations to help listeners see God working through committed believers.

Where do we start, and how do we proceed? Future preachers or teachers, or those already preaching and teaching, could devote a portion of weekly study time. We can grow incrementally, improving our understanding and expanding our tools for application. We might even set aside a concentrated part of the study year to studying historic preaching, which, though likely difficult to achieve, would be highly rewarding.

Systematic Theology

Systematic theology is the careful articulation of Christian teachings in an organized, integrated, doctrine-by-doctrine system. Careful systematics views each subject, or topic, or area of doctrinal explanation, from two major perspectives: what the Scriptures say about the topic, and what the church has taught about the topic. In the process, systematic theologians use reason and experience to describe the inner unity of the faith. They interpret the biblical, historic truths of God within the hermeneutical para-

> Theology must move among three poles—the biblical gospel, the heritage of the church and the thought forms of the contemporary world.
>
> **STANLEY GRENZ AND**
> **ROGER OLSON**

digms of the culture. In other words, they make the truths of God accessible to their audience.

Faith groups that embrace apostolic succession have always sought to wed Scripture and tradition, believing that Tradition (now with a capital T) itself is revelation. Orthodox and Roman Catholic theologians have produced extensive works in systematic theology. They continue to write hundreds of single volumes, each investigating one systematic topic and closely related issues. They find it difficult to isolate particular doctrines without integrating those doctrines into the entire system. Fewer Protestants have attempted massive works in systematics, though several recent multivolume works stand out.[6]

Bible-focused Protestants place more emphasis on Scripture, believing that God inspired the Scripture but not necessarily the tradition. They have confidence that God has worked through the tradition, but that we are responsible to evaluate what was done by God's design and what was not. For this reason, Bible-focused Protestants have usually appealed primarily to the Bible in their systematic theologies; for them, explaining what Scripture says about systematic topics *is* systematic theology. Historical explanations, though illustrative, fall under another area, which some label "historical theology."[7]

How do historic partners and mentors in Christian history help Bible-focused Christians in systematic theology? While we affirm the primacy of Scripture, we need tradition to help us understand Scripture. Even if we could confine our study to what the Scriptures teach about a particular subject, we would need the history of interpretation on those passages, for theologians throughout history often cited the same passages as they addressed systematic topics. Since all of us bring presuppositions and theological understandings to Scripture, Christians need each other to bring accountability to our understanding. We cannot build a balanced systematic theology without historical theology.

Knowing how Christianity developed throughout the centuries acquaints us with doctrinal discussions as they emerged in their particular contexts. In the process, we see what is at stake in the doctrines themselves. Christology, for example, impacts soteriology (and much more). Christ is both divine and human, raising human nature to a new level and becoming our atoning sacrifice. Being fully human makes him the "first fruits of those who have died" (1 Cor 15:20 NRSV). These are essential elements of our salvation. We learn this from many writers throughout the centuries, but they were important in the fourth- and fifth-century discussions eventually leading to the Chalcedonian Definition in 451. Knowing those events and arguments frames our study of Christology, soteriology and the topics with which they are interwoven.

Historical theology also helps us use theological language more carefully. When explaining the Trinity, for example, beginners often speak of "God," "Jesus" and "Holy Spirit," by which they mean "Father," "Son" and "Holy Spirit." Theologically speaking, "God" refers to the three divine persons either individually or as the triune God. "Jesus" refers to the Son, but after the incarnation. Jesus has two natures: he is fully human and fully divine. Before the incarnation, the Son was only divine, but after the incarnation, the Son, who is now Jesus, is divine and human. Less careful vocabulary tends to perpetuate theological confusion, but careful terminology helps us convey truth more responsibly.

Christian history brings accountability to our own systematic theology. Because "all theological systems reflect the particular cultural grid in which they were originally written,"[8] including historic positions, we need transtemporal accountability through the study of ancient, medieval, Reformation and post-Reformation resources. When we find agreement across cultures, continents and centuries, we are confident in our conclusions. When we do not find agreement, we humbly evaluate the evidence and prayerfully incline to the most likely options.

Historical theology helps the student develop particular standards by which to evaluate comprehensive systematic theologies and volumes on particular subjects. Historical theology also helps pastors or laypersons, with limited time to devote to the study of systematics, to choose which resources to read.

What process should you follow? Decide from personal interest or community need what topic needs to be studied, and then look to the Scriptures. What does the Bible teach about this topic? Tap historical-critical, Reformation, medieval and ancient perspectives to evaluate carefully using the biblical interpretations of other believers, past and present.

Then consult other believers, both historic and contemporary, from your own culture and other cultures. I recommend authors who not only study the Scriptures carefully but also cite historic theologians and their positions.

SPIRITUALITY

Christian history's greatest impact on my life is in spirituality, and for this I am indebted to God and to Christians across the centuries. I always had a hunger for spirituality, stemming from God's gift of creating humans in the divine image. My pastors and teachers encouraged regular Bible reading and prayer, which I did in spurts for many years. I practiced some of the spiritual disciplines when Richard Foster first published *Celebration of Discipline* in 1978.[9] I studied and memorized Scripture, but my spirit wanted more.

> *The lack of a credible and distinctive spirituality is one of the greatest weaknesses facing evangelicalism today.*
>
> **ALISTER McGRATH**

Historical theology introduced me to spiritual masters across the centuries. I first noticed that nearly every great church leader or theologian of the early period also practiced a strict, highly disciplined ascetic life, most often as a monk or in clerical community. They connected theological understanding with spirituality. Later I realized that the great leaders of the church whom I had come to respect most, whether early, medieval, Reformation or recent, were committed to disciplined spirituality.

I was blessed to study John Cassian, who became my spiritual mentor. As I read Cassian's report of conferences with the great monks of Egypt,[10] I wanted a deeper spirituality, and those monks could teach me how. Reading and journaling through the Scriptures and through the desert fathers became a daily staple for me, with periodic prayers encouraging daily spiritual rhythm. Soon I was offering students assignment options for being mentored by one or more spiritual masters from the period or subject being studied. History of Christian spirituality grew popular among students.

The purpose of my story is this. Why does church history matter? Because Christian history helps develop our spirituality. How? There we
find the great spiritual masters, who integrated life, theology, ministry
and spirituality into a singular life of submission to God. They teach us
means for overcoming our vices and for developing the virtues. They
mentor our development, providing models and instructions on how
to proceed along the path, with clarifications, safeguards and assurances all along the way. They teach us how to face our spiritual battles
and the enemies who inflict them. They teach us humility. We are partners with them on the path to God. Each time I study a spiritual master,
I realize that I am a beginner on a long path. But most importantly, I
am indeed on the path.

Interest in Christian spirituality has exploded in the last thirty years.
Bible-focused Christians, hungering for the deeper walk with the transcendent God, who is ever present, are turning to mentors, sometimes in
person, often through writings. The most common entry point focuses on
the spiritual disciplines—reading popular authors such as Dallas Willard,
Richard Foster and Scot McKnight. Soon spiritual travelers realize that
spiritual disciplines are tools for the journey and not ends in themselves,
and they turn to the great spiritual masters from across the centuries.

Christian history, therefore, is foundational to Christian spirituality.
Reading historic spiritual masters inspires us to embark on the journey, to
take additional steps that move us toward God. Listening to their wisdom
empowers us to develop a plan for spiritual growth that is both intentional
and intense. Once we step onto the path, their experiences and instruction
stretch us to love God more deeply and to obey God more consistently. Can
we also learn this from contemporary teachers? Certainly. But the corporate
wisdom of spiritual masters from twenty centuries is confirmed by the spiritual masters of our own time, who guide us to the historic spiritual masters
for deeper wisdom and greater learning.

Spiritual directors, past and present, consistently teach that we cannot
understand the truths of spirituality apart from practicing disciplined spirituality. Real knowledge, for them, is assimilated, primarily through experience. Information apart from practice often leads to misunderstanding, or

worse, to pride that we are mature when we are not. In order to understand spirituality, we must practice spirituality.

So where do we begin? I am not a spiritual master, to be sure. The suggestions that follow arise from my experience over several years—failure and progress, disobedience and surrender, but steady movement forward on the path toward God.

Start by making a plan. Set a daily time and place. Then choose what to read; design a routine for reading Scripture and reading a spiritual master. Scripture reading might follow a structured plan through the whole Bible or through the Old Testament or the New Testament. Certain periods of the year might specialize in particular passages, such as the penitential psalms or the passion narratives during the weeks leading up to Resurrection Sunday; these could replace or be added to the other plan. In choosing a spiritual master, perhaps there is one who has already had an influence on you, or perhaps someone has recommended a good master with whom to start.

Consider journaling. We read more closely, reflect on what we will write, compose carefully what we do write, and pray reflectively. Read the Scripture, summarizing the passage and writing key passages. Then write reflective prayer, targeting personal changes from the Scripture and seeking God's help. Repeat the same process from the spiritual master, including summary, helpful quotations and reflective prayer. This plan gives priority to Scripture, God's Word, yet allows us to learn from the Christian community as well.

Once you are comfortable with a daily time of encounter, plan to pray at various times throughout the day, using psalms or historic prayers modeled by spiritual masters or adopted for specific spiritual needs. Most historic mentors teach how to do this, targeting spiritual sins and temptations strongest in one's own life. Periodic prayer reminds us of God's presence, empowers us to fight temptation, and brings spiritual rhythm to our day.

Continuing on the journey, decide whether to learn from several spiritual masters over a shorter period of time or from one spiritual mentor over an extended period. The former allows breadth, teaching several approaches to spirituality; the latter fosters depth, forming spiritual practice in a unified, historically proven method.

Finally, employ other spiritual disciplines as helpful or necessary; in other words, choose the tools proper to the occasion or need. If the plan includes a spiritual director, choose one who is seasoned, and consider the type of spirituality to be employed. When you fail, do not be legalistic; remember that spiritual disciplines, and corresponding personal application, are tools— means to help us grow pure in heart. When you fail, or when life interrupts the routine, start again the next day. But stay on the path. God will help.

Hundred of books have been published on historic Christian spirituality. Some examine spirituality within a faith group (e.g., Roman Catholic, Orthodox, Anabaptist) or within a monastic school of thought (e.g., Franciscan, Cistercian, Ignatian). Others consider themed spiritual models (e.g., Russian, Celtic) or particular emphases in spirituality (e.g., continual prayer, mysticism, desert fathers). Still others deal with specific time periods. Historic spiritual works of historic Christians and volumes on individual spiritual masters, including contemporary authors, have been and continue to be published each year. If we add recent volumes on contemporary spirituality, the list explodes. Hopefully, the "Recommended Resources for Ministry" at the end of this book will simplify the process.

WORSHIP

Each generation grows up worshiping in the forms used by their preceding generations, which adopted forms passed on from their preceding generations. The earliest Christians borrowed worship forms from their Jewish roots.[11] In most faith groups each generation reconstitutes worship, combining those forms with other forms in order to experience worship more appropriately. They knowingly or unknowingly adopt elements from previously generations. This is true for individual and corporate worship. Worship mirrors tradition; worship embodies tradition.

> The way into the future . . . is not an innovative new start for the church; rather, the road to the future runs through the past.
>
> **ROBERT E. WEBBER**

Christian history emphasizes the enormous importance of worship. Persecuted Christians throughout the centuries risked torture and death to gather for worship; this continues today. Medieval communities sacrificed labor and materials, over multiple generations, to erect elaborate church buildings; they worshiped God through sacrificial labor to build a place of worship for future generations. Christians have been willing to lay down time, possessions and even life so that they could continue to worship appropriately in a sacred place.

What do our historic worship partners and mentors teach us? Christian history broadens worship horizons and fills gaps in our worship practice in several ways. Studying worship from other eras adds breadth and depth to the elements of worship already familiar to us. We affirm current forms, but we become aware of other forms: divine liturgy, prescribed liturgy, alternate methods of prayer, sacramental practices and many others.

Knowing the history of worship helps us recover or reemphasize the historic centers of worship—the persons of God and the redemptive work of God. Historic Christian worship emphasizes God's presence—Father, Son, Holy Spirit. We embrace mystery. We experience God as both transcendent and immanent—too exalted to be present, yet very present. We experience in word and sacrament what we clearly appreciate but can never fully understand. Historic Christian worship retells God's redemptive story—from eternity to eternity, from creation to re-creation. Historic Christian worship, therefore, focuses on eschatological hope. Historic Christian worship remembers the past, experiences the present, and anticipates the future.

Today we see broad evidence of Christians seeking these historic Christian experiences in worship. Tired of market-oriented approaches that seem to focus on self-improvement of finances, relationships and self-image, many cry out to be held near by the transcendent God, to experience a piece of what they can never fully experience here, and to be transformed into what God created them to become. Often their Bible-focused churches incorporate these elements into their corporate gatherings. When they do not, some venture outside their faith group to seek help. Studying the central emphases of historic Christian worship can deepen our worship by helping worship leaders and worshipers find centuries-tested elements of worship.

Christian history also helps us celebrate our shared identity and find assurance in community with Christians across cultures, continents and centuries. When we share in the prayers of the church, or in the Lord's Supper, or in corporate affirmations of our faith, we celebrate our identity with Christians across the centuries. As we affirm them and are affirmed by them, we sense a deep connectedness with the whole church. As we evaluate their practices, we embrace those that we consider proper and helpful, but we reject those that we do not. When we see a gap in our practice, we move to recover a neglected focus.

How can Bible-focused Christians allow historic Christian worship to inform—and transform—our worship? How do we proceed? Once again, start by becoming familiar with literature on the history of Christian worship. In the process, evaluate your own congregational worship. Ask several key questions. Is God the central focus of each element of worship? Do we intentionally exalt Father, Son *and* Holy Spirit through our praise, prayer, preaching and the Lord's Supper? Do we emphasize God's transcendence and presence? Do we include elements of God's redemptive story, from eternity to eternity? Do we highlight God's gift of hope, now and for eternity? Apply these same questions to personal worship.

Then, add historic elements of worship to those that the worshipers already know. Plan in this way to expand and deepen the worship experience. Remember, these are not essentials of the faith; they are simply suggestions that could enhance worship for Bible-focused Christians.

Add worship forms that could deepen the experience of worship. The possibilities here are as many as the historic times that we investigate. Some are already present for many Bible-focused Christians. Consider adding others, such as readings from the lectionary (helps us to include all of Scripture in the annual worship plan), praying historic prayers, employing congregational response, and many more.

Where helpful, add elements from the liturgical calendar to the congregation's annual worship cycle. Most Bible-focused Christians already celebrate major events of the Christian calendar, such as Advent season (Christmas) or Resurrection season (Easter), some more broadly than others. So we have a place for celebrating Christian holidays. Why not consider expanding this? When we practice the major seasons of the church year, we are in sync with the annual rhythm of Christians across cultures, continents and centuries.

Celebrate the Lord's Supper, the Eucharist, more often and more attentively. Christians across the centuries nearly everywhere centered the events of their Sunday worship on the Lord's Supper—every Sunday. In fact, for over fifteen hundred years there was almost universal consensus. Also, consider praying historic eucharistic prayers. We may differ about the nature of the event, but in the Lord's Supper we celebrate God's presence, mystery and transcendence. Why miss this opportunity?

EXPANSION: MISSION

The church began as a small group of Christians in Palestine. Today Christians are present in nearly every corner of the planet. The history of this expansion, sometimes called by various names, is a key part of the Christian tradition. We partner with historic Christians in God's Great Commission to bring the gospel to all nations (see Mt 28:19; Mk 16:15), taking our place in God's cosmic scheme of redemption, confident that we are part of God's continually unfolding story from eternity to eternity.

> *We look at missions and missionaries in the past that we may know ourselves better in the present: both what we should and should not be.*
>
> **ALAN TIPPET**

Heroic examples of sacrifice by dedicated evangelists, missionaries and church planters across the centuries inspire us to greater sacrifice and service. In the seventh and eighth centuries Willibrord, for example, brought most of Frisia into Christianity because of his dedicated tenacity and fearless encounter.[12] In 723 Boniface openly felled the oak of Thor (Donar) and built a chapel with the wood; many embraced Christianity.[13] In 1956 Jim Elliot and four others were martyred in Ecuador by Waodani warriors; the ongoing work of his wife, Elisabeth, and others brought many Waodani to Christ.[14]

Historic missionary methods become models to imitate or to avoid, depending on how theologically appropriate and how effective the methods were. As we analyze their approaches, we adopt those that help and reject those that do not. We learn from their mistakes, and we capitalize on their successes. The ninth-century missionary success of Cyril and Methodius is well known, and their methods became models for centuries to come, even today. They worked in the Slavonic language of the people; they invented an alphabet, developed a grammar, translated the Scriptures, and introduced a Slavonic liturgy. They founded a school that taught written Slavonic and developed an indigenous clergy. Furthermore, they immersed the enterprise in prayer.[15] The remarkable stories of many other missionaries can help contemporary missionaries: consider the creativity of nineteenth- and twentieth-century missionary pioneers who spread the gospel throughout the world. Why not learn from their methods?

Christian history also gives contemporary missiology credibility by holding us accountable. Christian history, particularly mission history, invites us to consider our own missiology in the light of twenty centuries of missionary outreach. This includes more recent developments in non-Western cultures and the fresh perspectives that globalization brings to the faith.[16]

Christian history also helps us challenge others to embrace world mission. Knowing the mission history of our own faith group, or of a region that our church supports, connects the congregation with that work. Countless illustrations from mission history help us challenge believers to help by providing financial and prayer support. Some may decide to become missionaries.

How do we learn the history of Christian mission? Resources in the history of Christian mission are helpful. These may include Christian expansion in particular regions or countries. Biographies of historic Christian evangelists and missionaries yield effective illustrations for preaching and teaching. They also provide inspiration, shared mission identity and a sense of mission community.

ETHICS

Christians in every century have faced moral and ethical questions, sometimes personal, sometimes societal. We can learn from their actions. Often their biblical and theological arguments are persuasive, and these are available to us. We evaluate them, but we also hold ourselves accountable to them. When we face ethical issues, we can invite historic believers to the table. When we find consensus, we have confidence in our position. When we do not, we may realize that historic positions were more culture-driven than God-driven and have confidence nonetheless. But we may also discover that our own position is more culture-driven than God-driven and thus be led to reassess it in light of our cultural biases.

> By reading Clement, Gregory of Nyssa, Basil, and Augustine, Christians hope to learn again how to live faithfully.
>
> **STANLEY HAUERWAS AND SAMUEL WELLS**

Some moral behaviors have been rejected by Christians across the continents and centuries. Kidnapping, for example, is condemned in most situations. Other ethical discussions reoccur every generation. The ethics of Christians fighting in war, for example, has been debated in nearly every culture and century. Still other issues are emerging in our own generation and thus were never faced by earlier Christians, at least not directly. Today, for example, for the first time the church is discussing the ethics of cloning, genetic engineering, human trait selection and various forms of mind control.

How can studying ethical decisions of the past help us? When we face similar ethical issues, we see how previous generations of Christian handled these issues, we evaluate their views and actions, and we allow them to evaluate us. We apply the criteria that we use to evaluate them to our own options. If a long-settled issue presents itself in new forms, such as the capturing of African children to make them child soldiers, we can apply principles for slavery and child abuse. When we are facing the very same issues that others have faced, such as whether to oppose government-sponsored racism, we can apply principles learned from events surrounding the American Civil War or World War II. When new issues emerge, we can examine prior applications of moral principles to help us determine the moral foundation from which to decide.

A hot topic today is the implantation of devices to enhance natural intelligence. We can examine precedents. On one hand, we already sustain or enhance natural life with pacemakers, artificial valves, knee replacements and organ transplants. On the other hand, we have consistently opposed manipulative mind control. As we consider the moral implications of implanting thought and memory devices, what principles will we use to make those decisions? The point here is that we must study the Scriptures, consult the living church, and research through Christian thinkers of the past for historic theological principles to help us make those decisions.

Historic ethical debates can open our minds to possibilities that we have not considered. Whether we change our thinking or not, positions of past Christians compel us to rethink our own. In a simple example, Christians in many centuries, including our own, have debated whether it is ever proper to lie or to break promises. Many Christians say no, but many other Christians argue that lying is sometimes necessary in order to achieve a greater good—for example, a psychiatrist professing ignorance about something said in confidence by a client, or even Peter pretending that he did not know Ananias and Sapphira's conspiracy (Acts 5:1-11). John Cassian and Augustine exchanged literary work on this very subject in the fifth century, with godly supporters on both sides.[17] Roman Catholics later developed teaching on "mental reservation," or "mental equivocation," used at first to keep secrets faithfully, but later for subversive purposes. Eventually the more severe forms were condemned.[18] Considering their reasons and motives helps us decide.

Often the past shows us that the right ethical option is less clear than we anticipated. We do not always find agreement among historic Christians; sincere believers have disagreed, both in the same period and from one period to another. Christians initiated the Crusades, yet today most Christians reject the very concept. In the Spanish Empire, the subsequent British Empire and the antebellum United States Christians argued both for and against slavery from the same Bible, yet few Christians today believe that slavery is ethical. Studying their positions and actions helps us make more informed ethical decisions.

As we see historic processes for making ethical decisions, we plan more strategically for making ethical decisions in the present. Certainly we reject unilateral enforcement such as that undertaken by the Inquisition, which tortured hundreds in order to exact confessions and information. Yet we embrace theological debate, reading ethical publications, gathering experts for open discussion, attending academic conferences, and many other historic processes.

When we consider the ethical questions of our own day—personhood, abortion, racism, ethnicism, homosexuality, women in ministry, pacifism, genocide, neurotheology, cyber implants, and more—Bible-focused Christians need more than their own culture-informed understanding. The purpose of this book is not to answer each of these ethical questions. The point is this: with twenty centuries of believers sharing our Christian identity, community and accountability, we need each other as we consider ethical questions.

COMPASSION

The Christian centuries boast hundreds of compassionate pastors. When we consider major areas of ministry, benevolent work, or pastoral work in a congregation, these pastors are once again our partners and mentors. Their lives of vision and sacrificial service encourage us.[19] Who could read Mother Teresa's story without being inspired? She risked her own life to obey Christ; first she cared for outcaste lepers, then the poor, unwed mothers, orphaned children, many others.

> *The history of pastoral care is a history of the Christian Church in action.*
>
> **G. R. EVANS**

Her international voice still echoes in many hearts.[20] Eric Liddell, willing to sacrifice Olympic gold in order to obey Christ, won his medal, but he surrendered privilege so that he could walk and bicycle in rural China to share God's love. He died showing compassion to others in a World War II Japanese concentration camp, speaking his final words to a camp nurse, "It's complete surrender."[21]

Historic acts of Christian compassion model priorities for us. Augustine of Hippo tells of devoting significant time to pastoral issues—resolving financial conflict, church discipline, moral lapses among clergy, kidnapping and human trafficking, assigning employment.[22] Basil of Caesarea sold his possessions, fed the hungry, and preached openly about sharing with the poor.[23] Pope Gregory I "regularly gave whatever money he had to relieve the poor."[24]

We partner with these historic Christian servants, sometimes by initiating efforts similar to theirs, other times by continuing their ministries. Besides helping the poor, for example, Vincent de Paul in the seventeenth century worked with galley ship convicts who became ill, and then he started hospitals, organized local groups for charity, sent aid to slaves, and rescued homeless babies abandoned in the streets. He founded the Congregation of the Mission (priests) and the Sisters of Charity (nuns) to multiply his service, which spread throughout France and to several foreign lands.[25] Today similar ministries continue, and his two organizations continue to serve. Hundreds of other inspiring models of ministry could be mentioned.

Once again, we evaluate their methods, rejecting those that we find problematic and embracing those that effectively carried out God's will. We evaluate our own methods by theirs, asking how they might advise us to be more godly in our ministries. In this way we share connected identity as God's servants, enjoy community of faithful service, and share accountability across the centuries. We broaden horizons and fill gaps in our service.

What process should we follow, and what resources should we consult? In Christian history courses or planned reading note particular examples of Christian leaders who showed Christian compassion. This will develop a sensitivity for helping those in need. Challenge other believers by telling their heroic stories and the life-changing results.

UNITY

Christian unity is God's gift to the church, an ever-present reality, whether Christians act like it or not. We have one Father, one Savior, one Spirit, one fellowship in the Spirit. We are destined for one heaven. We share the Scriptures, and we share the same rich Christian tradition. Jesus prayed in John 17 that, based on God's truth, his disciples would be one, so that the world would believe. Christians, especially Bible-focused Christians, embrace Christ's desire and prayer, strategizing how we can demonstrate our Christian unity to a world that desperately needs Christ.

> I ask . . . that they may all be one . . . so that the world may know that you have sent me and have loved them even as you have loved me.
>
> **JESUS OF NAZARETH,**
> **JOHN 17:20-23 NRSV**

Prior to the Reformation, Christian unity was assumed. Even when Christians separated, visible Christian unity was considered the norm. After the Reformation, distinct groups proliferated. Today, with thousands of Christian denominations and organizations, we must be intentional about our efforts to demonstrate Christian unity.[26]

The nineteenth century brought renewed concern for Christian unity. The Stone-Campbell movement in the United States, for example, sought unity of all Christians based on a common faith in the Scriptures "so that the world may believe."[27] By the end of the nineteenth century many other cries for ecumenicity had emerged. Missionaries realized that their message was compromised by the credibility gap caused by a visibly divided, competing church.

Formal organizations were started to promote cooperation in bringing Christian faith to others, initially among missionary and benevolent ministries. A number of faith group mergers also occurred. Sometimes denominational family groups united or reunited. Other times previously unrelated groups merged to form new denominations. Eventually ecumenical leaders sought to unite mainline denominations into single church bodies, regionally and globally. More recently, ecumenical efforts concentrate more on cooperation than merger. We see many efforts at dialogue.

The last few decades have also evidenced a growing, broader mutual acceptance among by Bible-focused Christians. Believers, unaware or less concerned about doctrinal distinctives, move freely from one faith group to another. National organizations include very diverse members. Christians labor together in home building, disaster relief, food pantries, homeless shelters, clothing banks and other ministries, with little regard for faith group membership. Believers cross theological lines to practice spirituality with other Christians.

When Christians differ on what they consider core beliefs, they may not be able to partner with integrity in some forms of ministry. But in scores of ministries we can cooperate without compromising what we believe to be true. When we do partner with one another, we respond to New Testament teaching about Christian unity, particularly the prayer of Jesus in John 17. How does studying Christian history help us to express Christian unity?

Christian history certainly teaches us the need for practicing Christian unity. How did we end up with hundreds and hundreds of faith groups, each with distinctives, some thinking that they are the most correct Christians? In Christian history we learn the reasons for divisions, whether theological, sociological, political or all of the above. We discover what motives and emphases formed new movements.

Christian history, therefore, helps Christians from various backgrounds understand each other. When we understand the depth of and reasons for our distinctives, we have a framework for dialogue, cooperative ministries and mutual affection. Even when we disagree, we value one another because we understand each other.

Christian history also provides ecumenical mentors. We share their vision. We embrace them in shared identity, community and accountability.

We learn from their successes and failures, evaluating their projects and approaches. For example, the ecumenical movement began by focusing on cooperation, then moved to merger, but then returned to cooperation. Why repeat the process? We can scrutinize ourselves through their eyes. In other words, we hold them accountable, and we allow them to hold us accountable. This provides motivation, but also safeguards.

How does knowing Christian history help ecumenical endeavor? When we understand major movements and the theological, sociological and political reasons behind our divisions, we are ready to engage the ecumenical process. Reading the works of historic ecumenists or theologians of Christian unity reinforce our motivations. We intentionally engage activities that reflect Christian unity as we initiate or join ecumenical dialogue, and as we participate in ecumenical projects.

CULTURAL ENGAGEMENT

Christian efforts to transform culture stand on a wide continuum. One pole embraces culture in order to change culture, winning credibility by identifying with culture, yet introducing Christian principles where they differ. The opposite pole rejects culture, or stands in radical contrast to culture, juxtaposing Christian values with cultural values. Most Christians, historic and contemporary, live somewhere between

> *Only the Church—past, present, and future—can correct private presuppositions and cultural bias.*
>
> **ROBERT T. JOHNSTON**

these poles. Sometimes we choose where to stand, but more often we simply assume the positions of family, friends or church leaders. The profile that we take can have huge impact on our effectiveness. How can Christian history help us in our efforts to transform culture?

Earlier Christians give us models for cultural engagement. As we reflect on their interactions with culture, we see positions that we have not considered. We find radicals at the end of the cultural-engagement spectrum, but we also find Christians who strategized between the poles. We see the effectiveness or lack of effectiveness of each profile that we study. We learn how to discern which social and cultural concerns we have borrowed from culture and which run across cultures, continents and centuries. This in turn helps us to exegete culture.[28]

This process of expanding our possibilities helps us to be intentional about where we will position ourselves on the cultural-engagement spectrum, and which particular issues we will confront. Rather than simply adopting the positions of those in our closest circles of inquiry, we are better equipped to develop strategies and make form informed choices.

Furthermore, the courage and faithfulness of Christians across the centuries who often surrendered rank and privilege for the sake of the gospel inspires us to take a stand. Moved by past heroes, we muster the courage to begin something that we sense God wants us to do, perhaps sometimes a calling that we have ignored for many years.

Christian history also teaches us criteria for evaluating our own positions. We more easily evaluate past Christians, for we have the advantage of seeing their results. We reject positions with negative outcomes. The challenge comes when we allow the past to critique us. For example, we quickly decide that some Christians in Nazi Germany, or those who supported the Dred Scott decision by the US Supreme Court, were wrong to let government set the standards for Christians. But we rarely ask how great Christians throughout the centuries would evaluate the current inclination to let government set their standards on issues such as abortion, homosexual marriage, cloning and other divisive moral questions. "To criticize the theology of past generations is relatively painless. To admit the possibility of similar cultural and ecclesiological limitations in ourselves is more difficult."[29]

Finally, by studying the past we learn to be cautious. We could misunderstand God's will and take a wrong position, sometimes with disastrous results. Consider three closely related examples. In the first, Thomas Müntzer led peasants in the famous Peasants' War in 1524 in Germany. Müntzer and his followers believed that God was leading them to rebel against the princes. They were slaughtered at the Battle of Frankenhausen, and Müntzer was captured, tortured and executed.[30] Similarly, in the second, Radical Reformers established a theocracy in 1534 in Münster, deposing the magistrates, but the leaders were later defeated and executed.[31] In the third, Melchior Hoffman, who helped inspire the Münster affair, believed an old man's prophecy meant that he would be Elijah for Christ's second coming in 1533 after six months' imprisonment. He provoked his own arrest, was imprisoned, and died there ten years later.[32]

Inspired by historic examples of influential Christians, what approaches might we take today to change our culture? Sometimes we will follow those who openly confronted or criticized leaders. We have already noted John Chrysostom's confrontation of Eudoxia and Arcadius. Ambrose, in the fourth century, on several occasions defied the emperor, critiquing cruelty, promising to withhold Christian rites, and openly refusing to surrender the basilica to Arians.[33] When Basiliscus usurped the imperial crown in 475 and promoted Monophysitism (the view that after the incarnation, Jesus Christ had only a divine nature), Daniel the Stylite[34] objected, later dismounted his pillar, and preached that he should be overthrown. Basiliscus withdrew his edict and later resigned.[35] Martin Luther's open opposition to indulgences, his publishing the *Ninety-Five Theses*, and his "Here I stand" refusal to submit to the Diet of Worms are well known.[36]

Other times we follow Christians who transformed culture by choosing to live simple lives in contrast with the materialistic values of their time. At the more radical end, great thirteenth-century leaders such as Francis of Assisi and Clare of Assisi, or Domingo de Guzman (Dominic), imitated Christ's poverty by becoming the poorest of the poor. Thomas Aquinas (thirteenth century) and Ignatius of Loyola (sixteenth century) abandoned power and family privilege to serve Christ alone. In the nineteenth century Catherine and William Booth preached to London's most needy, feeding the hungry and caring for the homeless; from this work came the Salvation Army.[37]

Still other times we oppose culture, or government, by disobeying the law because of our integrity. We have already noted Christian responses to American slavery. Although some Christians defended slavery, many Christians disobeyed the Fugitive Slave Law, risking imprisonment and property seizure; they helped slaves escape, harbored them, ran Underground Railroad stations, and conspired with others to do so.[38] Under Nazi domination in the Netherlands, Dutch Christian Casper ten Boom had his family wear the Jewish star and illegally hid Jews in their home during the Holocaust. Casper died in a concentration camp, but their story lives on.[39] Dietrich Bonhoeffer refused to submit to Nazi laws by working in the German underground church, possibly participating in the plot to assassinate Adolf Hitler.[40] Karol Józef Wojtyla in Poland secretly studied for the priesthood, escaped Nazi arrest, and helped many Polish Jews. As archbishop of Kraków, he became the symbol of opposition to atheistic communism. In 1978 he became Pope John Paul II, and in 1979 he visited Poland as pope. Researchers disagree about the extent, but they unanimously credit him with aiding the fall of communism in Eastern Europe.[41]

We also engage culture by responding to needs of society. We had already noted revival preachers addressing the problem of alcoholism on the early nineteenth-century American frontier, and Vincent de Paul prompting hundreds to serve in multiple ministries. Christian history is filled with additional examples. William Wilberforce's conversion led him to work to end slavery, leading to the English Parliament prohibiting slave trade (1807) and slavery (1833).[42] James Gibbons, Baltimore's archbishop from 1877 to 1921, advised US presidents, but he also encouraged laborers to organize in the face of church opposition.[43]

We also confront culture when we challenge others to take action to correct a wrong. When Walter Rauschenbush saw massive poverty, he challenged Christians to spread the gospel by living in Christlike service. He helped ignite the theologically diverse social gospel movement.[44] Gustavo Gutiérrez lived among the poor of Lima, Peru, where he believed that the poor were systematically oppressed through an unjust social structure. As a biblical advocate of social justice, Gutiérrez, through his book *A Theology of Liberation*, launched liberation theology.[45] Martin Luther King Jr. motivated a nation to embrace civil rights, speaking boldly and sacrificing his life.[46]

Yes, we partner with historic Christians to transform culture. We sometimes find problems in elements of their theology, but nevertheless they are our coworkers and mentors. When we consider their approaches, they open our minds to new vision and fill in holes in our understanding. When we adopt approaches similar to theirs, they help us live in fuller Christian community and celebrate our shared identity. When we are too radical or not radical enough, they confirm or confront us, holding us accountable as they reach across cultures and centuries.

MAKING A PLAN

Each student of Christian history walks a unique path in his or her Christian development. Some will appreciate the benefits of Christian history while working in employment not directly related to ministry. Others will serve as Sunday school teachers, small group leaders or youth sponsors. Still others will serve as pastors or professors. So the path to deeper encounters with Christians from the past will differ from ministry to ministry. But, sooner or later, most of us will ask, "With my busy schedule, and the demands of work, family and ministry, what areas should I plan to study further?"

No one ever becomes familiar with everything, and certainly that which we do become familiar with does not come to us all at once. We all choose distinct means to deeper understanding that fit our particular lives and ministry. The best way to do that is to consider our options. Those who incline to higher education can take a course at a nearby college or seminary or online. Others might choose a single resource to read, which might lead to other resources (several can be found in the "Recommended Resources for Ministry" below). Still others may prefer to set aside a portion of their weekly study to increase their understanding of the people, teachings, controversies and developments of the church across the centuries. Still others may work through historic sources in a group study, perhaps with those who specialize in their own area of interest or ministry. As we do, we embrace additional values, and we develop a way of thinking that naturally asks the historical questions. We study the Bible, and at the same time we are curious to know what believers throughout the centuries have taught—how they understood the Scriptures, and what they believed about the issues we are considering.

Whatever our station in life, or our present avenue of Christian service, or our future ministry, we maximize our potential when we are intentional about embracing the whole Christian community. As our knowledge of Christian history steadily increases, our pool of ministry resources also increases. We make friends across the centuries—partners and mentors. We expand our ideas by those tested through time and experience. We learn from their models and methods, their successes and failures. We become aware of dangers. We sharpen our criteria for evaluating the past and the present. We articulate the truth more carefully. We are better ministers, for their sacrificial service inspires us to deeper surrender, and we in turn inspire others.

CELEBRATE THE BODY OF CHRIST

Why does church history matter? Those ready to explore this question stand at the door of fascination and fulfillment, questions and answers, foes and friends. This doorway opens to a whole new world—a world daring us to enter, offering us an invitation to love and learn from our past. When we cross the threshold, we will never be the same. We meet people and discover places that we never knew existed. A new way of thinking permeates everything that we consider, and everything that we do. The previous pages have guided us to this surprising, yet curiously welcoming world. We pause here to look back at how we came to this place.

Part 1, "How We Understand the Tradition," first showed us how Christians across the centuries have understood the tradition. From the beginning of the church, believers looked to history to understand truth. The earliest Christians knew that they continued the story of God's people, the Hebrews, whom God had prepared for the Christ. Jesus had transformed the message, and the Holy Spirit now filled the Christians, but God's plan of redemption continued. Throughout Christian history, believers continued to look to their predecessors—to the revealed Scriptures and to those who followed God in truth. Eventually some abused parts of tradition to promote ideas opposed to the tradition. Century after century produced efforts to restore important aspects of Christianity, the most widespread being the sixteenth-century Reformation, which produced a variety of understandings about Christianity. Next we examined how today's faith group families view tradition, including those accepting apostolic succession, those who are more Bible-focused in their perspective, and others. We likely located our own journey on this map, reinforced some commitments and opened our minds to others.

Part 2, "Expanding Circles of Inquiry," got to the heart of the title, *Why Church History Matters.* When we study church history, we expand our circles of inquiry from Christians most like us to believers who are very different. Expanding circles break down lines of demarcation. As we include believers of other cultures and other centuries, our circles become transcultural, global and transtemporal. We discover better who we are, and we appreciate the identity that we share with the other Christians. We draw assurance from the fact that we are part of the eternal community of believers. We hold past and present believers accountable, and we hold ourselves accountable to them. They broaden our horizons, suggesting to us entire vistas that we never before considered. They fill gaps in our theology that we never realized we had. They excite us with possibilities that we had not considered.

In the process, we seek consensus across the centuries—*consensus fidelium.* When we find consensus, we grow more certain that we stand in the truth. When we do not find consensus, we still grow more confident, not because our answers are superior to others, but because truth has enlightened our position and relaxed our former inflexibility. We sense authenticity, for we have tried to include all of the Christians—the whole church—across cultures, continents and centuries.

Part 3, "Tradition Serving the Church," showed us how Christian history helps us minister more effectively. We partner in with historic Christians, who provide models, methods and resources to make us better at what we do. By consulting the Christians across cultures and time, we increase our understanding of Scripture; we have better text, better translation, better exegesis. We incorporate former methods or the conclusions of those who used them well into our own biblical understanding. We also ask these partners and mentors to teach us how to do ministry more effectively—whether preaching, teaching, systematics, spirituality, worship, mission, ethics, compassion, ecumenicity, cultural engagement, and others not here considered.

Why does church history matter? Church history helps us celebrate the body of Christ! As we walk through that doorway we embrace the whole body of Christ—our entire extended family, in the plan of the triune God, from eternity to eternity. As God redeems the cosmos, from before creation until Christ's second coming and beyond, God works through believers; we stand in this mighty flood of surrendered theology and service. They are our brothers and sisters. And although family can be messy, we are God's family. Yes, this great cloud of witnesses includes our friends, advisors, partners, mentors and models. As we cross the threshold, they travel with us through this foreign land we call earth, and yet they wait for us in our eternal home.

Recommended Resources
for Ministry

Resources marked *** are recent, more easily accessible works for introductory students.

History of Christianity

Histories

***Cairns, Earle Edwin. *Christianity Through the Centuries: A History of the Christian Church*. 3rd ed. Grand Rapids: Zondervan, 1996.

Cambridge History of Christianity. 9 vols. Cambridge: Cambridge University Press, 2006-2012.

Dowley, Tim, et al., eds. *Introduction to the History of Christianity*. Rev. ed. Minneapolis: Fortress, 2006.

***González, Justo L. *The Story of Christianity*. Rev. ed. 2 vols. New York: HarperOne, 2010. [In Spanish, *Historia del Cristianismo*. 2 vols. Miami: Editorial Unilit, 1994.]

Latourette, Kenneth Scott. *A History of Christianity*. Rev. ed. 2 vols. New York: Harper & Row, 1975.

McManners, John, ed. *The Oxford Illustrated History of Christianity*. Oxford: Oxford University Press, 1990.

Walker, Williston, et al. *A History of the Christian Church*. 4th ed. New York: Scribner, 1985.

Historical Biography

Foxe, John. *Foxe's Book of Martyrs: A History of the Lives, Sufferings, and Trium-

phant Deaths of the Early Christian and the Protestant Martyrs. Edited by
William Byron Forbush. Peabody, MA: Henrdrickson, 2004. Original available
as *The Unabridged Acts and Monuments Online* (Sheffield: HRI Online Publica-
tions, 2011) at www.johnfoxe.org; also available at www.jesus.org.uk/christian
-classics/john-foxe; free ebook available at www.gutenberg.org/ebooks/22400.
***Galli, Mark, and Ted Olsen. *131 Christians Everyone Should Know.* Nashville:
Broadman & Holman, 2000.
***Tucker, Ruth. *Parade of Faith: A Biographical History of the Christian Church.*
Grand Rapids: Zondervan, 2011.
Tucker, Ruth, and Walter L. Liefeld. *Daughters of the Church: Women and Min-
istry from New Testament Times to the Present.* Grand Rapids: Academie
Books, 1987.

Preaching and Teaching

Edwards, O. C., Jr. *A History of Preaching.* 2 vols. Nashville: Abingdon, 2004.
Fant, Clyde E., Jr., and William M. Pinson Jr. *20 Centuries of Great Preaching: An
Encyclopedia of Preaching.* 13 vols. Waco, TX: Word, 1971.
Kienzle, Beverly Mayne, and Pamela J. Walker, eds. *Women Preachers and
Prophets Through Two Millennia of Christianity.* Berkeley: University of Cal-
ifornia Press, 1998.
Larsen, David L. *The Company of the Preachers: A History of Biblical Preaching
from the Old Testament to the Modern Era.* 2 vols. Grand Rapids: Kregel, 1998.
Old, Hughes Oliphant. *The Reading and Preaching of the Scriptures in the
Worship of the Christian Church.* 7 vols. Grand Rapids: Eerdmans, 1998-2010.
***Wilson, Paul Scott. *A Concise History of Preaching.* Nashville: Abingdon, 1992.

Systematic Theology

Protestant

Barth, Karl. *Church Dogmatics.* Edited by G. W. Bromiley and T. F. Torrance.
Translated by G. W. Bromiley. 14 vols. London: T & T Clark, 2004.
Bray, Gerald. *God Is Love: A Biblical and Systematic Theology.* Wheaton, IL:
Crossway, 2012.
Brunner, Emil. *Dogmatics.* 3 vols. Translated by Olive Wyon. London: Lutter-
worth, 1949-1962.
Erickson, Millard. *Christian Theology.* 3rd ed. Grand Rapids: Baker Academic,
2013.

Jenson, Robert. *Systematic Theology*. 2 vols. New York: Oxford University Press, 1997-1999.

***McGrath, Alister. *Christian Theology: An Introduction*. 4th ed. Malden, MA: Wiley-Blackwell, 2006.

***Oden, Thomas. *Systematic Theology*. 3 vols. Peabody, MA: Hendrickson, 2006.

Pannenberg, Wolfhart. *Systematic Theology*. 3 vols. Translated by Geoffrey W. Bromiley. Grand Rapids: Eerdmans, 1988-1994.

Tillich, Paul. *Systematic Theology*. 3 vols. Chicago: University of Chicago Press, 1951-1963.

Eastern Orthodox

***Lossky, Vladimir. *Orthodox Theology: An Introduction*. Crestwood, NY: St. Vladimir's Seminary Press, 2001.

Meyendorff, John. *Byzantine Theology: Historical Trends and Doctrinal Themes*. 2nd ed. New York: Fordham University Press, 1979.

Staniloae, Dumitru. *The Experience of God: Orthodox Dogmatic Theology*. 3 vols. Translated and edited by Ioan Ionita and Robert Barringer. Brookline, MA: Holy Cross Orthodox Press, 1994-2011.

***Ware, Timothy. *The Orthodox Church*. 2nd ed. London: Penguin, 1993.

Roman Catholic

Balthasar, Hans Urs von. *The Glory of the Lord: A Theological Aesthetics*. Edited by Joseph Fessio and John Riches. Translated by E. Leiva-Merkakis. 2nd ed. 7 vols. San Francisco: Ignatius Press, 2009.

———. *Theo-Drama*. Translated by Graham Harrison. 5 vols. San Francisco: Ignatius Press, 1988-1998.

———. *Theo-Logic*. Translated by Adrian J. Walker. 3 vols. San Francisco: Ignatius Press, 2000-2005.

Fiorenza, Francis Schüssler, and John P. Galvin, eds. *Systematic Theology: Roman Catholic Perspectives*. 2nd ed. Minneapolis: Fortress, 2011.

Rahner, Karl. *Foundations of Christian Faith: An Introduction to the Idea of Christianity*. Translated by William V. Dych. New York: Crossroad, 1982.

***Ratzinger, Joseph [Pope Benedict XVI]. *Introduction to Christianity*. Translated by J. R. Foster. 2nd ed. San Francisco: Ignatius Press, 2004.

Thomas Aquinas. *The Summa Theologica of Thomas Aquinas*. Translated by Fathers of the English Dominican Province. New York: Benziger Brothers, 1948. Reprint, Notre Dame, IN: Christian Classics, 1981.

CHRISTIAN SPIRITUALITY

Introductions

Maas, Robin, and Gabriel O'Donnell, eds. *Spiritual Traditions for the Contemporary Church.* Nashville: Abingdon, 1990.

***McGrath, Alistair. *Christian Spirituality: An Introduction.* Oxford: Blackwell, 1999.

Sheldrake, Philip. *Explorations in Spirituality: History, Theology, and Social Practice.* New York: Paulist Press, 2010.

***Tyson, John R., ed. *Invitation to Christian Spirituality: An Ecumenical Anthology.* New York: Oxford University Press, 1999.

Webber, Robert E. *The Divine Embrace: Recovering the Passionate Spiritual Life.* Grand Rapids: Baker, 2006.

Histories

Bouyer, Louis, François Vandenbrouke and Jean Leclerq. *History of Christian Spirituality.* Translated by Mary P. Ryan. 3 vols. New York: Seabury, 1963-1969.

***Holmes, Urban T., III. *A History of Christian Spirituality: An Analytical Introduction.* New York: Seabury, 1980. Reprint, Harrisburg, PA: Morehouse, 2002.

McGinn, Bernard, et al., eds. *Christian Spirituality.* 3 vols. New York: Crossroad, 1987-1991.

***Mursell, Gordon, ed. *The Story of Christian Spirituality: Two Thousand Years, from East to West.* Minneapolis: Fortress, 2001.

Pourrat, Pierre. *Christian Spirituality.* Translated by W. P. Mitchell and S. P. Jacques. 4 vols. London: Burns, Oates & Washbourne, 1922-1927. Reprint, Charleston, SC: Forgotten Books, 2009-2010.

WORSHIP

***Bradshaw, Paul. *Early Christian Worship: A Basic Introduction to Ideas and Practice.* Collegeville, MN: Liturgical Press, 1996.

Hurtado, Larry W. *At the Origins of Christian Worship: The Context and Character of Earliest Christian Devotion.* Grand Rapids: Eerdmans, 2000.

Jones, Cheslyn, et al., eds. *The Study of Liturgy.* Rev. ed. London: SPCK; New York: Oxford University Press, 1992.

Lang, Bernhard. *Sacred Games: A History of Christian Worship.* New Haven: Yale University Press, 1997.

Martin, Ralph. *Worship in the Early Church.* Rev. ed. Grand Rapids: Eerdmans, 1974.

Senn, Frank. *Christian Liturgy: Catholic and Evangelical*. Minneapolis: Fortress, 1997.

Wainwright, Geoffrey, and Karen Westerfield Tucker, eds. *The Oxford History of Christian Worship*. Oxford: Oxford University Press, 2006.

***Webber, Robert E. *Ancient-Future Worship: Proclaiming and Enacting God's Narrative*. Grand Rapids: Baker, 2008.

————, ed. *Twenty Centuries of Christian Worship*. Vol. 2 of *The Complete Library of Christian Worship*. Peabody, MA: Hendrickson, 1995.

White, James F. *A Brief History of Christian Worship*. Nashville: Abingdon, 1993.

EXPANSION: MISSION

Histories

Latourette, Kenneth Scott. *Christianity in a Revolutionary Age: A History of Christianity in the Nineteenth and Twentieth Centuries*. 5 vols. New York: Harper, 1958-1961. Reprint, Grand Rapids: Zondervan, 1969.

————. *A History of the Expansion of Christianity*. 7 vols. New York: Harper & Brothers, 1937-1945. Reprint, Grand Rapids: Zondervan, 1970.

***Neill, Stephen. *A History of Christian Missions*. 2nd ed. London: Penguin, 1986.

Pierson, Paul E. *The Dynamics of Christian Mission: History Through a Missiological Perspective*. Pasadena, CA: William Carey International University Press, 2009.

Missionary Biography

Robert, Dana L. *American Women in Missions: A Social History of Their Thought and Practice*. Macon, GA: Mercer University Press, 1996.

***Tucker, Ruth. *From Jerusalem to Irian Jaya: A Biographical History of Christian Missions*. 2nd ed. Grand Rapids: Zondervan, 2004.

————. *Guardians of the Great Commission: The Story of Women in Modern Missions*. Grand Rapids: Zondervan, 1994.

ETHICS

***Hauerwas, Stanley, and Samuel Wells. *The Blackwell Companion to Christian Ethics*. 2nd ed. Malden, MA: Wiley-Blackwell, 2011.

COMPASSION

***Evans, G. R., ed. *A History of Pastoral Care*. New York: Cassell, 2000.

UNITY

Amanze, James. *A History of the Ecumenical Movement in Africa*. Gaborone, Botswana: Pula Press, 1999.

Calkins, Gladys Gilkey. *Follow Those Women: Church Women in the Ecumenical Movement; A History of the Development of United Work Among Women of the Protestant Churches in the United States*. New York: United Church Women, 1961.

***Fitzgerald, Thomas E. *The Ecumenical Movement: An Introductory History*. Westport, CT: Greenwood, 2004.

Koshy, Ninan, ed. *A History of the Ecumenical Movement in Asia*. 2 vols. Geneva: World Alliance of YMCAs, 2004-2010.

Rouse, Ruth, et al., eds. *A History of the Ecumenical Movement*. 3 vols. Geneva: World Council of Churches, 1993-2004.

***Snaitang, O. L. *A History of the Ecumenical Movement: An Introduction*. Bangalore: BTESSC/SATHRI, 2006.

CULTURAL ENGAGEMENT

Moore, T. M. *Culture Matters: A Call for Consensus on Christian Cultural Engagement*. Grand Rapids: Baker, 2007.

***Niebuhr, H. Richard. *Christ and Culture*. 50th anniversary ed. San Francisco: Harper & Row, 2001.

Notes

INTRODUCTION

[1]My recent survey of master of divinity programs found that Protestant seminaries generally require two or three courses in church history, with one of those courses being a history of their particular faith group. Christian history consistently ranges from 5 to 10 percent of the requirements. If the denominational history requirement is excluded, programs generally require 2 to 7 percent. Even some Roman Catholics have complained that their seminaries have reduced their Christian history requirements.

CHAPTER 1: WHAT IS THE TRADITION?

[1]For example, Arthur Schlesinger Jr. cites New York's curriculum guide for eleventh-grade American history as instructing teachers to teach students the three ideological foundations for the American Constitution, one of which is "The Haudenosaunee political system of the Iroquois tribe" (*The Disuniting of America: Reflections on a Multicultural Society* [2nd ed.; New York: W. W. Norton, 1992], 54). Deborah E. Lipstadt tells of recent contentions that the Holocaust never occurred (*Denying the Holocaust: The Growing Assault on Truth and Memory* [New York: Free Press, 1993]).

[2]*The Report of the Theological Commission on Tradition and Traditions*, Faith and Order Paper 40 (Geneva: World Council of Churches, 1963), 17-18.

[3]D. H. Williams, *Evangelicals and Tradition: The Formative Influence of the Early Church* (Grand Rapids: Baker Academic, 2005), 50.

[4]George Tavard, *Holy Writ or Holy Church: The Crisis of the Protestant Reformation* (New York: Harper, 1959), 3.

[5]Harold O. J. Brown, "Proclamation and Preservation: The Necessity and Temptations of Church Tradition," in *Reclaiming the Great Tradition: Evangelicals, Catholics and Orthodox in Dialogue*, ed. James S. Cutsinger (Downers Grove, IL: InterVarsity Press, 1997), 85.

[6]Stanley J. Grenz and John R. Franke observe, "The Protestant movement in general and evangelicalism in particular have rightly maintained that the Spirit speaking in and through Scripture is the norming norm for Christian faith and life. Although Scripture retains the position of primacy, the tradition of the community provides a crucial and indispensable (re)source for theology. Tradition forms the hermeneutical context and trajectory for the construction of a contemporary theology that is faithfully Christian" ("Theological Heritage as Hermeneutical Trajectory: Toward a Nonfoundationalist Understanding of the Role of Tradition in Theology," in *Ancient and Postmodern Christianity: Paleo-Orthodoxy in the 21st Century; Essays in Honor of Thomas C. Oden*, ed. Kenneth Tanner and Christopher A. Hall [Downers Grove, IL: InterVarsity Press, 2002], 239).

CHAPTER 2: HOW HAVE WE UNDERSTOOD TRADITION HISTORICALLY?

[1]See Irenaeus, *Against All Heresies* 3.4 (ANF 1:330, 347).

[2]F. F. Bruce, *Tradition Old and New* (Eugene, OR: Wipf & Stock, 1970), 117-18.

[3]Irenaeus, *Against All Heresies* 3.4 (ANF 1:417).

[4]Among many examples, note that the third-century Novatianism dispute, over the proper bishop of Carthage and the validity of sacraments administered outside the realm of the proper bishop, and later the fourth-century Donatism dispute, over the proper bishop of Rome, went on in North Africa for three centuries. Note also that Nicene orthodoxy was seen as unnecessary by most of the bishops for five decades after the Council of Nicaea.

[5]Vincent of Lérins, *Commonitory* 1.2.5 (NPNF[2] 11:132).

[6]Vincent of Lérins, *Commonitory* 1.29.76 (NPNF[2] 11:153).

[7]Vincent of Lérins, *Commonitory* 1.2.6 (NPNF[2] 11:132).

[8]Gabriel Moran, *Scripture and Tradition: A Survey of the Controversy* (New York: Herder & Herder, 1963), 32.

[9]George Tavard, *Holy Writ or Holy Church: The Crisis of the Protestant Reformation* (New York: Harper, 1959), 10-11. Tavard, cited often in this chapter, provides possibly the most complete historical survey of positions held by key theologians on Scripture and tradition.

[10]Consider, for example, the Paschal controversy in the second century. Ephesus (allied with Carthage) celebrated Christ's death, burial and resurrection on the Passover (Nisan 14), and Rome (allied with Alexandria) celebrated them the first Sunday after Passover. Rome traced its practice to the apostles Peter and Paul, while Ephesus traced its practice to the apostle John and to Mary the mother of Jesus. For an excellent description, see Giorgio LaPiana, "The Roman Church at the End of the Second Century," *HTR* 18 (1925): 201-77; idem, "Foreign Groups in Rome During the First Centuries of the Empire," *HTR* 20 (1927): 183-403.

[11]D. H. Williams, "Scripture, Tradition, and the Church: Reformation and Post-Reformation," in *The Free Church and the Early Church: Bridging the Historical and Theological Divide*, ed. D. H. Williams (Grand Rapids: Eerdmans, 2002), 107. See others whom he cites: A. N. S. Lane, "Scripture, Tradition and Church: An Historical Survey," *VE* 9 (1975): 37-55; Richard Bauckham, "Tradition in Relation to Scripture and Reason," in *Scripture, Tradition, and Reason: A Study in the Criteria of Christian Doctrine; Essays in Honour of Richard P. C. Hanson*, ed. Richard Bauckham and Benjamin Drewery (Edinburgh: T & T Clark, 1988), 117-45.

[12]John Scotus Eriugena, *On the Divine Nature* 1.64 (translation from Tavard, *Holy Writ or Holy Church*, 12-13).

[13]Rupert of Deutz, *On God's Omnipotence* 27 (translation from Tavard, *Holy Writ or Holy Church*, 13).

[14]Hugh of St. Victor, *On Scripture and the Sacred Writings* 6 (translation from Tavard, *Holy Writ or Holy Church*, 16).

[15]Ibid.

[16]See Paul de Vooght, *Les sources de la doctrine chrétienne d'après les théologiens du XIVe siècle et du début du XVe: Avec le texte intégral des XII premières questions de la Summa inédite de Gérard de Bologne (1317)* (Bruges: Desclée de Brouwer, 1954), 149. See also Johannes von Beumer, "Das katholische Schriftprinzip in der theologischen Literatur der Scholastik bis zur Reformation," *Scholastik* 16 (1941): 24-52.

[17]Thomas Aquinas, *Summa theologiae*, article 8. Quoted from A. C. Pegis, ed. and trans., *Basic Writings of Saint Thomas Aquinas* (New York: Random House, 1945), 15.

[18]For a detailed table showing Thomas's use of the fathers, see Leo J. Elders, "Thomas Aquinas and the Fathers of the Church," in *The Reception of the Church Fathers in the West: From the Carolingians to the Maurists*, ed. Irena Backus (2 vols.; Leiden: Brill, 1997), 1:341.

[19]Henry of Ghent, *Commentary on the Sentences*, prologue 10.1.4-10.

[20]See Tavard, *Holy Writ or Holy Church*, 22-28.

[21]Marsilius of Padua, *Defender of the Peace* 2.19. See Marsilius of Padua, *The Defender of the Peace*, ed. and trans. Annabel Brett (CTHPT; Cambridge: Cambridge University Press, 2005), 360-66.

[22]See Tavard, *Holy Writ or Holy Church*, 36-37.

[23]Quoted from Walter Ullmann, *Medieval Papalism: The Political Theories of the Medieval Church* (London: Methuen, 1949), 50-55, 89, 99-100.

[24]Tavard, *Holy Writ or Holy Church*, 79.

[25]Tavard (ibid., 52-54) says that Gerson lists these six in several places, citing Gerson's *Declaratio Veritatum* as a good epitome.

[26]See Brian Gogan, *The Common Corps of Christendom: Ecclesiological Themes in the Writings of Sir Thomas More* (SHCTh 26; Leiden: Brill, 1982), 47-48.

[27]John Wycliffe, *On the Truth of Sacred Scripture* 21.33-34. See John Wycliffe, *John Wyclif: On the Truth of Holy Scripture*, trans. Ian Christopher Levy (Kalamazoo, MI: Medieval Institute Publications, 2001), 61.

[28]See Gerald Bray, "Scripture and Tradition in Reformation Thought," *ERT* 19 (1995): 158.

[29]John Huss, *On the Church* 16. See John Huss, *The Church*, trans. David S. Schaff (1915; repr., Westport, CT: Greenwood, 1974), 163.

[30]Jan den Boeft, "Erasmus and the Church Fathers," in Backus, *Church Fathers in the West*, 2:537.

[31]See Manfred Schulze, "Martin Luther and the Church Fathers," in Backus, *Church Fathers in the West*, 2:597-609.

[32]See also Tavard, *Holy Writ or Holy Church*, 83.

[33]John Calvin, *Institutes* 4.10.18; 4.10.23.

[34]John Calvin, "Reply to Cardinal Sadoleto," in *A Reformation Debate: Sadoleto's Letter to the Genevans and Calvin's Reply*, ed. John C. Olin (New York: Harper & Row, 1966), 62.

[35]Bruce, *Tradition Old and New*, 144.

[36]Silva, *Has the Church Misread the Bible?* 96. See also Daniel B. Clendenin, "Orthodoxy on Scripture and Tradition: A Comparison with Reformed and Catholic Perspectives," *WTJ* 57 (1995): 389.

[37]Timothy George, "An Evangelical Reflection on Scripture and Tradition," *Pro Ecclesia* 9, no. 2 (2000): 191.

[38]For extensive treatment of the Radical Reformers, see George Huntston Williams, *The Radical Reformation* (3rd ed.; SCES 15; Kirksville, MO: Sixteenth Century Journal Publishers, 1992).

[39]See Tavard, *Holy Writ or Holy Church*, 123, 177. Tavard refers to Sylvester Prierias, *Dialogue on the Power of the Pope*; Johann von Eck, *On the Primacy of Peter Against Luther* (published 1521); Johann Cochläus, *On the Authority of the Church and Scripture Against Luther* (published 1524).

[40]Gabriel Moran explains that these theologians argue that Trent declared a double means (Scripture and tradition) but avoided declaring a double source and successfully left the issue undecided (*Scripture and Tradition: A Survey of the Controversy* [New York: Herder & Herder, 1963], 37-38). Moran (ibid., 108n63) cites Callahan, Oberman, O'Hanlon, Rahner, Küng, Daniélou, Congar, Semmelroth, Bouyer, Dubarle, Liégé and Schmaus as modern theologians with this understanding of Trent.

[41]See A. Spindeler, "*Pari pietatis affectu*: Das Tridentinum über Heilige Schrift und apostolische Überlieferung," *TGl* 51 (1961): 179; B. C. Butler, *The Church and the Bible* (Baltimore: Helicon, 1960), 47; G. Van Noort, *The Sources of Revelation: Divine Faith*, trans. and rev. W. R. Murphy and J. J. Castelot (Westminster: Newman, 1961), 153; Maurice Bénevot, "Tradition, Church and Dogma," *HeyJ* 1 (1960): 39-41;

Gerard Owens, "Is All Revelation Contained in Sacred Scripture?" *SMR* 1 (1958): 60; Henry Lennerz, "Scriptura Sola," *Gregorianum* 40 (1959): 52.

[42]Note that some say that post-Tridentine theologians originated the modern two-source theory. See, for example, J. R. Geiselmann, "Das Konzil von Trient über das Verhältnis der Heiligen Schrift und der nicht geschriebenen Traditionen," in *Die mündliche Überlieferung: Beiträge zum Begriff der Tradition*, ed. Michael Schmaus (Munich: Max Hueber, 1957), 123-206; V. Moran, "Scripture and Tradition: A Current Debate," *ACR* 38 (1961): 21-22.

[43]Stanley J. Grenz and John R. Franke, "Theological Heritage as Hermeneutical Trajectory: Toward a Nonfoundationalist Understanding of the Role of Tradition in Theology," in *Ancient and Postmodern Christianity: Paleo-Orthodoxy in the 21st Century; Essays in Honor of Thomas C. Oden*, ed. Kenneth Tanner and Christopher A. Hall (Downers Grove, IL: InterVarsity Press, 2002), 221.

[44]See the introduction in Albert C. Outler, ed., *John Wesley* (New York: Oxford University Press, 1964).

[45]United Methodist Church, *The Book of Discipline of the United Methodist Church* (Nashville: United Methodist Publishing House, 2004), 77.

[46]See *Scripture, Tradition and Traditions*, Faith and Order Paper 42 (Geneva: World Council of Churches, 1963).

[47]See the full text in Walter M. Abbott, ed., *The Documents of Vatican II*, translation ed. Joseph Gallagher (New York: Guild Press, 1966), 114-18.

[48]Richard J. Foster, *Celebration of Discipline: The Path to Spiritual Growth* (San Francisco: Harper & Row, 1978).

[49]Robert E. Webber, *Common Roots: A Call to Evangelical Maturity* (Grand Rapids: Zondervan, 1978).

[50]Robert E. Webber and Donald Bloesch, eds., *The Orthodox Evangelicals: Who They Are and What They Are Saying* (Nashville: Thomas Nelson, 1978), 11.

[51]Chris Armstrong, "The Future Lies in the Past," *ChrTo* 52 (2008): 25. Lovelace writes, "We need to listen to history—the history of our own movement, and the body of tradition that has nourished other movements. The early fathers, the medieval mystics, the spiritual doctors of the Reformation and Counter-Reformation, the leaders of the awakening eras, the uneven prophets of liberal social reform—all of these can force us back toward Biblical balance and authentic spirituality" (Richard F. Lovelace, "Evangelical Spirituality: A Church Historian's Perspective," *JETS* 31 [1988]: 35).

[52]Thomas C. Oden, "Then and Now: The Recovery of Patristic Wisdom," *ChrCent* 107 (1990): 1166.

[53]Thomas C. Oden, *After Modernity . . . What? Agenda for Theology* (Grand Rapids: Zondervan, 1990), 34.

[54]For a current list of volumes available in the Ancient Christian Commentary on Scripture series, see www.ivpress.com.

[55]Augustine, *Confessions* 1.1 (available in many editions and translations).

CHAPTER 3: HOW DO WE UNDERSTAND THE TRADITION TODAY?

[1]Vladimir Lossky, *In the Image and Likeness of God*, ed. John H. Erickson and Thomas E. Bird (Crestwood, NY: St. Vladimir's Seminary Press, 1974), 148.

[2]Timothy Ware, *The Orthodox Church* (2nd ed.; London: Penguin, 1993), 197.

[3]Constantine N. Callinicos, *The Greek Orthodox Catechism* (New York: Greek Archdiocese of North and South America, 1960), 6.

[4]Lossky, *Image and Likeness of God*, 151-52.

[5]Ware, *The Orthodox Church*, 196 (with further description on pp. 198-206). See also James Stamoolis, "Scripture and Tradition in the Orthodox Church," *ERT* 19 (1995): 133.

[6]John Meyendorff, *The Orthodox Church* (4th ed.; Crestwood, NY: St. Vladimir's Seminary Press, 1996), 4.

[7]Ware, *The Orthodox Church*, 197.

[8]See also Daniel B. Clendenin, "Orthodoxy on Scripture and Tradition: A Comparison with Reformed and Catholic Perspectives," *WTJ* 57 (1995): 394-96.

[9]Lossky, *Image and Likeness of God*, 149.

[10]Ware, *The Orthodox Church*, 202.

[11]For a list and brief description, see ibid., 203.

[12]Ibid., 204.

[13]These are the Divine Liturgy of John Chrysostom (most common, used most Sundays and most Eucharistic holy days), the Divine Liturgy of St. Basil the Great (used on Sunday during Lent and several Christian holidays), the Liturgy of the Presanctified Gifts (extended Vespers service distributing Eucharist consecrated the previous Sunday) and the Liturgy of St. James (used in specific locations on the feast day of James, Christ's brother).

[14]Ware, *The Orthodox Church*, 204.

[15]Ibid., 206.

[16]Ibid.

[17]Aleksei Stepanovich Khomyakov, "On the Western Confessions of Faith," in *Ultimate Questions: An Anthology of Modern Russian Religious Thought*, ed. Alexander Schmemann (Crestwood, NY: St. Vladimir's Seminary Press, 1977), 29-69.

[18]John Meyendorff, *Catholicity and the Church* (Crestwood, NY: St. Vladimir's Seminary Press, 1983), 97.

[19]John Meyendorff, *Living Tradition: Orthodox Witness in the Contemporary World* (Crestwood, NY: St. Vladimir's Seminary Press, 1978), 44.

[20]See Sergius Bulgakov, *The Orthodox Church* (Crestwood, NY: St. Vladimir's Seminary Press, 1988), 11-12, 24; Thomas Hopko, *All the Fullness of God: Essays on Orthodoxy, Ecumenism and Modern Science* (Crestwood, NY: St. Vladimir's Seminary Press, 1982), 49; Ware, *The Orthodox Church*, 207-8; Lazarus Moore, *Sacred Tradition in the Orthodox Church* (Minneapolis: Light & Life, 1984), 5-8.

[21]Georges Florovsky, *Bible, Church, Tradition: An Eastern Orthodox View* (Belmont, MA: Nordland, 1972), 48.

[22]Isaac Melton, "A Response to Harold O. J. Brown," in *Reclaiming the Great Tradition: Evangelicals, Catholics and Orthodox in Dialogue*, ed. James S. Cutsinger (Downers Grove, IL: InterVarsity Press, 1997), 91-92.

[23]*Canons and Decrees of the Council of Trent*, trans. H. J. Schroeder (St. Louis: Herder, 1941), 17.

[24]Yves Congar, *Tradition and Traditions: An Historical and a Theological Essay*, trans. Michael Naseby and Thomas Rainborough (New York: Macmillan, 1966), 169.

[25]Norman L. Geisler and Ralph E. MacKenzie, *Roman Catholics and Evangelicals: Agreements and Differences* (Grand Rapids: Baker, 1995), 180. See, for example, Ludwig Ott, *Fundamentals of Catholic Dogma*, ed. James Bastible, trans. Patrick Lynch (St. Louis: Herder, 1954), 1-10; John Henry Newman, *On the Inspiration of Scripture*, ed. J. Derek Holmes and Robert Murray (Washington: Corpus Books, 1967); Joseph Ratzinger, *God's Word: Scripture, Tradition, Office*, ed. Peter Hünermann and Thomas Söding, trans. Henry Taylor (San Francisco: Ignatius Press, 2005), especially part 2, "The Question of the Concept of Tradition," and part 3, "Biblical Interpretation in Conflict"; Yves Congar, *The Meaning of Tradition*, trans. A. N. Woodrow (San Francisco: Ignatius Press, 2004), especially chapter 3, "The Content of Tradition: Tradition and Scripture"; Louis Bouyer, *The Meaning of Sacred Scripture*, trans. Mary Perkins Ryan (Liturgical Studies 5; Notre Dame: University of Notre Dame Press, 1958), 1-3.

[26]Avery Dulles, "Revelation as Basis for Scripture and Tradition," *ERT* 21 (1997): 118-20.

[27]Abbott, *Documents of Vatican II*, 114-18.

[28]See *Catechism of the Catholic Church* (2nd ed; Liguori, MO: Liguori Publications, 1997), paragraphs 80-82. Official version at www.scborromeo.org/ccc.htm.

[29]Ibid., paragraph 83.

[30]Ibid., paragraph 95.

[31]Richard P. McBrien says that this has always been the singular criterion, for "*Scripture is itself a product of Tradition*," for "Tradition comes *before* and *during*, and not just *after*, the writing of Sacred Scripture" (*Catholicism* [rev. ed.; San Francisco: HarperCollins, 1994], 62-63).

[32]See *Canons of the Church of England* (6th ed., with 1st and 2nd supplements; London: Church House Publishing, 2000), 3-10; also available at www.churchofengland.org/about-us/structure/churchlawlegis/canons.aspx. See also *The Book of Common Prayer: 1662 Version* (London: David Campbell, 1999), which contains the *Thirty-Nine Articles of Religion*.

[33]William H. Van de Pol, *Anglicanism in Ecumenical Perspective*, trans. Walter van de Putte (Pittsburgh: Duquesne University Press, 1965), 46.

[34]James A. Pike and W. Norman Pittenger, *The Faith of the Church: The Church's*

Teaching (Church's Teaching Series 3; Greenwich, CT: Seabury, 1951), 19.

[35]Van de Pol, *Anglicanism in Ecumenical Perspective*, 47.

[36]*Book of Common Prayer*, 449, 454.

[37]Van de Pol, *Anglicanism in Ecumenical Perspective*, 47.

[38]F. F. Bruce, *Tradition Old and New* (Eugene, OR: Wipf & Stock, 1970), 169.

[39]J. A. T. Robinson, "Not Radical Enough?" *ChrCent* 86 (1969): 1446.

[40]Peter Kreeft, *Fundamentals of the Faith: Essays in Christian Apologetics* (San Francisco: Ignatius Press, 1988), 272-73.

[41]Geisler and MacKenzie, *Roman Catholics and Evangelicals*, 179-80.

[42]D. H. Williams, *Evangelicals and Tradition: The Formative Influence of the Early Church* (Grand Rapids: Baker Academic, 2005), 57.

[43]Stephen R. Holmes, *Listening to the Past: The Place of Tradition in Theology* (Grand Rapids: Baker Academic, 2002), xi.

[44]See Geisler and MacKenzie, *Roman Catholics and Evangelicals*, 196.

[45]Kreeft, *Fundamentals of the Faith*, 272.

[46]D. H. Williams, *Retrieving the Tradition and Renewing Evangelicalism: A Primer for Suspicious Protestants* (Grand Rapids: Eerdmans, 1999), 29. See also Frances Young, "A Cloud of Witnesses," in *The Myth of God Incarnate*, ed. John Hick (Philadelphia: Westminster, 1977), 13-47; Maurice Wiles, *The Remaking of Christian Doctrine* (London: SCM Press, 1974).

Chapter 4: Who Am I? Christian History and Christian Identity

[1]Thomas Oden, "Then and Now: The Recovery of Patristic Wisdom," *ChrCent* 107 (1990): 1164-68.

[2]Oden reflects this emphasis in several of his works: *After Modernity . . . What? Agenda for Theology* (Grand Rapids: Zondervan, 1990); *The Rebirth of Orthodoxy: Signs of New Life in Christianity* (San Francisco: HarperSanFrancisco, 2003); *How Africa Shaped the Christian Mind: Rediscovering the African Seedbed of Western Christianity* (Downers Grove, IL: InterVarsity Press, 2007); *Classic Christianity: A Systematic Theology* (New York: HarperOne, 2009); *The African Memory of Mark: Reassessing Early Church Tradition* (Downers Grove, IL: InterVarsity Press, 2011); *Early Libyan Christianity: Uncovering a North African Tradition* (Downers Grove, IL: InterVarsity Press, 2011). See also Thomas C. Oden, Kenneth Tanner and Christopher A. Hall, *Ancient and Postmodern Christianity: Paleo-Orthodoxy in the 21st Century; Essays in Honor of Thomas C. Oden* (Downers Grove, IL: InterVarsity Press, 2002).

[3]For "the rule of truth," see Irenaeus, *Against All Heresies* 1.22.1 (ANF 1:347). The concept is clear in Irenaeus, *Against All Heresies* 1.10.1: "The Church . . . has received from the apostles and their disciples this faith" (ANF 1:330); and in Irenaeus, *Against All Heresies* 3.2.2: "We refer them to that tradition which originates from the apostles, which is preserved by means of the succession of presbyters in the Church. . . .

[T]hese men do now consent neither to Scripture nor to tradition" (ANF 1:415).

[4]Tertullian, *Prescription Against Heretics* 1:12-13, challenges believers to seek truth only from Christians, which will not impair "the rule of faith" and immediately introduces the creed with these words: "Now, with regard to this rule of faith—that we may from this point acknowledge what it is which we defend" (ANF 3:249).

[5]Particular references in the writings of these and other early church writers abound. For Augustine, for example, see William S. Babcock, "Grace, Freedom, and Justice: Augustine and the Christian Tradition," *PSTJ* 26, no. 4 (1973): 1-15; for Augustine's dealings with synergist Julian of Eclanum, see Mathijs Lamberigts, "Augustine's Use of the Tradition in His Reaction to Julian of Aeclanum's *Ad Turbanitium: Contra Iulianum I-II*," *AugStud* 41, no. 1 (2010): 183-200. For Cyril, see, for example, Christopher A. Beeley, "Cyril of Alexandria and Gregory Nazianzen: Tradition and Complexity in Patristic Christology," *JECS* 17 (2009): 381-419.

[6]See, among many others, Francis of Assisi, *The Earlier Rule* and *The Later Rule* 1, 4, 6, in *Francis of Assisi*, ed. Regis J. Armstrong, J. A. Wayne Hellman and William J. Short, vol. 1, *The Saint: Early Documents* (Hyde Park, NY: New City Press, 1999), 63-64, 100-103. See also, for example, Guy Bedouelle, "Dominic and Apostolic Poverty," in *Saint Dominic: The Grace of the Word*, trans. Mary Thomas Noble (San Francisco: Ignatius Press, 1994), chapter 8.

[7]For Evagrius, see Palladius, "Evagrius," in *Palladius: The Lausiac History*, trans. Robert T. Meyer (ACW 34; New York: Newman Press, 1964), 110-14; Tim Vivian, trans., *Four Desert Fathers: Pambo, Evagrius, Macarius of Egypt, and Macarius of Alexandria; Coptic Texts Relating to the Lausiac History of Palladius* (Crestwood, NY: St. Vladimir's Seminary Press, 2004), 69-92. For Cassian, see John Cassian and Boniface Ramsey, *John Cassian: The Conferences* (ACW 57; New York: Newman Press, 1997); John Cassian and Boniface Ramsey, *John Cassian: The Institutes* (ACW 58; New York: Newman Press, 2000).

[8]Benedict of Nursia, *The Rule of St. Benedict* 42.3, 73.

[9]See, for example, Manfred Schulze, "Martin Luther and the Church Fathers," and Johannes Van Orrt, "John Calvin and the Church Fathers," in *The Reception of the Church Fathers in the West: From the Carolingians to the Maurists*, ed. Irena Backus (2 vols.; Leiden: Brill, 1997), 2:597-609, 2:661-700.

[10]Rowan Williams, *Why Study the Past? The Quest for the Historical Church* (Grand Rapids: Eerdmans, 2005), 27.

[11]See Williams's monographs *Evangelicals and Tradition: The Formative Influence of the Early Church* (Grand Rapids: Baker Academic, 2005); *Retrieving the Tradition and Renewing Evangelicalism: A Primer for Suspicious Protestants* (Grand Rapids: Eerdmans, 1999); and edited volumes *The Free Church and the Early Church: Bridging the Historical and Theological Divide* (Grand Rapids: Eerdmans, 2002); *Tradition, Scripture, and Interpretation: A Sourcebook of the Ancient Church* (Grand Rapids: Baker Academic, 2006).

[12]For his autobiographical account, see John Henry Newman, *Apologia pro vita sua* (New York: Robert Appleton, 1865). See also William Barry, "John Henry Newman," in *The Catholic Encyclopedia*, vol. 10 (New York: Robert Appleton, 1911), 794-800 (available at www.newadvent.org/cathen/10794a.htm).

[13]John Henry Newman, *The Idea of a University: Defined and Illustrated* (1852; repr., London: Longmans, Green, 1899).

[14]See Williams, *Why Study the Past?* 23-24.

CHAPTER 5: A GREAT CLOUD OF WITNESSES: *CHRISTIAN COMMUNITY ACROSS THE CENTURIES*

[1]Recent books include Stanley Grenz, *Theology for the Community of God* (Grand Rapids: Eerdmans, 1994); Paul Janowiak, *Standing Together in the Community of God: Liturgical Spirituality and the Presence of Christ* (Collegeville, MN: Liturgical Press, 2011); Scot McKnight, *A Community Called Atonement: Living Theology* (Nashville: Abingdon, 2007); Philip Francis Esler, *New Testament Theology: Communion and Community* (Minneapolis: Fortress, 2005); Eddie Giffs and Ryan K. Bolger, *Emerging Churches: Creating Christian Community in Postmodern Cultures* (Grand Rapids: Baker Academic, 2005).

[2]See Harold O. J. Brown, "Proclamation and Preservation: The Necessity and Temptations of Church Tradition," in *Reclaiming the Great Tradition: Evangelicals, Catholics and Orthodox in Dialogue*, ed. James S. Cutsinger (Downers Grove, IL: InterVarsity Press, 1997), 74-76.

[3]N. T. Wright, *Simply Christian: Why Christianity Makes Sense* (San Francisco: HarperSanFrancisco, 2006), 203.

[4]For critique of this loss of community, see Jeffrey Bingham, "Evangelicals, Irenaeus, and the Bible," in *The Free Church and the Early Church: Bridging the Historical and Theological Divide*, ed. D. H. Williams (Grand Rapids: Eerdmans, 2002), 27-46; David F. Wells, *No Place for Truth; or, Whatever Happened to Evangelical Theology?* (Grand Rapids: Eerdmans, 1993); Michael Scott Horton, *Made in America: The Shaping of Modern American Evangelicalism* (Grand Rapids: Baker, 1991), especially 166-71; Stanley J. Grenz, *Revisioning Evangelical Theology: A Fresh Agenda for the Twenty-first Century* (Downers Grove, IL: InterVarsity Press, 1993), 50-54; Peter Toon, "Is a Personal Relationship with Jesus What I Really Want?" *Touchstone* 11, no. 5 (1998): 13-14.

[5]Stanley Hauerwas, *Dispatches from the Front: Theological Engagements with the Secular* (Durham, NC: Duke University Press, 1994), 18.

CHAPTER 6: ACCOUNTABILITY PARTNERS: *SHARING ACCOUNTABILITY WITH HISTORIC CHRISTIANS*

[1]The name has been changed.

[2]Clark H. Pinnock, "Tradition Can Keep Theologians on Track," *ChrTo* 26 (1982): 26.

[3]Grant R. Osborne, *The Hermeneutical Spiral: A Comprehensive Introduction to Biblical Interpretation* (2nd ed.; Downers Grove, IL: IVP Academic, 2006), 353.

[4]For perspectives on open theism, see Paul Helm et al., *Perspectives on the Doctrine of God: 4 Views* (Nashville: B & H Academic, 2008). For proponents, see Richard Rice, *The Openness of God: The Relationship of Divine Foreknowledge and Human Free Will* (Nashville: Review & Herald Publishing, 1980); Clark H. Pinnock, *Most Moved Mover: A Theology of God's Openness* (Carlisle: Paternoster, 2001); Clark H. Pinnock et al., *The Openness of God: A Biblical Challenge to the Traditional Understanding of God* (Downers Grove, IL: InterVarsity Press, 1994); Gregory Boyd, *God of the Possible: A Biblical Introduction to the Open View of God* (Grand Rapids: Baker, 2000).

[5]Eusebius of Caesarea lauds Constantine as a great Christian in *Hist. eccl.* 9.9-11; 10.1-9 (NPNF[2] 1:363-87); in *Life of Constantine* (NPNF[2] 1:481-559); and in *Oration of Eusebius* [often called *Panegyric of Constantine*], especially 1-10 (NPNF[2] 1:582-95). Since then, historians have varied in their assessments; see summary in Timothy D. Barnes, *Constantine and Eusebius* (Cambridge, MA: Harvard University Press, 1981), 272-75. Some argue in favor of Constantine, such as Norman H. Baynes, *Constantine the Great and the Christian Church* (London: Humphrey Milford, 1929). Recently, Peter J. Leithart, in *Defending Constantine: The Twilight of an Empire and the Dawn of Christendom* (Downers Grove, IL: IVP Academic, 2010), sees Constantine positively, but in chapter 14 he lists more recent detractors.

[6]This is the Vincentian canon mentioned in part 1. See Vincent of Lérins, *Commonitory* 2.5.

CHAPTER 7: MENTORS AND FRIENDS: *HISTORIC CHRISTIANS BROADEN OUR HORIZONS AND FILL GAPS IN OUR UNDERSTANDING*

[1]See the following works by Webber: *Ancient-Future Faith: Rethinking Evangelicalism for a Postmodern World* (Grand Rapids: Baker, 1999); *Ancient-Future Evangelism: Making Your Church a Faith-Forming Community* (Grand Rapids: Baker, 2003); *Ancient-Future Time: Forming Spirituality Through the Christian Year* (Grand Rapids: Baker, 2004); *Ancient-Future Worship: Proclaiming and Enacting God's Narrative* (Grand Rapids: Baker, 2008). See also his *Common Roots: A Call to Evangelical Maturity* (Grand Rapids: Zondervan, 1978); revised edition, *Common Roots: The Original Call to an Ancient-Future Faith* (Grand Rapids: Zondervan, 2009).

[2]Williams wrote *Retrieving the Tradition and Renewing Evangelicalism: A Primer for Suspicious Protestants* (Grand Rapids: Eerdmans, 1999); *Evangelicals and Tradition: The Formative Influence of the Early Church* (Grand Rapids: Baker Academic, 2005). He edited *The Free Church and the Early Church: Bridging the Historical and Theological Divide* (Grand Rapids: Eerdmans, 2002); *Tradition, Scripture, and Interpretation: A Sourcebook of the Ancient Church* (Grand Rapids: Baker Academic, 2006).

[3]Quoted in Chris Armstrong, "The Future Lies in the Past," *ChrTo* 52 (2008): 23.

[4]For Cassian's presentation, see John Cassian, *Conferences* 3, 13. For Orthodox

writers, see Timothy Ware, *The Orthodox Church* (2nd ed.; London: Penguin, 1993), 218-25; Vladimir Lossky, *The Mystical Theology of the Eastern Church* (Crestwood, NY: St. Vladimir's Seminary Press, 1976), 198-216; John Meyendorff, *Byzantine Theology: Historical Trends and Doctrinal Themes* (2nd ed.; New York: Fordham University Press, 1979), 138-46.

[5]For example, for Erasmus, see *On the Freedom of the Will*, in E. Gordon Rupp and Philip S. Watson, ed. and trans., *Luther and Erasmus: Free Will and Salvation* (LCC 17; London: SCM Press, 1969), 35-97, esp. 81-84; for Melanchthon, see Gregory B. Graybill, *Evangelical Free Will: Philipp Melanchthon's Doctrinal Journey on the Origins of Faith* (OTM; Oxford: Oxford University Press, 2010).

PART THREE INTRODUCTION

[1]For more comprehensive histories of interpretation, see Henning Graf Reventlow, *History of Biblical Interpretation*, vol. 1, *From the Old Testament to Origen*, trans. Leo G. Perdue; vol. 2, *From Late Antiquity to the End of the Middle Ages*, trans. James O. Duke; vol. 3, *Renaissance, Reformation, Humanism*, trans. James O. Duke; vol. 4, *From the Enlightenment to the Twentieth Century*, trans. Leo G. Perdue (RBS 50, 61-63; Atlanta: Society of Biblical Literature, 2009-2010); Alan J. Hauser and Duane Frederick Watson, eds., *A History of Biblical Interpretation*, vol. 1, *The Ancient Period*; vol. 2, *The Medieval Through the Reformation Period* (Grand Rapids: Eerdmans, 2003-2009); William Yarchin, *History of Biblical Interpretation: A Reader* (Grand Rapids: Baker Academic, 2011); Frederic W. Farrar, *History of Interpretation* (Grand Rapids: Baker, 1962). See also Henri de Lubac, *Medieval Exegesis: The Four Senses of Scripture*, trans. Mark Sebanc and E. M. Macierowski (4 vols.; Ressourcement; Grand Rapids: Eerdmans; Edinburgh: T & T Clark, 1998-2009).

CHAPTER 8: RIGHTLY DIVIDING THE WORD OF TRUTH

[1]For example, Greeks already used allegory to interpret Homer, Jews to interpret the OT Scriptures.

[2]See Leonhard Goppelt, *Typos: The Typological Interpretation of the Old Testament in the New*, trans. Donald H. Madvig (Grand Rapids: Eerdmans, 1982); Christopher R. Seitz, *Figured Out: Typology and Providence in Christian Scripture* (Louisville: Westminster John Knox, 2001); see also Patrick G. Barker, "Allegory and Typology in Galatians 4:21-31," *SVTQ* 38 (1994): 193-209.

[3]See also Donald H. Juel, "Interpreting Israel's Scriptures in the New Testament," in *A History of Biblical Interpretation*, ed. Alan J. Hauser and Duane Frederick Watson (2 vols.; Grand Rapids: Eerdmans, 2003-2009), 1:283-303.

[4]Irenaeus's *Against All Heresies* is most easily available in English in ANF 1. For Irenaeus's interpretative method, see also Reventlow, *History of Biblical Interpretation*, 1:153-74.

[5]Irenaeus, *Against All Heresies* 4.32.1 (ANF 1:506).

[6]Irenaeus, *Against All Heresies* 1.22.1 (ANF 1:347); this rule is described without the actual term in 1.10.1 (ANF 1:330-31).

[7]See Frances Young, "Alexandrian and Antiochene Exegesis," in Hauser and Watson, *History of Biblical Interpretation*, 1:334-54. Note also Moisés Silva, *Has the Church Misread the Bible? The History of Interpretation in the Light of Current Issues* (Grand Rapids: Academie, 1987), 54-55.

[8]James Kugel, *How to Read the Bible: A Guide to Scripture Then and Now* (New York: Free Press, 2007), 14-16, 20-21.

[9]Origen, *On First Principles* 4.2.4 (ANF 4:359, cited in ANF as 4.1.11).

[10]Origen, *On First Principles* 4.2.6 (ANF 4:360, cited in ANF as 4.1.12).

[11]Origen, *On First Principles* 4.3.4 (ANF 4:367, cited in ANF as 4.1.18).

[12]John Cassian, *Conferences* 8.3.1-6; 8.4.1-2 (translation from Boniface Ramsey, ed. and trans., *John Cassian: The Conferences* [ACW 57; New York: Newman Press, 1997], 292-94; see also NPNF[2] 11:376-77).

[13]John Cassian, *Conferences* 14.1-2 (NPNF[2] 11:435).

[14]John Cassian, *Conferences* 14.8 (NPNF[2] 11:437-38).

[15]Augustine, *On Christian Doctrine* 3.15 (NPNF[1] 1:563).

[16]Augustine, *On Christian Doctrine* 30-37. For more on Augustine's exegesis, see Reventlow, *History of Biblical Interpretation*, 2:76-94; Hauser and Watson, *History of Biblical Interpretation*, 1:380-408.

[17]D. H. Williams, ed., *Tradition, Scripture, and Interpretation: A Sourcebook of the Ancient Church* (Grand Rapids: Baker Academic, 2006), 33.

[18]Peter J. Leithart, *Deep Exegesis: The Mystery of Reading Scripture* (Waco, TX: Baylor University Press, 2009), 207.

[19]See Gregory the Great's *Commentary on Job*, which uses this method throughout the commentary (the Latin title is *Magna moralia*). See also Reventlow, *History of Biblical Interpretation*, 2:100-26, 146-47, 164-69, 174-78, 195-201, 250; Mary A. Mayeski, "Early Medieval Exegesis: Gregory I to the Twelfth Century," in Hauser and Watson, *History of Biblical Interpretation*, 2:86-112.

[20]See also Silva, *Has the Church Misread the Bible?* 54-55; Kugel, *How to Read the Bible*, 22-23.

[21]See Rainer Berndt, "The School of St. Victor in Paris," in *Hebrew Bible, Old Testament: The History of Its Interpretation*, ed. Magne Sæbø, vol. 1, part 2, *The Middle Ages* (Göttingen: Vandenhoeck & Ruprecht, 2000), 490-92. See also Boyd Taylor Coolman, *The Theology of Hugh of St. Victor: An Interpretation* (Cambridge: Cambridge University Press, 2010), 124-37.

[22]Bonaventure, *Breviloquium* prologue 4.1 (translation from George Tavard, *Holy Writ or Holy Church: The Crisis of the Protestant Reformation* [New York: Harper, 1959], 17).

[23]For more on scholastic biblical interpretation, see Christopher Ocker, "Scholastic Interpretation of the Bible," in Hauser and Watson, *History of Biblical Interpretation*, 2:254-79.

[24]*Textus Receptus* (Received Text) is the name given to the Greek NT text resulting from later editions of Erasmus's work; it was the standard critical NT text until the nineteenth century, when alternatives began to be produced.

[25]Reventlow, *History of Biblical Interpretation*, 3:34-35.

[26]Ibid., 3:39-46, 56-63.

[27]From WA 5:645 (in Latin). See also Manfred Schulze, "Martin Luther and the Church Fathers," in *The Reception of the Church Fathers in the West: From the Carolingians to the Maurists*, ed. Irena Backus (2 vols.; Leiden: Brill, 1997), 2:615-17.

[28]From *Luther's Works*, vol. 54, *Table Talk*, ed. and trans. Theodore G. Tappert (Philadelphia: Fortress, 1967), 406. There are excellent sections on Luther in Reventlow, *History of Biblical Interpretation*, 3:69-87; Mark D. Thompson, "Biblical Interpretation in the Works of Martin Luther," in Hauser and Watson, *History of Biblical Interpretation*, 2:299-318.

[29]Reventlow, *History of Biblical Interpretation*, 3:103-15.

[30]Note that Calvin opposes allegory even when commenting on Paul's use of allegory in Galatians 4:21-26 (*The Epistles of Paul the Apostle to the Galatians, Ephesians, Philippians, and Colossians*, ed. David W. Torrance and Thomas F. Torrance, trans. T. H. L. Parker [Calvin's Commentaries 11; Grand Rapids: Eerdmans, 1994], 84-88).

[31]John Calvin, preface to *Institutes of the Christian Religion* (1539 edition).

[32]See Reventlow, *History of Biblical Interpretation*, 3:119-37; Barbara Pitkin, "John Calvin and the Interpretation of the Bible," in Hauser and Watson, *History of Biblical Interpretation*, 2:341-71.

[33]For extensive treatment of the Radical Reformers, see George Huntston Williams, *The Radical Reformation* (3rd ed.; SCES 15; Kirksville, MO: Sixteenth Century Journal Publishers, 1992); for briefer introduction, see George H. Williams and Angel M. Mergal, eds., *Spiritual and Anabaptist Writers* (LCC 25; Philadelphia: Westminster John Knox, 1957), 19-35.

[34]For more on Anabaptist exegesis, see Stuart Murray, "Biblical Interpretation Among the Anabaptist Reformers," in Hauser and Watson, *History of Biblical Interpretation*, 2:403-27.

[35]See Guy Bedouelle, "Biblical Interpretation in the Catholic Reformation," in Hauser and Watson, *History of Biblical Interpretation*, 2:428-49.

[36]This was discussed in part 1. See Jaroslav Pelikan, *Obedient Rebels: Catholic Substance and Protestant Principle in Luther's Reformation* (London: SCM Press, 1964), 27-104; A. N. S. Lane, "Calvin's Use of the Fathers and the Medievals," *CTJ* 16 (1981): 149-205.

[37]See Heinrich Heppe, *Reformed Dogmatics Set Out and Illustrated from the Sources*, trans. G. T. Thomson, rev. and ed. Ernst Bizer (Grand Rapids: Baker, 1978), 30-31.

[38]See Anthony N. S. Lane, "*Sola Scriptura*? Making Sense of a Post-Reformation Slogan," in *A Pathway into the Holy Scripture*, ed. Philip E. Satterthwaite and David F. Wright (Grand Rapids: Eerdmans, 1994), 323-24.

[39]See de Lubac's massive contribution, *Medieval Exegesis: The Four Senses of Scripture*, trans. Mark Sebanc and E. M. Macierowski (4 vols.; Ressourcement; Grand Rapids: Eerdmans; Edinburgh: T & T Clark, 1998-2009). He sees progress in critical exegesis but cautions that we need the fuller picture that ancient exegesis affords.

[40]See, for example, John Locke, *Essay Concerning Human Understanding* (1689), especially book 4, chapter 18 ("Of Faith and Reason, and Their Distinct Provinces"), paragraphs 3-5.

[41]See, for example, John Toland, *Christianity Not Mysterious* (1696), especially the preface, and section 2 ("That the Doctrines of the Gospel Are Not Contrary to Reason").

[42]Sterrett recommends consulting other Christians, particularly younger consulting older, but with no mention of the works of departed Christians (*How to Understand Your Bible* [2nd ed.; Downers Grove, IL: InterVarsity Press, 1974], 14-15). Step 11a of Stuart's methodology ("Investigate what others have said about the passage") could be construed to include historic Christians, though not explicitly (*Old Testament Exegesis: A Primer for Students and Pastors* [2nd ed.; Philadelphia: Westminster, 1984], 39). Fee, in step 13 of his methodology, concurs, and he recommends wide reading in a broad bibliography, but the recommended authors are almost exclusively contemporaries (*New Testament Exegesis: A Handbook for Students and Pastors* [rev. ed.; Louisville: Westminster John Knox, 1993], 182-86). Note that elsewhere Fee says that personal exegesis "must finally be the product of the Christian community at large . . . indebted to that long history of orthodox consensus" ("Exegesis and the Role of Tradition in Evangelical Hermeneutics," *ERT* 17 [1993]: 433).

[43]A. Berkeley Mickelsen, *Interpreting the Bible* (Grand Rapids: Eerdmans, 1963); I. Howard Marshall, ed., *New Testament Interpretation: Essays on Principles and Methods* (Grand Rapids: Eerdmans, 1977); Walter C. Kaiser and Moisés Silva, *Introduction to Biblical Hermeneutics: The Search for Meaning* (Grand Rapids: Zondervan, 1994); William W. Klein, Craig L. Blomberg and Robert L. Hubbard Jr., *Introduction to Biblical Interpretation* (rev. ed.; Nashville: Thomas Nelson, 2004), 171-200 discuss the possibility of levels of meaning, but they do so without considering patristic and medieval methods; J. Scott Duvall and J. Daniel Hays, *Grasping God's Word: A Hands-On Approach to Reading, Interpreting, and Applying the Bible* (2nd ed.; Grand Rapids: Zondervan, 2005); Andreas J. Köstenberger and Richard D. Patterson, *Invitation to Biblical Interpretation: Exploring the Hermeneutical Triad of History, Literature, and Theology* (Grand Rapids: Kregel, 2011) ignore historic Christian interpretations, except to point out problems.

[44]See Duvall and Hays, *Grasping God's Word*, 184-96.

[45]C. S. Lewis, *Surprised by Joy: The Shape of My Early Life* (New York: Harcourt Brace, 1955), 201.

[46]Grant R. Osborne, *The Hermeneutical Spiral: A Comprehensive Introduction to Biblical Interpretation* (Downers Grove, IL: InterVarsity Press, 1991), 12-14.

[47]Grant R. Osborne, *The Hermeneutical Spiral: A Comprehensive Introduction to Biblical Interpretation* (2nd ed.; Downers Grove, IL: InterVarsity Press, 2006), 351-52.

[48]Moisés Silva, *Explorations in Exegetical Method: Galatians as a Test Case* (Grand Rapids: Baker, 1996).

[49]Moisés Silva, *Interpreting Galatians: Explorations in Exegetical Method* (Grand Rapids: Baker Academic, 2001), 15-16.

[50]Ibid., 17.

[51]David C. Steinmetz, "The Superiority of Pre-Critical Exegesis," *ThTo* 37 (1980): 27-38.

[52]Robert Stein, "The Interpretation of the Parable of the Good Samaritan," in *Scripture, Tradition, and Interpretation: Essays Presented to Everett F. Harrison by His Students and Colleagues in Honor of His Seventy-Fifth Birthday*, ed. W. Ward Gasque and William Sanford LaSor (Grand Rapids: Eerdmans, 1978), 278-95.

[53]Christopher A. Hall, *Reading Scripture with the Church Fathers* (Downers Grove, IL: InterVarsity Press, 1998).

[54]Ronald E. Heine, *Reading the Old Testament with the Ancient Church: Exploring the Formation of Early Christian Thought* (Grand Rapids: Baker Academic, 2007).

[55]John L. Thompson, *Reading the Bible with the Dead: What You Can Learn from the History of Exegesis That You Can't Learn from Exegesis Alone* (Grand Rapids: Eerdmans, 2007), 11.

[56]Matthew Levering, *Participatory Biblical Exegesis: A Theology of Biblical Interpretation* (Notre Dame, IN: University of Notre Dame Press, 2008); Leithart, *Deep Exegesis*; J. Todd Billings, *The Word of God for the People of God: An Entryway to the Theological Interpretation of Scripture* (Grand Rapids: Eerdmans, 2010).

[57]Robert F. Rea, "A Critical Study of the Gospel of John in Minuscule 1216," M.Div. thesis, Emmanuel School of Religion, 1978.

[58]See F. F. Bruce, *The New Testament Documents: Are They Reliable?* (6th ed.; Downers Grove, IL: InterVarsity Press, 1981), 9-15.

[59]Exceptions might include the ending of Mark 16, the ending of the Lord's Prayer in Matthew 6, the story of the adulterous woman in John 7:53–8:11.

[60]Bruce M. Metzger and Bart D. Ehrman, *The Text of the New Testament: Its Transmission, Corruption, and Restoration* (4th ed.; New York: Oxford University Press, 2005), 319-21, 322-27.

[61]Note this comment by Kurt Aland and Barbara Aland: "New Testament textual criticism must always keep in mind and consider the implications of what has been learned from studies in the history of the canon and from early Church history if its conclusions are to be sound" (*The Text of the New Testament*, trans. Erroll F. Rhodes [2nd ed.; Grand Rapids: Eerdmans, 1989], 67).

[62]Ceslas Spicq says that *kenoō* means "to empty, evacuate" and hence "purge," and that in Philippians 2:7 it could be well translated as "annihilated himself" and is thereby "reduced to nothing" (*TLNT* 2:308-10). A. Oepke defines the adjectival form (*kenos*) as "empty," "without content," and says that Philippians 2:7 teaches that Christ "negated himself, deprived himself of his worth, denied himself" (*TDNT* 3:659-62). E. Tiedke and H.-G. Link offer "to empty, and thus destroy, render void," saying that Philippians 2:7 literally means "he emptied himself," but they quote J. Jeremias (*TDNT* 5:711) that it should be translated "he poured out his life" (*NIDNTT* 1:546-48). Colin Brown concludes, "The emptying of v. 7 is the outpouring of himself in life and also on the cross" (*NIDNTT* 1:548-49).

[63]Mark J. Edwards, ed., *Galatians, Ephesians, Philippians*, gen. ed. Thomas C. Oden (ACCSNT 8; Downers Grove, IL: InterVarsity Press, 2005), 241-45.

[64]To research the issue further, see the following: K.-H. Bartels, *NIDNTT* 2:723-25; J. A. Fitzmyer, *EDNT* 2:440; Dale Moody, "God's Only Son: The Translation of John 3:16 in the Revised Standard Version," *JBL* 74 (1953): 213-19; T. C. de Kruijf, "The Glory of the Only Son (John 1:14)," in *Studies in John: Presented to Professor Dr. J. N. Sevenster on the Occasion of His Seventieth Birthday* (NovTSup 24; Leiden: Brill, 1970), 113-23; Frederick C. Grant, "'Only Begotten'—A Footnote to the R.S.V.," *BT* 17 (1966): 11-14; Gerard Pendrick, "ΜΟΝΟΓΕΝΗΣ," *NTS* 41 (1995): 587-600 argue for "only." F. Büchsel, *TDNT* 4:737-41; Barnabas Lindars, *The Gospel of John* (Grand Rapids: Eerdmans, 1972), 96; John V. Dahms, "The Johannine Use of Monogenēs Reconsidered," *NTS* 29 (1983): 222-32; James M. Bulman, "The Only Begotten Son," *CTJ* 16 (1981): 56-79 contend for "only begotten." D. A. Fennema, "John 1:18: 'God the Only Son,'" *NTS* 31 (1985): 124-35 argues for more than "only" depending on context. Richard N. Longenecker, "The One and Only Son," in *The NIV: The Making of a Contemporary Translation*, ed. Kenneth L. Barker (Grand Rapids: Zondervan, 1986), 119-26, supports "one and only Son."

[65]For example, in John 1:14 the NRSV has "glory as of a father's only son," displacing the historic understanding that this passage reflects the *divine* glory shared by the Father and the Son.

[66]The name has been changed.

[67]Roman Catholic scholars have debated the fuller meaning (*sensus plenior*) of Scripture since the 1940s. Andrea Fernández coined the term in Alberto Vaccari, J. Ruwet and Andrea Fernández, *De S. Scriptura in universum* (Rome: Pontifical Biblical Institute, 1925). For excellent history, see Raymond E. Brown, "The History

and Development of the Theory of a Sensus Plenior," *CBQ* 15 (1953): 141-62; "*The Sensus Plenior* of Sacred Scripture" (S.T.D. diss., St. Mary's University, 1955); "The *Sensus Plenior* in the Last Ten Years," *CBQ* 25 (1963): 262-85.

[68]For examples, see Gordon Fee, "Exegesis and the Role of Tradition in Evangelical Hermeneutics," *ERT* 17 (1993): 421-36.

[69]Silva, *Interpreting Galatians*, 32-33.

[70]For example, one might be tempted to ignore great thinkers such as John Chrysostom or Martin Luther because they have been labeled as anti-Semitic, or to exclude Calvin and Zwingli because they approved the killing of Anabaptists.

[71]James L. Kugel, *How to Read the Bible: A Guide to Scripture, Then and Now* (New York: Free Press, 2007) models the integration of modern conclusions about OT accounts with those of ancient interpreters.

CHAPTER 9: TRADITION AND MINISTRY

[1]Thomas C. Oden says, "One of the practical goals of the ACCS is the renewal of contemporary preaching in the light of the wisdom of ancient Christian preaching" (general introduction in Andrew Louth, ed., *Genesis 1–11* [ACCSOT 1; Downers Grove, IL: InterVarsity Press, 2001], xxxi).

[2]See Athanasius's report of Arius's *Thalia* in Athanasius, *On the Synods of Ariminum and Seleucia* 15 (NPNF[2] 4:457-58; or Stuart Hall's translation in J. Stevenson, ed., *A New Eusebius: Documents Illustrating the History of the Church to AD 337*, rev. W. H. C. Frend [2nd ed.; London: SPCK, 1987], 330-32).

[3]See NPNF[2] 7:284-334. See also Gregory of Nazianzus, *On God and Christ: The Five Theological Orations and Two Letters to Cledonius*, trans. Frederick J. Williams and Lionel R. Wickham (Crestwood, NY: St. Vladimir's Seminary Press, 2002), 25-148.

[4]See NPNF[1] 9:331-489; Franz van de Paverd, *St. John Chrysostom, the Homilies on the Statues: An Introduction* (OCA 239; Rome: Pont. Institutum Studiorum Orientalium, 1991); see also www.documenta-catholica.eu/d_0345-0407-%20 Iohannes%20Chrysostomus%20-%20Homilies%20on%20Statues%20-%20EN.pdf.

[5]Excerpts from versions of the sermon are available at www.fordham.edu/halsall /source/urban2-5vers.html.

[6]See "Recommended Resources for Ministry" at the end of the book.

[7]This is evident in, for example, Wayne Grudem, *Systematic Theology: An Introduction to Biblical Doctrine* (Leicester: Inter-Varsity Press; Grand Rapids: Zondervan, 1994); Jack Cottrell, *The Faith Once for All: Bible Doctrine for Today* (Joplin, MO: College Press, 2002). Note also Gregg Allison, *Historical Theology: An Introduction to Christian Doctrine; A Companion to Wayne Grudem's Systematic Theology* (Grand Rapids: Zondervan, 2011), which seeks to complete Grudem's volume in parallel chapters providing quotations from historic Christians.

[8]Mark W. Karlberg, "Doctrinal Development in Scripture and Tradition: A Reformed Assessment of the Church's Theological Task," *CTJ* 30 (1995): 402.

[9]See Richard J. Foster, *Celebration of Discipline: The Path to Spiritual Growth* (3rd ed.; San Francisco: HarperSanFrancisco, 1998).

[10]See John Cassian, *Institutes*, at NPNF² 11:201-290, or Boniface Ramsey, ed. and trans., *John Cassian: The Institutes* (ACW 58; New York: Newman Press, 2000); John Cassian, *Conferences*, at NPNF² 11:291-546, or Boniface Ramsey, ed. and trans., *John Cassian: The Conferences* (ACW 57; New York: Newman Press, 1997). Benedictines and others note that Benedict of Nursia (*The Rule of St. Benedict* 42.3, 73) made Cassian's *Conferences* regular mealtime reading.

[11]See Paul F. Bradshaw, *The Search for the Origins of Christian Worship: Sources and Methods for the Study of Early Liturgy* (New York: Oxford University Press, 1992), 1-29.

[12]See Alcuin, "The Life of Saint Willibrord," trans. C. H. Talbot, in *Soldiers of Christ: Saints and Saints' Lives from Late Antiquity and the Early Middle Ages*, ed. Thomas F. X. Noble and Thomas Head (University Park, PA: Pennsylvania State University Press, 1995), 189-214; also available at www.fordham.edu/halsall/basis /Alcuin-willbrord.asp; see also Bede, *Ecclesiastical History* 5.10, in Judith McClure and Roger Collins, eds., *Bede: The Ecclesiastical History of the English People* (Oxford: Oxford University Press, 1994).

[13]See Willibald's account in Talbot, *The Anglo-Saxon Missionaries in Germany* (New York: Sheed & Ward, 1954), 45-56; also available at www.fordham.edu/halsall/basis /willibald-boniface.html. See also Ruth A. Tucker, *From Jerusalem to Irian Jaya: A Biographical History of Christian Missions* (2nd ed.; Grand Rapids: Zondervan, 2004), 47-51.

[14]See Elisabeth Elliot, *Shadow of the Almighty: The Life and Testament of Jim Elliott* (San Francisco: HarperCollins, 1989); Elisabeth Elliot, *Through Gates of Splendor* (Wheaton, IL: Tyndale House, 1981); "Go Ye and Preach the Gospel," *Life*, January 30, 1956, 10-19 (available at books.google.com/books?id=gT8EAAAAMB AJ&lpg=PA10&dq=life%20magazine%20jim%20elliot&pg=PA10#v=onepage&q& f=false). See also "Papers of Philip James Elliot—Collection 277," Billy Graham Center, Wheaton College.

[15]For more on Cyril and Methodius, see Anthony-Emil N. Tachiaos, *Cyril and Methodius of Thessalonica: The Acculturation of the Slavs* (Crestwood, NY: St. Vladimir's Seminary Press, 2001); Francis Dvornik, *Byzantine Missions Among the Slavs: SS. Constantine-Cyril and Methodius* (New Brunswick, NJ: Rutgers University Press, 1970); Michael Lacko, *Saints Cyril and Methodius* (2nd ed.; Rome: Slovak Editions "Sts. Cyril and Methodius," 1969); Francis Dvornik, "The Significance of the Missions of Cyril and Methodius," *Slavic Review* 23 (1964): 195-211; Cyril J. Potoček, *Saints Cyril and Methodius, Apostles of the Slavs* (New York: P. J. Kennedy & Sons, 1941).

[16]See, for example, Lamin O. Sanneh, *Disciples of All Nations: Pillars of World Christianity* (OSWC; New York: Oxford University Press, 2008); Philip Jenkins, *The*

Next Christendom: The Coming of Global Christianity (3rd ed.; New York: Oxford University Press, 2011).

[17]See John Cassian, *Conferences* 17; Augustine *On Lying* and *Against Lying*. See also Boniface Ramsey, "Two Traditions on Lying and Deception in the Ancient Church," *The Thomist* 49 (1985): 504-33.

[18]See *Catholic Encyclopedia* (New York: Robert Appleton, 1911), s.v. "Mental Reservation" (available at www.newadvent.org/cathen/10195b.htm).

[19]Note what Thomas Oden says of the Ancient Christian Commentary on Scripture series: "Another intensely practical goal of the ACCS is to renew our readers' awareness of the ancient tradition of pastoral care and ministry to persons. Among the leading Fathers who excel in pastoral wisdom and application of the Bible to the work of ministry are Gregory of Nazianzus, John Chrysostom, Augustine, and Gregory the Great" (general introduction in Louth, *Genesis 1–11*, xxxii).

[20]See Kathryn Spink, *Mother Teresa: A Complete Authorized Biography* (New York: HarperCollins, 1997); Navin Chawla, *Mother Teresa: The Authorized Biography* (Darby, PA: Diane Publishing, 1992); Meg Greene, *Mother Teresa: A Biography* (Westport, CT: Greenwood, 2004); Anne Sebba, *Mother Teresa: Beyond the Image* (2nd ed.; New York: Doubleday, 1997).

[21]See David McCasland, *Eric Liddell: Pure Gold; A New Biography of the Olympic Champion Who Inspired Chariots of Fire* (Grand Rapids: Discovery House, 2001). See also Julian Wilson, *Complete Surrender: A Biography of Eric Liddell, Olympic Gold Medalist and Missionary* (2nd ed.; Milton Keynes: Authentic Media Limited, 2012); Janet and Geoff Benge, *Eric Liddell: Something Greater Than Gold* (Seattle: YWAM Publishing, 1999).

[22]See Henry Chadwick, "New Letters of St. Augustine," *JTS* 34 (1983): 425-52.

[23]See, for example, Basil of Caesarea, *Sermon to the Rich*, trans. Peter Gilbert, bekkos .wordpress.com/st-basils-sermon-to-the-rich; also available with translations of four similar sermons in C. Paul Schroeder, *On Social Justice: St. Basil the Great* (PP 38; Crestwood, NY: St. Vladimir's Seminary Press, 2009).

[24]Bede, *Ecclesiastical History* 2.1, available at www.fordham.edu/halsall/source/bede -greggrea.asp and www.fordham.edu/halsall/basis/bede-book2.asp.

[25]*Catholic Encyclopedia* (New York: Robert Appleton, 1911), s.v. "St. Vincent de Paul," available at www.newadvent.org/cathen/15434c.htm. See also F. A. Forbes, *St. Vincent de Paul* (Rockford, IL: Tan Books, 1998).

[26]In 2011 the Pew Research Center reported forty-one thousand Christian denominations and organizations around the world, though denominations in more than one country were counted once for each country (Pew Forum on Religion and Public Life, *Global Christianity: A Report on the Size and Distribution of the World's Christian Population* [Washington, DC: Pew Research Center, 2011] 95); also available at www.pewforum.org/uploadedFiles/Topics/Religious_Affiliation

/Christian/Christianity-fullreport-web.pdf.

[27]See, for example, D. Newell Williams, Douglas A. Foster and Paul M. Blowers, eds., *The Stone-Campbell Movement: A Global History* (St. Louis: Chalice Press, 2013). See also Henry E. Webb, *In Search of Christian Unity: A History of the Restoration Movement* (2nd ed.; Abilene, TX: Abilene Christian University Press, 2003); Leroy Garrett, *The Stone-Campbell Movement: The Story of the American Restoration Movement* (2nd ed.; Joplin, MO: College Press, 2002).

[28]I have avoided lengthy discussion of models of interaction. The best-known description of models of interaction is H. Richard Niebuhr, *Christ and Culture* (San Francisco: Harper, 1951). Others who question Niebuhr include D. A. Carson, *Christ and Culture Revisited* (Grand Rapids: Eerdmans, 2008); Craig A. Carter, *Rethinking Christ and Culture: A Post-Christendom Perspective* (Grand Rapids: Brazos, 2006).

[29]Robert T. Johnston, "The Role of Women in Church and Home: An Evangelical Test Case in Hermeneutics," in *Scripture, Tradition, and Interpretation: Essays Presented to Everett F. Harrison by His Students and Colleagues in Honor of His Seventy-Fifth Birthday*, ed. W. Ward Gasque and William Sanford LaSor (Grand Rapids: Eerdmans, 1978), 254.

[30]See George Huntston Williams, *The Radical Reformation* (3rd ed.; SCES 15; Kirksville, MO: Sixteenth Century Journal Publishers, 2000), 137-74. See also Tom Scott and Robert W. Scribner, eds. and trans., *The German Peasants' War: A History in Documents* (Atlantic Highlands, NJ: Humanities Press, 1991); Peter Blickle, *The Revolution of 1525: The German Peasants' War from a New Perspective*, trans. Thomas A. Brady Jr. and H. C. Eric Midelfort (Baltimore: Johns Hopkins University Press, 1981).

[31]See Williams, *Radical Reformation*, 553-88; Anthony Arthur, *The Taylor-King: The Rise and Fall of the Anabaptist Kingdom of Münster* (New York: St. Martin's Press, 1999). See also sixteenth-century author Hermann von Kerssenbrock, *Narrative of the Anabaptist Madness: The Overthrow of Münster, the Famous Metropolis of Westphalia*, trans. Christopher S. Mackay (SHCTr 132; Leiden: Brill, 2007).

[32]See Williams, *Radical Reformation*, 387-93, 408-10, 422-25; see also William R. Estep, *The Anabaptist Story: An Introduction to Sixteenth-Century Anabaptism* (3rd ed.; Grand Rapids: Eerdmans, 1975), 151-56. For more on Hofmann, see Klaus Deppermann, *Melchior Hoffman: Social Unrest and Apocalyptic Visions in the Age of Reformation*, ed. Benjamin Drewery (Edinburgh: T & T Clark, 1987).

[33]Of several examples for Ambrose, consider three: (1) in 384 he told Valentinian II that if he returned the Altar of Victory to the senate house, the emperor would find no priest to serve him at church (see Ambrose, *Epistle* 17 [NPNF² 10:411-414]); (2) in 385 and again in 386 he refused to surrender the Milan basilica for the use of Arians, despite Valentinian II's order (Ambrose, *Epistle* 20; *Epistle* 21 [NPNF² 10:422-29]); (3) after Theodosius I slaughtered seven thousand at Thessalonica in

390, Ambrose instructed him to repent or be denied the Eucharist (Ambrose, *Epistle* 51 [NPNF² 10:450-51]).

[34]Stylites (from the Greek word *stylos*, meaning "pillar") were monks who lived on pillars, supported by other monks yet serving as peacemakers, arbitrators and changers of society because of their respected holiness. The practice began in the fifth century and lasted into the fifteenth.

[35]See Elizabeth A. S. Dawes and Norman H. Baynes, trans., *Three Byzantine Saints: Contemporary Biographies of St. Daniel the Stylite, St. Theodore of Sykeon, and St. John the Almsgiver* (2nd ed.; Crestwood, NY: St. Vladimir's Seminary Press, 1977). The section on Daniel the Stylite is available at www.fordham.edu/halsall /basis/dan-stylite.asp.

[36]See James M. Kittelson, *Luther the Reformer: The Story of the Man and His Career* (Minneapolis: Augsburg, 1986); James A. Nestingen, *Martin Luther: A Life* (Minneapolis: Augsburg, 2003); or the classic Roland H. Bainton, *Here I Stand: A Life of Martin Luther* (New York: Abingdon, 1950; repr., Peabody, MA: Hendrickson, 2009).

[37]See Roy Hattersley, *Blood and Fire: William and Catherine Booth and Their Salvation Army* (New York: Doubleday, 2000); Roger J. Green, *Catherine Booth: A Biography of the Cofounder of the Salvation Army* (Grand Rapids: Baker, 1996); Roger J. Green, *The Life and Ministry of William Booth: Founder of the Salvation Army* (Nashville: Abingdon, 2005); Trevor Yaxley, *William and Catherine: The Life and Legacy of the Booths, Founders of the Salvation Army* (Minneapolis: Bethany House, 2003).

[38]See David W. Blight, *Passages to Freedom: The Underground Railroad in History and Memory* (Washington, DC: Smithsonian Books, 2004); Fergus M. Bordewich, *Bound for Canaan: The Underground Railroad and the War for the Soul of America* (New York: Amistad, 2005); Ann Hagedorn, *Beyond the River: The Untold Story of the Heroes of the Underground Railroad* (New York: Simon & Schuster, 2004).

[39]See Corrie ten Boom, John L. Sherrill, and Elizabeth Sherrill, *The Hiding Place: The Triumphant True Story of Corrie ten Boom* (35th anniversary ed.; Grand Rapids: Chosen Books, 2006).

[40]See Eric Metaxas, *Bonhoeffer: Pastor, Martyr, Prophet, Spy* (Nashville: Thomas Nelson, 2010); Eberhard Bethge, *Dietrich Bonhoeffer: A Biography*, rev. and ed. Victoria J. Barnett, trans. Eric Mosbacher et al. (rev. ed.; Minneapolis: Fortress, 2000); Ferdinand Schlingensiepen, *Dietrich Bonhoeffer 1906-1945: Martyr, Thinker, Man of Resistance*, trans. Isabel Best (London: T & T Clark, 2010).

[41]See George Weigel, *Witness to Hope: The Biography of Pope John Paul II* (2nd ed.; New York: HarperCollins, 2005). See also Garry O'Connor, *Universal Father: A Life of Pope John Paul II* (London: Bloomsbury, 2005); Edward Stourton, *John Paul II: Man of History* (London: Hodder & Stoughton, 2006); Tadeusz Szulc, *Pope John Paul II: The Biography* (New York: Scribner, 1995); Jonathan Kwitny, *Man of the Century: The Life and Times of Pope John Paul II* (New York: Henry Holt, 1997).

[42]See Eric Metaxas, *Amazing Grace: William Wilberforce and the Heroic Campaign to End Slavery* (New York: HarperCollins, 2007); Kevin Belmonte, *Hero for Humanity: A Biography of William Wilberforce* (Colorado Springs, CO: NavPress, 2002); John Pollock, *Wilberforce* (New York: St. Martin's Press, 1977); David J. Vaughan, *Statesman and Saint: The Principled Politics of William Wilberforce* (Nashville: Cumberland House, 2002); Robin Furneaux, *William Wilberforce* (London: Hamish Hamilton, 1974).

[43]See Bernard B. Galway, "Cardinal Gibbons and the Labor Movement in the United States" (M.A. thesis, Fordham University, 1939). For an extensive biography, see John T. Ellis, *The Life of James Cardinal Gibbons: Archbishop of Baltimore, 1834-1921* (2 vols.; Milwaukee: Bruce, 1952; repr., Westminster, MD: Christian Classics, 1987).

[44]See Walter Rauschenbusch, *Christianity and the Social Crisis* (1907) and *Theology for the Social Gospel* (1917); Christopher Hodge Evans, *The Kingdom Is Always But Coming: A Life of Walter Rauschenbusch* (Grand Rapids: Eerdmans, 2004; Waco, TX: Baylor University Press, 2010); Paul M. Minus, *Walter Rauschenbusch: American Reformer* (New York: Macmillan, 1988); Dores Robinson Sharpe, *Walter Rauschenbusch* (New York: Macmillan, 1942).

[45]See Gustavo Gutiérrez, *A Theology of Liberation: History, Politics and Salvation*, trans. and ed. Caridad Inda and John Eagleson (rev. ed.; Maryknoll, NY: Orbis, 1988); in Spanish, *Teología de la liberación: Perspectivas* (Lima: CEP, 1971).

[46]See Martin Luther King Jr., *The Autobiography of Martin Luther King, Jr.*, ed. Clayborne Carson (New York: Time Warner, 1998); John A. Kirk, *Martin Luther King Jr.* (Harlow: Pearson Longman, 2005); Thomas F. Jackson, *From Civil Rights to Human Rights: Martin Luther King, Jr., and the Struggle for Economic Justice* (Philadelphia: University of Pennsylvania Press, 2007); David J. Garrow, ed., *Martin Luther King, Jr.: Civil Rights Leader, Theologian, Orator* (3 vols.; Brooklyn, NY: Carlson, 1989); Coretta Scott King, *My Life with Martin Luther King, Jr.* (rev. ed.; New York: Puffin Books, 1993).

SOURCES FOR PULL QUOTES

Walter M. Abbott, ed., *The Documents of Vatican II*, translation ed. Joseph Gallagher (New York: Guild Press, 1966), 114-18.

G. R. Evans, ed., preface to *A History of Pastoral Care* (New York: Cassell, 2000), ix.

Georges Florovsky, *Bible, Church, Tradition: An Eastern Orthodox View* (Belmont, MA: Nordland, 1972), 80.

Stanley J. Grenz and John R. Franke, "Theological Heritage as Hermeneutical Trajectory: Toward a Nonfoundationalist Understanding of the Role of Tradition in Theology," in *Ancient and Postmodern Christianity: Paleo-Orthodoxy in the 21st Century; Essays in Honor of Thomas C. Oden*, ed. Kenneth Tanner and

Christopher A. Hall (Downers Grove, IL: InterVarsity Press, 2002), 221.

Stanley Grenz and Roger E. Olson, *Twentieth-Century Theology: God and the World in a Transitional Age* (Downers Grove, IL: InterVarsity Press, 1992), 9.

Stanley Hauerwas and Samuel Wells, *The Blackwell Companion to Christian Ethics* (2nd ed.; Malden, MA: Wiley-Blackwell, 2011), 34.

Robert T. Johnston, "The Role of Women in Church and Home: An Evangelical Test Case in Hermeneutics," in *Scripture, Tradition, and Interpretation: Essays Presented to Everett F. Harrison by His Students and Colleagues in Honor of His Seventy-Fifth Birthday*, ed. W. Ward Gasque and William Sanford LaSor (Grand Rapids: Eerdmans, 1978), 10.

Peter Kreeft, *Fundamentals of the Faith: Essays in Christian Apologetics* (San Francisco: Ignatius Press, 1988), 273.

Alister E. McGrath, "Borrowed Spiritualities," *ChrTo* 37 (1993): 20.

Michael Pasquarello III, *Christian Preaching: A Trinitarian Theology of Proclamation* (Grand Rapids: Baker Academic, 2006), 79.

J. A. T. Robinson, "Not Radical Enough?" *ChrCent* 86 (1969): 1446.

Albert Schweitzer, *The Quest of the Historical Jesus*, trans. W. Montgomery (London: Adam & Charles Black, 1910), p. 399.

Moisés Silva, *Has the Church Misread the Bible? The History of Interpretation in the Light of Current Issues* (Grand Rapids: Academie, 1987), 95.

Moisés Silva, *Interpreting Galatians: Explorations in Exegetical Method* (Grand Rapids: Baker Academic, 2001), 17.

Thomas Aquinas, *Summa theologiae*, article 8. Quoted from A. C. Pegis, ed. and trans., *Basic Writings of Saint Thomas Aquinas* (New York: Random House, 1945), 15.

Alan R. Tippett, *Introduction to Missiology* (Pasadena, CA: William Carey Library, 1987), 251.

Vincent of Lérins, *Commonitory* 1.2.5 (NPNF² 11:132).

Robert E. Webber, *Ancient-Future Evangelism: Making Your Church a Faith-Forming Community* (Grand Rapids: Baker, 2003), 204.

Robert E. Webber, *Ancient-Future Worship: Proclaiming and Enacting God's Narrative* (Grand Rapids: Baker, 2008), 20.

D. H. Williams, *Retrieving the Tradition and Renewing Evangelicalism: A Primer for Suspicious Protestants* (Grand Rapids: Eerdmans, 1999), 17-18.

Name and Subject Index

Abelard, Peter, 139

abortion, 182, 187

absolute truth, 26, 46, 75, 86, 109, 111

  See also objectivity

accountability. *See* tradition: and accountability

Act of Supremacy (1534), 67

Act of Supremacy (1559), 67

Africa Bible Commentary, 150, 163

Against All Heresies, 135

Against the Arians, 169

Albigensian crusade, 104

Alcuin, 139

Alexandria, 37-38, 152, 202n10

  See also Alexandrian school

Alexandrian school, 135-36, 159

allegory. *See under* Scripture: and spiritual meanings

Ambrose, 43, 91, 167, 188, 221n33

Amish, 103

Ammonius, 152

Anabaptist(s), 49-50, 72, 104, 108, 114, 142-43, 170, 176

anagogy. *See under* Scripture: and spiritual meanings

Ancient Christian Commentary on Scripture, 56, 85-86, 149, 163, 220n19

Ancient Christian Doctrine series, 120-21

Ancient-Future series, 56, 120

Ancyra, 38

Andreae, Johannes, 46

Anglicans, Anglican Church. *See* Church of England

Anglo-Catholic Movement, 92-93

anointing (ceremonial), 63

Antioch, 37-38

  See also Antiochene school

Antiochene school, 136-37, 159

apologists, 104

apophatic theology, 124-25

apostles, apostolic, 16, 28-31, 36-37, 39-47, 51, 60-70, 73, 91, 135, 137, 151, 158, 164, 171, 191

  and apostolic succession, 60-70, 171, 191

Apostles' Creed, 48

apostolic succession. *See under* apostles

Aquinas. *See* Thomas Aquinas

Arcadius, Roman emperor, 169, 188

archbishop(s), 37, 39, 42, 91, 189

Arian(s), Arius, Arianism, 102, 116, 155, 168-69, 188

Aristotle, 111, 165

Arminianism. *See* grace, theologies of

Armstrong, Chris, 56

ascetic(s), asceticism, 92, 101, 108, 124, 140, 143, 173

  See also spirituality: desert fathers; spirituality: mysticism

Asia Bible Commentary series, 150, 163

Athanasian Creed, 48

Athanasius, 48, 155

atonement. *See under* Jesus Christ; soteriology/salvation

Augustine, 43, 48, 58, 91, 116, 125-26, 137, 148, 167, 180, 182-83

Augustinianism. *See* grace, theologies of

authenticity. *See under* tradition

authority of Scripture. *See* Scripture

autonomous free-willism. *See* grace, theologies of

baptism, 39, 63, 106

Baptist(s), 92

Barth, Karl, 106

Basel-Ferrara-Florence, Council of (1431–1439), 63

Basil of Caesarea, 180, 183

Basiliscus, Roman emperor, 188

Bede, 43, 139

Benedict XVI, pope, 65

Benedict of Nursia, 91

Bernard of Clairvaux, 139

Bible Belt, 169

"Bible-focused"

  and accountability, 110

  Bible-focused Protestants, 70-74, 191-92

  definition of, 17

  and desire for/interest in community, 98, 101, 150

  and desire for deeper, historical meaning, 57

  and exegetical method, 147

  and historical method, 27, 29, 33-34, 101, 103, 114

  and ministry, 166-89

  and need for/dependence on

tradition, 77, 86, 88, 95, 122

  and neglect/distrust of tradition, 17-19, 58, 72-74, 93, 95

  and recent interest in tradition, 55-58, 120-21

Billings, J. Todd, 149

bishop(s), 36-39, 41-42, 45, 51, 60, 62-63, 66, 69, 91, 116, 169, 189

Blomberg, Craig, 147

Bonaventure, 139-40

Bonhoeffer, Dietrich, 103, 188-89

Boniface, missionary, 179

Book of Common Prayer, 68

Book of Concord, 48

Book of Discipline, 54

Booth, Catherine and William, 188

Bouyer, Louis, 65

Brown, Harold, 31

Bruce, F. F., 36, 49, 69

Cajetan, Thomas, cardinal, 143

calendar, Christian, 16, 121, 178

Callinicos, Constantine, 61

Calvin, John, 17, 48-49, 70, 91, 104, 126-27, 142-43

  and *Institutes of the Christian Religion*, 49, 142

  and *Reply to Cardinal Sadoleto*, 49

Calvinism. *See* Calvin, John; grace, theologies of

canon law(yer), 46-47, 63

Canons of the Church of England, 68

Cappadocians, 95, 125, 155

  Basil of Caesarea, 180, 183

  Gregory of Nazianzus, 148, 169

  Gregory of Nyssa, 180

Carson, D. A., 158

Cassian, John, 25, 91-92, 101-2, 127, 136, 138, 173, 182

  See also grace, theologies of

Catechism of the Catholic Church, 67

catena(e), 139

Catholics, Catholicism. *See* Roman Catholic Church

celibacy, 73, 123

certainty. *See under* tradition

Chalcedon, Council of (451), 38, 94, 172

Chalcedonian Definition, 172

charismatic, 60, 72, 77
child abuse, 181
Christ. *See* Jesus Christ
Christian history, definitions of.
   See under tradition: definitions
Christology. *See under* Jesus
   Christ
Chrysostom, John. *See* John
   Chrysostom
church history, definitions of.
   See under tradition: definitions
Church of England (Anglicans),
   60, 67-69, 71, 77, 93
   and Scripture, tradition and
   reason, 68-69
Church's Bible series, 150, 163
Cistercian spirituality. *See*
   spirituality
civil rights, US, 189
Civil War, American, 181
Clare of Assisi, 188
Clement II, pope, 169
Clement of Alexandria, 152, 180
clergy, 67-68, 71, 169, 183
   See also archbishop(s);
   bishop(s); metropolitan;
   patriarch(s); Roman
   Catholic Church: and
   magisterium
Clermont, Council of (1095), 169
cloning, 181, 187
Cochläus, Johann, 50
Commentary on Job, 138
Communion. *See* Eucharist
communism, 104, 189
community. *See* tradition: and
   community
compassion, 166, 183-84, 192
Complutensian Polyglot, 140
conciliar movement, 45-46
Congar, Yves, 65
consensus fidelium, consensus, 29,
   56, 83, 85, 96, 101, 103, 115-18,
   128-29, 163, 178, 180, 192
Constantine I, Roman emperor,
   25, 38, 42, 94, 116
Constantinople, 37-38, 42, 62,
   125, 169
Constantinople, Council of (381),
   37-38, 125
cross. *See* Jesus Christ: and cross,
   crucifixion, death
Crusades, 104, 114, 169, 182
cultural engagement, 186-89, 192
"cultures, continents and centuries"
   as a concept, 15-16, 20, 35,
   56-57, 77, 81-84, 86-93,

95-97, 100-101, 115, 117-19,
   121, 149-50, 169, 172-73,
   177-84, 186-87, 189-92
   as an expression, 81-82, 90-92,
   96, 119, 129, 150, 161,
   163-64, 172, 177-78, 187, 192
Curtis, Ken, 55
cyber implants, intelligence,
   181-82
Cyprian, 104
Cyril, missionary, 179
Cyril of Alexandria, patriarch, 91
Daniel the Stylite, 188
Decius, Roman emperor, 104
deconstruction, reconstruction, 27
*Decree Concerning the Canonical
   Scriptures*, 65
Dei Verbum, 64-67
deism, deist(s), 145
Denzinger, Henry, 65
desert fathers. *See under*
   spirituality: forms of
determinism. *See* grace,
   theologies of
Didymus the Blind, 152
Diet of Worms, 170, 188
Diocletian, Roman emperor, 104
*Dogmatic Constitution on Divine
   Revelation*. *See Dei Verbum*
Dominic (Domingo de Guzman,
   founder of Dominicans), 91,
   188
Dominicans, 114
Donation of Constantine, 42
Donatism, 202n4
Dred Scott, US Supreme Court
   decision, 187-88
Dulles, Avery, 65-66
Duvall, J. Scott, 147
Eastern Orthodoxy, 17, 19, 25, 55,
   59, 73, 77, 108, 122
   and apophatic theology, 124-
   25
   and canon law, 63
   and ecumenical councils,
   62-63
   and Great Schism, 42, 62-63
   and icons, 61, 63
   and liturgies, 63, 206n13
   and papacy, 42
   and Scripture, 60-64, 144
   and spirituality, 176
   and synergism, 25, 127-28
   and systematic theology, 171
   and view(s) of tradition,
   28-29, 60-64
Eck, Johann von, 50
ecumenism, 184-86, 192

Ehrman, Bart, 151-52
ekklēsia, 153-54
Elizabeth I, queen of England,
   67-68
Elliot, Jim and Elisabeth,
   missionaries, 179
Enlightenment, 51-53, 109, 124,
   144-46, 149, 158, 160, 163
Ephesus, Council of (431), 38
Episcopalians, 67
   See also Church of England
Erasmus, Desiderius, 48, 140-41
Eriugena, John Scotus, 42-43,
   139
eschatology, 10, 125, 137-38, 140,
   157, 160-61, 166, 177-79, 184, 193
   See also Scripture: and
   spiritual meanings, anagogy
eternal life. *See* eschatology
ethics, 18-19, 34, 144, 180-82, 192
ethnicism, 182
ethnicity, 100
Eucharist, 16, 31, 39, 97, 177-79
Eudoxia, empress, 169, 188
Eusebius of Caesarea, 116, 152
Euthymius Zigabenus, 152
Evagrius, 91
evangelical(s), evangelicalism,
   17-18, 55-56, 72, 77, 88, 100, 120
evangelism, evangelist(s), 114,
   179-80
Evans, G. R., 183
evolution, theory of, 52, 147
exegesis of Scripture. *See* Scripture
faith alone, justification by. *See*
   soteriology/salvation
Faith and Order Commission
   (National Council of Churches
   USA), 29, 54-55
   Third World Conference on
   Faith and Order, 54
   Fourth World Conference on
   Faith and Order, 29, 54-55
Fee, Gordon, 146-47
feminism. *See* women, roles
Five Theological Orations, 169
Florovsky, Georges, 60
Foster, Richard, 55-56, 173-74
Francis of Assisi, 91, 114, 116, 176,
   188
Franciscan spirituality. *See*
   spirituality
Franciscan(s), 114, 176
Franck, Sebastian, 142
Franke, John, 51-52
Fugitive Slave Law, US, 187-88
fundamentalist, 17, 77
Funk, Robert, 158

Geisler, Norman, 72
gender, 25, 100
genetic engineering, 181
Geneva, Switzerland, 143
genocide, 182
George of Athos, 152
Gerald of Bologna, 44
Germanus, monk, 101-2
Gerson, Jean, 46
Gibbons, James, cardinal, 189
Gillquist, Peter, 55
glossing, 139, 141, 149
Gnosticism, Gnostic(s), 91, 102, 135
Godfrey of Fontanis, 44
Gospels, 16, 36, 43, 151-52
gospel(s)
    false gospel, 31
    good news told, 30-32, 55, 62, 81, 144, 168, 170, 179-80, 187
    social gospel, 189
grace, theologies of, 126-28
Graham, Billy, 114
"great apostasy," 93-94
Great Commission, 179, 184-85
    See also mission/missions
Great Papal Schism. *See under* papacy
Great Schism (1054, between East and West), 42, 62-63
Grebel, Conrad, 49, 142
Gregory I, the Great, 43, 48, 81, 138, 180, 183
Gregory of Nazianzus, 148, 169
Gregory of Nyssa, 180
Grenz, Stanley, 51-52
Grudem, Wayne, 120
Guido Terreni of Perpignan (Guy de Perpignan), 45
Gutiérrez, Gustavo, 189
Hall, Christopher, 149
Hauerwas, Stanley, 101, 180
Hays, J. Daniel, 147
heaven. *See* eschatology
Heine, Ronald, 149
Henry VIII, king of England, 67
Henry of Ghent, 44
heresy, 45, 107, 115, 117, 168
    See also Arian(s); Gnosticism; modalism; monophysitism
Hick, John, 75
historical theology, definitions of. *See* tradition: definitions
historical-critical exegesis. *See under* Scripture
history, definitions of, 23-24
    See also tradition: definitions

Hoffman, Melchior, 187-88
Holmes, Stephen, 72
Holy Spirit
    and church authority, 44
    and inspiration of Scripture, 36-37, 60, 137, 142-43, 157
    and omnipresence, 125
    as a person of the Trinity, 26, 50, 102-3, 106-7, 112, 125, 155, 164-65, 172, 177-78, 184
    and revealing through tradition/church, 28, 36, 41, 47, 60-66
    and work in Christians (not revelation), 33, 74, 76-77, 87, 90, 110, 142, 191
    See also Trinity
Homilies on the Statues, 169
homosexuality, 182, 187
hope, eternal. *See* eschatology
Hosius of Cordova, 116
Hubbard, Robert, Jr., 147
Hübmaier, Balthasar, 49
Hugh of St. Victor, 43, 139
human trafficking, 183
Huss, John, 46-47, 141
icons, 61, 63
identity. *See under* tradition
Ignatian spirituality. *See* spirituality
Ignatius of Antioch, 37, 104
Ignatius of Loyola, 143, 188
individualism, 98-99, 101, 108, 121
indulgences, 70, 73, 93, 112-13, 188
inspiration of Scripture. *See under* Scripture
Inquisition, 104, 182
Institutes of the Christian Religion, 49, 142
Irenaeus of Lyons, 36-37, 91, 135, 137, 208n3
Isidore of Seville, 42-43, 139
Isidorean Decretals. *See* Pseudo-Isidorean Decretals
Israel, 16, 30, 35, 54
Jehovah's Witnesses, 102
Jerome, 43, 48, 152
Jesus Christ, 30-33, 36, 38, 41, 46, 54-55, 58-62, 64-65, 71-72, 81, 83, 86, 89, 99-100, 106-8, 115-17, 128-29, 134-38, 160, 166, 179, 183-85, 191-93
    and atonement, 52, 90, 122, 125, 157, 165
    and Christology, 28, 33, 50, 52, 59, 71, 74, 77, 92, 95, 102, 112-13, 123, 125, 138,

154-56, 165, 171-72, 188
    and cross, crucifixion, death, 16, 31, 63, 123-24
    and incarnation, 16, 30, 102, 112, 123, 125, 154, 165, 172, 175, 188
    and messianic prophecy, 157
    and second coming, 112, 188, 193
    and virgin birth, 30, 125, 157
    See also Eucharist; Trinity
Jew(s), Jewish, 114, 135, 137, 158, 176, 188-89
Joachim of Fiore, 139
John the Baptist, 157
John Chrysostom, 48, 91, 116, 162, 167, 169, 188, 206n13
John Paul II, pope, 104, 189
Johnston, Robert T., 186
Jones, Jim, 115
justification. *See under* soteriology/salvation
Justin Martyr, 152
kenoō, 154
Khomyakov, Aleksei, 63
kidnapping, 181, 183
King, Martin Luther, Jr., 189
Klein, William, 147
Koresh, David, 115
Köstenberger, Andreas, 147
Kreeft, Peter, 70-72, 74
Large Catechism, 48
lectionary, 178
Lefèvre, Jean, 141
Leithart, Peter, 149
Levering, Matthew, 149
Lewis, C. S., 148
liberalism, theological, 52-53, 55-56, 70, 74-76
liberation theology, 189
Liddell, Eric, 183
liturgy. *See* worship
Locke, John, 111
Lord's Supper. *See* Eucharist
Lossky, Vladimir, 60-62
Lovelace, Richard, 56
Lubac, Henri de, 144, 149
Luther, Martin, 13, 17, 19, 32, 48, 50, 70, 91, 104, 141, 143, 167, 170, 188
    and justification by faith alone, 48 (*see also* soteriology/salvation: justification)
    See also Scripture: and *sola scriptura*
Lutheran(s). *See* Luther, Martin
lying, 181-82

MacKenzie, Ralph, 72
magisterium. *See* Roman Catholic
    Church: and magisterium
Maldonado, Juan, 143
Manz, Felix, 142
Marshall, I. Howard, 147
Marsilius of Padus, 44-45
martyr(s), martyrdom. *See*
    persecution, martyrdom
Mary, mother of Jesus, 30, 51, 73,
    157, 168
Mary, queen of England, 67
McGrath, Alister, 173
McKnight, Scot, 174
Melanchthon, Philip, 48
Menno Simons, 49
Mennonites, 103
mental reservation, mental
    equivocation, 182
mentoring, mentor(s), 9, 15, 92,
    101-2, 106, 108, 120-29, 166-71,
    173-75, 177, 183, 185, 189-90,
    192-93
    See also tradition: and
    broadened horizons;
    tradition: and filling
    theological gaps in
    understanding
messianic prophecy. *See under*
    Jesus Christ
Metaphysics, 111
Methodius, missionary, 179
metropolitan, 37, 39
Metzger, Bruce, 151-52
Meyendorff, John, 61-64
Mickelsen, A. Berkeley, 147
mind control, 181
mission/missions, missionary,
    16-18, 33, 53, 114, 179-80,
    184-85, 192
modalism, 102, 106-7, 116
modernism, modernity. *See*
    Enlightenment
monk(s), monasticism. *See*
    ascetic(s), asceticism
monogenēs, 154-56
monophysitism, 188
Moody, Dwight L., 114
moral interpretation. *See* Scripture:
    and spiritual meanings
Moran, Gabriel, 40
Mother Teresa. *See* Teresa of
    Calcutta, Mother
Münster, 142, 187
Müntzer, Thomas, 142, 187
mysticism. *See under* spirituality
Nazism, 104, 187-89
Nesteros, abba, 136-37

neurotheology, 182
New Age, 102
Newman, John Henry, 65, 92-93
Nicaea, Council of (325), 38, 48,
    116, 125, 202n4
Nicene Creed, 48
Nicholas of Lyra, 139-40
Niebuhr, H. Richard, 103
Niebuhr, Reinhold, 103
Ninety-Five Theses, 188
nondeterminism. *See* grace,
    theologies of
Novatianism, 202n4
oak of Thor (Donar), 179
Oak, Synod of the (403), 169
objectivity, 24-28, 51, 53, 62, 74,
    86, 109, 124, 147, 158, 164
    and "objective enough,"
    26-27, 109, 164
Ockham. *See* William of Ockham
Oden, Thomas, 55-56, 85-86,
    120-21
On First Principles, 136
On the Truth of Sacred Scripture, 46
"only begotten (Son)." *See*
    monogenēs
open theism, 113-14
Origen, 43, 136, 148, 152, 167
Orthodox, Orthodox Church(es).
    See Eastern Orthodoxy
Osborne, Grant, 113, 148
Ott, Ludwig, 65
Outler, Albert C., 54
Oxford Movement. *See*
    Anglo-Catholic Movement
pacificism (and fighting in war),
    103, 181-82
papacy
    and antichrist, 51
    and authority, 41-42, 44-50,
    64, 70, 73, 76, 93, 141-42
    and Great Papal Schism, 45
    and Great Schism (East and
    West), 42
    and infallibility, 73
    and primacy, 42, 46
    and supremacy, 42, 46-50, 73,
    93
    *See also names of particular
    popes*
paradox, 83-84, 87, 125, 129
    See also apophatic theology
Paschal Controversy, 202n10
Pasquarello, Michael, III, 97
patriarch(s), 37-39, 42, 169
Patterson, Richard, 147
Peasants' War, peasant revolt, 142,
    187

Pelagianism. *See* grace, theologies
    of
persecution, martyrdom, 41, 51,
    68, 103-4, 114, 116, 169-70, 176,
    179, 182
Peter Aureolis, 44
Peter Lombard, 140
Pinnock, Clark, 111
Pius XII, pope, 104
Polycarp, 104, 170
pope. *See* papacy
postmodern(ism), 56, 109-11,
    124-25
    See also apophatic theology
prayer
    continual, 176
    corporate, 99, 151, 177-78
    historic, 16, 39, 58
    by Jesus, 106, 184-85
    monastic, 140
    personal, 86, 97, 102, 107,
    172-73, 175, 179-80
    to saints, 73
    *See also Book of Common
    Prayer*; spirituality
preaching, preacher(s)
    and gospel, 31, 33, 60, 157
    and historic preachers, 15,
    66, 114, 139, 167-70, 180,
    183, 188-89
    and identity, 87
    and ministry, 16, 18-19, 34,
    99, 166-70, 178, 192
    and spiritual meanings of
    Scripture, 162, 164, 167-68
    and theology/doctrine, 57,
    142
    See also teaching, teacher(s)
Prierias, Sylvester, 50
Procopius of Gaza, 139
promise breaking, 182
Protestant(s), Protestantism, 9,
    28, 30, 63, 67, 77, 93-94, 108,
    122-23, 141, 144, 171
    Bible-focused Protestants,
    70-74, 171, 191-92
    and *consensus fidelium*, 56
    definitions of, 71
    and definitions of tradition,
    17-18, 28
    liberal Protestants, 52, 70,
    74-76
    and neglect/distrust of
    tradition, 17-19, 31, 51, 73
    and recent interest in
    tradition, 120
    and *sola scriptura*, 50, 54-55,
    64, 143

Pseudo-Isidorean Decretals, 42
purgatory, 73, 113
racism, 181-82
Radical Reformers, 49-50, 142, 187
   See also Anabaptists
rationalism. *See* Enlightenment
Ratzinger, Joseph. *See* Benedict XVI, pope
Rauschenbush, Walter, 189
recapitulation, 135, 137
redemption. *See under* soteriology/ salvation
Reformation Commentary on Scripture, 150, 163
Reformation, Reformers
   and church fathers, 48-49, 91, 143
   and persecution, 104, 114
   and Roman Catholic response, 17, 50-51, 64, 142-43 (*see also* Trent, Council of)
   and Scripture/*sola scriptura*, 17, 47, 51, 64, 69-72, 91, 93, 140-44, 150, 158-60, 163
   and sixteenth-century objections/teachings, 17, 30, 47, 49, 51, 58, 70-73, 76, 93, 108, 112, 143, 160-61, 191
   and spirituality, 172-73
   and understanding of tradition, 47-51
   See also names of individual Reformers
Reformed theology. *See* grace, theologies of
relativism, relativity, 71, 101, 109
Renaissance, 140-41
Reno, R. R., 134
Renovaré, 56
Ressourcement series, 120
Reuchlin, Johannes, 140
Rimini, 38
Robinson, J. A. T., 67, 69
Roman Catholic Church, Roman Catholic(s)
   and apostolic succession, 60, 64-67
   and Church of England, 67-68
   and Great Schism, 42, 62-63
   and magisterium, 45, 47, 49, 67, 70, 72, 76
   and papacy, 42, 46
   and persecution, 104
   and response to Reformers, 17, 50-51, 64, 142-43 (*see also* Trent, Council of)
   and Scripture and tradition as

canon/revelation, 18-19, 40, 43, 48, 50-55, 64-67, 72-73, 141-42, 144
   and spirituality, 108, 176
   and systematic theology, 171
   and Tradition (capital T), 28-29
   See also individual Roman Catholics
Rome, 37-38, 41-42, 71
   See also papacy; Roman Catholic Church
rule of truth, rule of faith, 36-37, 40, 91, 135, 137-38, 144, 159, 161, 167-68, 208n3
Rupert of Deutz, 43
Sabellianism. *See* modalism
sacraments, sacramentology, 51, 64, 67, 71, 73, 142, 177, 202n4
   See also baptism; Eucharist
saint(s), 68, 73, 140
Salmerón, Alfonso, 143
salvation. *See* soteriology/ salvation
Salvation Army, 188
sanctification. *See under* soteriology/salvation
scholasticism, scholastics, 43, 139-40
schoolmen. *See* scholasticism
Schweitzer, Albert, 74
Scott, Dred, 187-88
Scripture
   and canon, 33, 36, 39, 41, 43-47, 51, 59, 61-62, 65, 72-74, 77, 95, 112
   and faith and interpretation, 144-46, 149, 159-60
   and historical-critical (theological-grammatical, historical-grammatical) exegesis, 133, 144-49, 156-59, 161-64, 172
      form criticism, 145, 157
      literary criticism, 145, 157
      motif criticism, 145, 157
      poststructuralism, 145, 157
      redaction criticism, 145, 157
      rhetorical criticism, 145
      source criticism, 145, 157
      structuralism, 145, 157
      textual criticism (*see below*)
   and history of interpretation, 134-50

and inspiration, 48, 51-52, 56-57, 66, 70, 72, 76, 112, 137, 142-43, 145-47, 157-58, 161, 164, 171
   and literal interpretation, 135-47, 152, 155, 157-58, 161-62, 167-69
   and myth, 52
   and participatory exegesis/ theological interpretation, 149
   and Rea's recommended exegesis, 160-64
   and *sensus plenior* (fuller meaning), 217n67
   and *sola scriptura*, 39-41, 46-50, 54, 64, 71-72, 93, 143-44
   and spiritual meanings, 135-40, 142, 148, 157-59, 162, 167-69
      allegory, 136-44, 146-48, 157-58, 160, 162, 167-69
      anagogy, 136-44, 147-48, 160, 162, 167-69
      tropology/moral interpretation, 136-44, 147-48, 157-58, 160, 162, 167-69
      typology, 135-44, 147-48, 157-58, 160, 162, 167-69
   and textual criticism, 19, 140-41, 150-52
   and tradition, 35-58, 113, 133-64, 191
   and translation, 150-56
Scripture, Tradition and Traditions, 54
Second Great Awakening, 114
Seleucia and Rimini, council of (359), 38
semi-Arians, 116
semi-Augustinianism. *See* grace, theologies of
semi-Pelagianism. *See* grace, theologies of
Sentences, 140
Separatism, 72
Serenus, abba, 136
sign of the cross, 63
Silva, Moisés, 47, 49, 147-49, 162
Simons, Menno. *See* Menno Simons
Sisters of Charity, 183
skepticism. *See* Enlightenment
slavery, 30, 181-83, 188-89

Small Catechism, 48
social gospel movement, 189
sola scriptura. *See under*
  Scripture
soteriology/salvation, 25, 61, 64,
  72-73, 86, 171-72
    atonement, 52, 122, 171-72
    incarnation, 123
    justification, 48-49, 123
    plan/path of salvation, 32-33,
      54, 68-70, 135, 138, 160,
      165, 172
    redemption, 16, 90, 99, 112,
      123, 125, 161, 166, 179, 191,
      193
    sanctification, 25, 97 (*see*
      also spirituality)
spiritual disciplines. *See*
  spirituality
spiritual formation. *See*
  spirituality
spirituality, 173-76, 185, 192
  forms of
    desert fathers, 91, 101-2,
      136, 138, 173, 176 (*see*
      also Cassian, John;
      Evagrius)
    Eastern Orthodox, 61, 176
    Protestant, 71, 74
    Roman Catholic, 176
    transcendentalist, 53
  mysticism, 143, 176
  need/desire/opportunities
    for, 16-17, 34, 53, 77, 87, 91,
    96, 114, 121-22, 137-40,
    149, 159, 162, 166, 173-76,
    185, 192
  recent interest in, 55-57, 120,
    149, 173-74
  spiritual masters, 15, 57, 91,
    104, 173-75 (*see also*
    individual spiritual
    masters)
  See also Scripture: and faith
    and interpretation
Stein, Robert, 149
Steinmetz, David, 149
Sterrett, T. Norton, 146
Stuart, Douglas, 146
Summa theologiae, 111
Sunday, Billy, 114
Sylvester I, pope, 42
synergism. *See* grace, theologies of
systematic theology, 18-19, 86,
  124, 148, 151, 170-73, 192
tabula rasa, 111
Tatian, 151-52
Tavard, George, 31, 40, 46, 50

teaching, teacher(s)
  and accountability, 112-14,
    117, 187
  and community, 100-102
  and doctrine/theology,
    14-15, 19-20, 23-24, 27-29,
    36-39, 43-45, 47, 63-64,
    66-74, 91, 93, 96, 102, 107,
    110, 112, 121, 125, 141, 153,
    161, 170-72
  and heresy/false teaching, 33,
    36, 44-45, 94, 103, 112
  and historic teachers, 15, 16
    (Jesus), 42, 46, 48-52, 57,
    60, 63-64, 76, 104, 117, 119,
    121-22, 136, 139-45,
    174-75, 177, 190
  and identity, 87-88
  and ministry, 16, 19, 34, 104,
    165-70, 180, 192
  and Scripture (*see* Scripture)
  and Tradition (capital T), 28,
    72-73
  See also mentoring; preaching
Ten Boom, Caspar, 188
Teresa of Ávila, 143
Teresa of Calcutta, Mother,
  114-15, 183
Tertullian, 91
textual criticism. *See under*
  Scripture
Textus Receptus, 140
Thirty-Nine Articles of Religion,
  68-69
Thomas Aquinas, 41, 44, 111,
  139-40, 148, 165, 188
Thompson, John L., 149
Tippet, Alan, 179
Totting, Heinrich, of Oyta, 45
tradition
  and accountability, 9, 15, 17,
    19, 23, 34, 50, 83-84, 92,
    99-119, 121, 129, 133, 142,
    150, 159-61, 164, 168-69,
    171-72, 180, 182, 184-86,
    189, 192
  and authenticity, 32, 58,
    83-84, 99, 104, 118-19,
    121-22, 128-29, 192
  and broadened horizons, 13,
    19, 83, 120-29, 164, 177,
    184, 192
  and certainty/confidence,
    36-37, 51, 66, 74, 83-84, 90,
    96, 100-101, 109-10, 118-19,
    125, 128-29, 145, 150-52,
    163-64, 166, 171, 180, 192
  and community, 9, 15, 17, 19,

    24, 27, 29, 31, 34, 50, 56-57,
    62-63, 74, 82-83, 88, 90, 92,
    96-105, 107-8, 110, 113, 116,
    118-22, 125, 129, 150-51,
    159-61, 164, 169, 172-73,
    175, 177, 180, 182, 184-86,
    189-90, 192
  and cultural engagement (*see*
    cultural engagement)
  current understandings, 59-77
  dangers of (or dangers of
    ignoring), 32-33, 50, 52, 96,
    107, 115, 117, 123-24, 128,
    150, 153, 155, 159, 164, 168,
    189-90
  definitions of
    synonyms (Christian
      tradition, church
      history, Christian
      history, historical
      theology), 19, 24, 28-29
    tradition, Tradition,
      traditions, traditioning,
      28-29, 54
  and ecumenism (*see*
    ecumenism)
  and ethics (*see* ethics)
  and filling theological gaps
    in understanding, 19, 57,
    83, 120-29, 164, 177, 184,
    189, 192
  history of, 35-58
  and identity, 9, 19, 23-24, 30,
    82-83, 85-99, 110, 113-14,
    116, 118-19, 121-22, 129,
    159-61, 164, 169, 177, 180,
    182, 184-86, 189, 192
  inevitability of, 30-32, 34, 59,
    62, 74
  and ministry, 9, 15, 17-19, 34,
    59, 90, 104, 114, 121, 129,
    133-90, 192-93
  and mission/missions (*see*
    mission/missions)
  oral tradition, 36, 42, 46, 50,
    60-62, 64-66, 73, 81
  and preaching (*see* preaching)
  prejudice against, 18-19, 121
  and Scripture (*see* Scripture:
    and tradition)
  and spirituality (*see*
    spirituality)
  and teaching (*see* teaching)
  Tradition (capital T)
    and Anglicans, 67-69
    and Bible-focused
      Protestants, 28, 70-74,
      171

and Eastern Orthodoxy,
28-29, 59-64, 171
and Roman Catholicism,
28-29, 41, 64-67, 171
tradition (lowercase t)
and Bible-focused
Protestants, 70-74, 171
and liberal Protestants,
74-76
and unity (*see*
ecumenism)
and worship (*see*
worship)
written tradition, 36
translation of Scripture. *See*
Scripture: and translation
Trent, Council of (1545–1563),
17-18, 50-51, 53, 64-65, 73, 142
Trinity
and apophatic theology, 125
and careful use of
terminology, 172
denials of traditional doctrine
of, 50, 106 (*see also* Arian(s);
Gnosticism)
and divine objectivity, 26
and ecumenism, 184
traditional doctrine of, 28, 33,
73-74, 95, 102, 112-13, 193

and worship, 177-78
See also Jesus Christ: and
Christology; Holy Spirit: as
a person of the Trinity;
Arians(s); Gnosticism;
modalism
tropology. *See under* Scripture:
and spiritual meanings
Tyconius, 137
typology. *See under* Scripture: and
spiritual meanings
Underground Railroad, 188
United Methodist Church, 54
United Pentecostal Church, 102
unity, Christian. *See* ecumenism
Valla, Lorenzo, 140
Vatican I, Council (1869–1870),
65, 73
Vatican II, Council (1962–1965),
54-55, 63-67
Vincent de Paul, 183, 189
Vincent of Lérins, 36, 39-40
Vincentian Canon. *See* Vincent of
Lérins
Waldensians, 114
Ware, Timothy (Kallistos), 60-62
Webber, Robert, 55-56, 120, 176
Wells, Samuel, 180
Wesley, Charles, 114

Wesley, John, 54, 114
Wesleyan quadrilateral, 54
Wheaton Theology Conference
(2007), 120
Wilberforce, William, 189
Wiles, Maurice, 75
Willard, Dallas, 174
William of Ockham, 45
Williams, D. H., 29-30, 41, 56, 72,
75, 92, 97, 120, 150
Williams, Rowan, 91-92, 97
Willibrord, 179
Wojtyla, Karol Józef. *See* John
Paul II
women, roles, 25, 182
World War II, 25, 144, 181, 183
worldview(s), 23-24, 31, 39, 86,
90, 110-11, 159
See also objectivity
worship, 18-19, 31-34, 39, 57-59,
61-63, 67, 74, 87, 93, 95, 99, 104,
121, 139, 176-79, 192, 206n13
Wright, N. T., 99
Wycliffe, John, 46, 141
Ximenes, Francisco, cardinal, 140
Young, Frances, 75
Zwingli, Ulrich, 17, 70, 104, 142

Scripture Index

OLD TESTAMENT
Genesis
16–18, *158*
21, *158*

Isaiah
7:14, *157*
40:3, *157*
54:1, *135*

Jeremiah
31:15, *157*

Hosea
11:1, *157*

Micah
5:2, *157*

Zechariah
9:9, *157*
11:12, *157*
12:10, *157*

NEW TESTAMENT
Matthew
1:22-23, *157*

2–3, *157*
16:16-19, *41*
21:5, *157*
27:9-10, *157*
27:46, *157*

Mark
15:34, *157*
16:15, *179*

Luke
1:26-30, *168*

John
1:14, *155*
1:18, *155*
1:29, *157*
3:16, *155*
3:18, *155*
17, *184, 185*
19:24, *157*
19:36, *157*
19:37, *157*

Acts
2, *168*

5:1-11, *182*

Romans
1:17, *141*
5, *135*
5:12-21, *157*
5:14, *135*

1 Corinthians
15:20, *172*
15:45, *157*

2 Corinthians
5:8, *100*
5:18, *165*
5:19, *166*

Galatians
1:8, *31*
4:21-31, *135, 158*
4:24, *158*

Ephesians
5:18-21, *107*

Philippians
2:5-11, *154*
2:7, *154*

2 Timothy
2:15, *134*

Hebrews
9, *157*
11, *100*
12:1, *97, 100*

James
5:16, *107*
5:20, *107*

2 Peter
3:2, *36*
3:16, *36*

1 John
4:9, *155*

Revelation
7, *100*